MAKING A DIFFERENCE

TEACHING BIBLICAL ADDICTION RECOVERY

RECOVERY SERIES

"AND OF SOME HAVE COMPASSION, MAKING A DIFFERENCE."
JUDE 22

Garland Mark Burgess

FOREWORD by DR. CLARENCE SEXTON

Making a Difference

Teaching Biblical Addiction Recovery

Garland Mark Burgess

First Edition

Published by

Copyright © March 2012
Garland Mark Burgess

Cover design by: KABU Graphics

All rights reserved. No part of this publication may be reproduced, copied, transmitted, or otherwise retained in any form, either electronic or mechanical, in part or in whole, except for brief quotations used in critical articles or reviews, without the prior written permission from the author/publisher.

ISBN-13: 978-0-9817474-1-5
ISBN-10: 0-9817474-1-8

LCCN: 2011919789

Printed in the USA

8 Making a Difference

Dedication

"Render therefore...honour to whom honour."

I dedicate this book to the following:

To my wife, for her encouragement, patience, counsel, prayers, and love. I would not have completed this work without her support.

To my parents, who have given their boys, now men, a godly heritage. My Dad's faithful leadership and consistent walk with the Lord and my Mom's virtue and loving care has made a lasting and significant impact on four generations - I honor them.

To my Aunt Linda, and in memory of my late, Uncle Dell, who the Lord used in a remarkable way to give us encouragement in a difficult time.

In memory of the late, Evangelist Lester Roloff. His life of faith, unyielding love, and ultimate sacrifice for those who were outcast, troubled, and unloved, left an indelible impression on me during my years as a young adult, traveling, singing, hunting, and flying, with him. His ministry was the seed from which the Lord used to begin a work in my own heart.

10 Making a Difference

Acknowledgements

First, to my Lord and Saviour, Jesus Christ, who is an ever-present help.

To my children for their patience and understanding in being denied time with Dad, and my own siblings for their support and prayers.

To my Pastor, Dr. Clarence Sexton, for being used by the Lord greatly to help me maintain a strictly biblical perspective. With the exception of my Dad, the Lord has used Dr. Sexton more than any other man to influence my understanding of truth.

I want to thank my friend, Dr. Gary Warren for many hours of editing; without whose help this project would not be successful.

I thank my friend, Dr. Donald N. Brandon for helping guide me through this process.

I also thank Dr. Charles Keen and his wife Mary for their kind friendship, support, and wise counsel.

12   Making a Difference

Preface

In Scripture, we find Jesus telling His listeners "the truth shall make you free." Later, standing before Pilate, Jesus was asked, "What is truth?" We hear people asking the same question as they seek the truth through reading books, or traveling to India or the Himalayas to be taught by gurus. In the 1960s, many of our youth were taught that truth could be found in LSD or other psychotropic drugs, only to find themselves dissatisfied, and their minds numbed or even destroyed through its use. Some people convinced that there is no truth, seek relief from life's difficulties in alcohol, or simply fall to viewing life with bitterness or anger.

It does not take a great mind to know that the truth we are searching for is not found in social or government programs, or even in the greatest wisdom devised by man. We only have to look around to see that having more freedoms does not result in the beneficiaries becoming freer. Perhaps the reason we have not found the truth that Jesus speaks of is because we have been looking in the wrong place. If it is not in the wisdom of man, or in government or secular programs, where is it?

Mark Burgess defines and provides a clear and well-marked runway in this jam-packed book, by which those in futile search for the truth can not only find it, but gain the freedom that Jesus promised to those that do find it.

For some, the search may be long and hard as they re-assess preconceived notions about life and relationships. Others may appreciate the help Mark provides in determining whether the "freedoms" we assume are ours to enjoy are, in fact, freedoms or illusions which lead to despair. In addition, what answer do we give to those who believe that change is not possible, or that the truth, which Jesus spoke of, is beyond their grasp?

In response, change requires that we choose to turn around and move in a different direction. The answer lies not in our past actions, but in our immediate choice to redirect our life. It is not only possible, but carries great rewards for those who, for once, put their faith in the One who promised a new life, and with Mark's guidance, taxi up to the runway for an adventure into the life Jesus promised to those who would heed Him.

Donald N. Brandon, PhD
Knoxville, Tennessee

Mark Burgess has a heart for God. He loves the Lord and he loves people. This book will prove to be a valuable tool in reaching and teaching a very needy group of people.

All of us know of precious ones who are in desperate need of help. What kind of help? The help we all need because of our sin. We need the Saviour, the Lord Jesus Christ and His power to make us whole.

May the Lord bless and use this effort in a mighty way.

> Clarence Sexton
> Acts 5:42

Foreword

Mark Burgess has a heart for God. He loves the Lord and he loves people. This book will prove to be a valuable tool in reaching and teaching a very needy group of people.

All of us know of precious ones who are in desperate need of help. What kind of help? The help we all need because of our sin. We need the Saviour, the Lord Jesus Christ and His power to make us whole.

May the Lord bless and use this effort in a mighty way.

Yvonne Sexton
Acts 5:14

Table of Contents

Introduction..21

Addictions Overview
Chapter
1. The Difference..29
2. Addiction..51
3. Recovery and Relapse..79
4. Recognizing Addictions......................................95
5. Effects of Addictions..121
6. Biblical Approach..137

Core Principles
Chapter
7. Truth..145
8. God–Belief System..167
9. Creation–Choices..187
10. Purpose–Significance......................................195
11. Accountability–Relationships............................207
12. Instruction–Obedience.....................................221

Our Response
Chapter
13. The Ministry of Recovery.................................241
14. Counsel and Restoration..................................253
15. Challenges and Goals......................................269

About the Author..289
About Transformed Life Ministries....................................291
Suggested Reading..297
Index..299

Introduction

Addictions and the problems they produce are not new to the world in which we live. People all over the world are in bondage to the sins of many different kinds of life-controlling habits. This group of people has become one of the largest unreached groups in all of modern societies. There is a sure answer for deliverance and victory. God has given us the answer to these problems in His Word.

The true Church of the living God has the ability and the duty to make a difference in the lives of people. Our communities and the world need to hear that Christ is the answer. Having the vision to reach addicts around the world requires people of vision. The Church has a great opportunity to help people gain permanent victory over the sins of life-controlling habits. We cannot find this victory in programs and treatments, but only in the person of Jesus Christ.

Although there have been many different approaches to the problem of addictions, the only true cure from addictions is found in the power of the Gospel of Jesus Christ. We must apply this truth in the life of the addict. Without this power, no one could live a life that is pleasing to God. God desires that we live according to His Word, becoming more like His Son as a result. Having a personal relationship with Christ is the only thing that can accomplish this.

If we are going to clear away the misconceptions and misunderstandings that surround addiction and recovery, we must learn what God has to say about them. If the problem of addictions and the supposed goal of recovery are misunderstood, there can only be a false sense of security in the answer for addiction problems.

God's Word has the answers for all things that touch our lives. Addictions are real, but so is the right answer for dealing with addictions. Our attempt with this work is to unveil the false assumptions and expose addiction behaviors for what they really are. By doing so, we will help the reader discover the truth about the cure for life-controlling habits. It is our desire to give this insight from nowhere, but the Word of God, regarding the permanent cure for addiction problems.

One of the motivating factors the Lord used in laying on my heart the necessity of yet another text dealing with addictions was the realization of the absence of a truly Biblical work being available. Over the course of directing several residential recovery facilities, I examined many different sources of curriculum material. The realization that most addiction recovery programs, even within the Christian community, uses material based upon the AA (Alcoholics Anonymous) 12-Step program, became very apparent.

The attempt to free someone from addiction based upon the memorization of a list of twelve ideals, is a misguided notion that man can free himself from life-controlling habits. In my opinion, the AA 12-Step program is a humanistic attempt to free man from his self-created slavery. The results of such teaching are simply adding one bondage to another – that of going to meetings.

In these programs, the success of the addict gaining recovery, hinges upon the addict memorizing the 12 steps and utilizing them when they are tempted to act out there addiction. They also rely heavily upon going to meetings as a way of preventing relapse.

Relying upon our flesh in any form can only result in failure. God tells us in His Word to "have no confidence in the flesh," including our own. No one can find true recovery in this way by his or her own admission. People in this situation always say they are "recovering." They are not able to say they have recovered because they have not.

Christian programs that use the 12-step model are falling into the same trap, even though they may use Scripture from the Bible to support the 12 steps. The emphasis is still upon the 12 steps instead of God's Word. If God's Word is sufficient, and it certainly is, why do we need the 12 steps? Another reason we do not use this approach is that recovery should not, and must not, be the goal. The goal should only be to please Christ through a life that is devoted to Him. The goal of a program determines the emphasis and the emphasis determines the results.

We must see addiction as God sees it, and our addiction recovery methods and message must begin and end with Biblical principles. When the Church adopts the methods and message of the world, there can never be what God can accomplish in the lives of people who are suffering from life-controlling behaviors. Psalm 127:1 says, "Except the LORD build the house, they labour in vain that build it: except the LORD keep the city, the watchman waketh but in vain." We must, begin with God and where God begins, when helping people overcome life-controlling habits.

As with any pioneering work, it takes time to gain acceptance. Most people do not like change. When previously accepted philosophies and methods are the main source of response to addictions, change is many times slow and difficult to attain. It is not my purpose to gain notoriety or recognition, only acceptance as a Biblical source for instruction in addiction recovery. The purpose of this work is to teach people, who have a desire to help others through a recovery ministry, the Biblical approach to teaching addiction recovery. The proper approach to teaching addiction recovery is a Systematic Teaching of Biblical Principles.

Some of the statements and assertions given in this text may be new to some people; some of whom have worked in the ministry of addiction recovery for many years. Many of these statements will challenge long-accepted and traditional methods. I ask the reader to open their mind and heart so the Holy Spirit may direct them toward the truth.

There is a two-fold purpose in my approach to teaching addiction recovery. First, I want to change Christian's mindset or thinking processes when it comes to the methods and message of the recovery ministry, and second, I want to bring the ministry of addiction recovery out of the shadows and into the light of mainstream ministry in our local churches. Life-controlling habits are increasing as our population increases. People need to look to God's Word for the answer to life-controlling habits. This text is the right start toward this goal and is simply the basis for a soul-winning effort.

There are several reoccurring themes throughout this book. These themes are necessary for correcting the thought patterns of people who wish to help those who are enslaved to life-controlling habits. Some of these themes overlap in several of the chapters. The intent is to teach the same principle from different perspectives, thereby giving the reader a complete view of the principle.

The Biblical view is that only God has the power to free someone from the bondage of addiction, not a vague, self-defined "higher power," conformity to a list of ideals, or manmade treatment protocols. Our belief is that the Word of God is the only source of power by which men become free from life-controlling habits. As this source, we rely solely upon it for the transformation needed in the lives of people. Any recovery program that does not use, the Word of God, as the basis for their recovery curriculum, will mistakenly lead people further into darkness.

Jesus said we are the light of the world. It is our duty, and should be our desire, to take the light of the glorious Gospel of Christ to the world. One way we can accomplish this is to reach and restore those who are in bondage to life-controlling habits. Jesus Christ gave His life for us on the cross at Calvary. There could be no better way for us to show our love to Him than to reach others with the Gospel.

Garland Mark Burgess
Acts 20:24

Addictions Overview

Chapter 1

The Difference

> "And of some have compassion, making a difference:"
> Jude 22

Nothing is more needful in the lives of people than to recognize they are sinners in need of the Saviour.

> "For what is a man profited, if he shall gain the whole world, and lose his own soul? or what shall a man give in exchange for his soul?" (Matthew 16:26)

The world around us is in great turmoil and fear because of many uncertainties. Christians have the best opportunity, right now, to carry the gospel to a lost and dying world than ever before. We have at our disposal many wonderful technologies and resources to get the Word of God to all the earth. We live in the greatest time of spiritual harvest that has ever existed since the creation of man. Over half of all the people that have been born on this earth are alive today. Jesus Christ commanded that we pray to the Lord of the harvest to send laborers into the harvest.

Our homes, communities, nation, and the world are in much need of Christians who are willing to give their lives to the cause of reaching others for Christ. There is no greater commitment Christians can make, than to a significant and meaningful relationship with Jesus Christ. Being a witness for Christ will occur naturally because of this relationship.

Laborers Needed

The fields are truly white unto harvest, but the laborers are very few. Generations of people are quite literally being lost to addictions. People who would otherwise be productive in our Christian communities are unreached because very few Christians have the knowledge and understanding necessary to effectively deal with addicts.

One of the most needed areas of Christian influence today is in this area of Addiction Recovery. We need Christians who have not just a greater knowledge, but also Biblical knowledge, and more than a better understanding, a Biblical understanding, of how to recognize and deal with addictions in the lives of others. They must be willing to help the addict find true freedom from the slavery and bondage of a life controlled by addictions. This is what will make the difference in the lives of addicts.

> **There is no greater commitment Christians can make, than to a significant and meaningful relationship with Jesus Christ.**

Addiction recovery is not the only area of ministry in need of laborers, but there are too few Christians who have enough burden and compassion for the addict to make this type of ministry their life's work. I say willing because even with God's calling there must be a willingness to endure disappointments and sacrifices that may be necessary to work in this area of ministry. In spite of these difficulties, Christians have the blessed opportunity to make a difference in the lives of many people today. As with any type of ministry, Christ alone must be the motive for giving one's life to a ministry such as this.

In many ways, this is a forgotten ministry. Many have forgotten that people who struggle with addictions are souls for whom Christ died; forgotten in the sense that churches have not realized the potential for adding souls to God's kingdom through the ministry of addiction recovery; and forgotten in the sense that few churches see the growing need of an addiction recovery ministry in their community. Therefore, the main purpose of the addiction recovery ministry must be as a soul-winning effort of the local church.

Addictions greatly affect churches and our society in general. One of the goals of this book is to raise awareness that addictions are a growing problem, not only in our Society, but in our Churches as well. As the Pillar and Ground of the Truth, churches have the answer for addiction problems. Many people are in bondage to life-controlling habits such as drugs, alcohol, pornography, and gambling. People are even addicted to many different types of sports activities. The time is right for the Church to make an impact on society through a ministry of addiction recovery.

People with life-controlling habits can receive permanent recovery through a systematic learning of Biblical truths. This approach to recovery is one of the things that separate this book from most others. If Christians understood the scope of biblical responsibilities given to the Church by God, there would be less secular involvement in many areas of need in our society. Addiction recovery is only one of these areas.

Different Approach
The government's involvement of taking care of the poor and needy is simply a response to, and reflection of, the failure of local churches to shoulder this responsibility. This failure on the part of local churches has not only opened the door for the government to create dependency upon itself, thereby validating in some people's minds the need for a large central government, but it has also minimized the effectiveness of the Church's ability to reach the lost for Christ. James 2:14-20 plainly reveals this truth.

"What doth it profit, my brethren, though a man say he hath faith, and have not works? Can faith save him? If a brother or sister be naked, and destitute of daily food, And one of you say unto them, Depart in peace, be ye warmed and filled; notwithstanding ye give them not those things which are needful to the body; what doth it profit? Even so faith, if it hath not works, is dead, being alone. Yea, a man may say, Thou hast faith, and I have works: shew me thy faith without thy works, and I will shew thee my faith by my works. Thou believest that there is one God; thou doest well: the devils also believe, and tremble. But wilt thou know, O vain man, that faith without works is dead?"

There *is* enough time, money, prayers, laborers, and material goods already at the disposal of God's people to take care of thousands of needy people in our communities through the local church. The reason most local churches are unable to offer assistance to the poor and needy is that its members are not obedient to God in the role of Biblical stewardship.

The same holds true of addiction recovery programs offered through our local churches. The world's economy cannot hold us hostage. The economic circumstances of the world do not limit God, but we limit His working in our lives by our lack of faith and obedience. Thus, we have come to realize that obedience is the key ingredient of stewardship. To be good stewards of God's resources, we must reach the world with the Gospel of Christ. This includes addiction recovery programs that teach the truth of God's Word as an effort to win souls.

My approach to addiction recovery is different from secular institutions and even many religious institutions. Their approach is to help a person recover from addictions through will power, change of environment, medical treatments, prolonged counseling sessions, therapy, reforming behaviors, and/or a combination of these, with some institutions using religion only as a cloak. My approach is to teach them that only God has the power to deliver a person from the bondage of addictions as He does with any sin. This power is only available to those who have trusted in Jesus Christ as their Saviour.

It is only through a personal relationship with Jesus Christ that a person can gain lasting recovery from the bondage of addiction. It is my conviction that when a person has this relationship with Christ, everything good in that person's life is a by-product of this relationship. Therefore, recovery from life-controlling habits becomes a result of this relationship as well.

> …anything that helps a person be productive in society has value to that society.

The desire to be obedient to God, the desire to serve Him, and the blessings enjoyed as a result, are all by-products of a meaningful relationship with Jesus Christ. A person who obeys Christ is given strength from God, through the Holy Spirit indwelling them, to not only overcome the desires of the flesh and any destructive activity that has control over them, but to understand what God's will is for them in this life. God's will in this world is not a mystery. Why would God not want His people to understand what His will is? He does! God has only one will in this world.

> "The Lord is not slack concerning his promise, as some men count slackness; but is longsuffering to us-ward, not willing that any should perish, but that all should come to repentance." (2Peter 3:9)

God desires that we know our place in His will. There are two things required for us to know our place in the will of God. First, we must have the kind of relationship with Christ that enables us to hear when He speaks to us through other Christians, circumstances, and most importantly, through reading and studying His Word. Secondly, when He does speak we must obey His commands. All Christians must live their lives on this foundation.

You will also notice that I do not use a "Twelve Step" emphasis in this text. It is my conviction that dependency on a 12-step program, or any program other than a Biblical one, is nothing more than just another addiction. It is my belief that when a program or curriculum places the emphasis on a list of ideals instead of on the Lord Jesus Christ and God's Word, they have lost the real power to free a man from life-controlling habits. Where we put the emphasis makes the difference.

This is not a point of contention and I do not intend to be divisive. I believe anything that helps a person be productive in society has value to that society. We should not condemn anything that helps people better themselves. However, my desire is to help people prepare for eternity. In helping a person prepare for eternity, we help them live free from life-controlling habits now. Therefore, I choose a purely Biblical approach to addiction recovery.

God has given us the answer to every problem and question we face in life. It is my desire to teach people how they can have victory over life-controlling habits, and in turn, have the ability to teach others what they have learned. However, we must begin with God and His Word.

The basis for creating this book on teaching biblical addiction recovery is the Word of God. This textbook will help anyone who desires to know more about a Biblical view of addiction recovery. It will also help local churches who desire to reach addicts by showing them how they can develop and run an addiction recovery ministry. Victory over addictions is obtained through the power of the gospel of Jesus Christ manifested in a Transformed Life.

On completion of this book, the reader should:

- Understand the problems addictions cause in our society and churches.

- Understand the proper biblical view of addictions.

- Understand how to establish a church ministry outreach that is both dynamic and relevant to those who have addiction problems today.

- Understand how to teach addiction recovery from a biblical perspective.

The concepts in this book are from the Word of God, which is the source of all truth. As Christians, we should understand and believe the Word of God to be the final authority for faith and practice. Many people claim this, but have very little faith in God and practice very little of what the Bible teaches.

This principle is basic to all Christian beliefs. It should be the desire of every individual to live by all the principles taught to us in the Word of God, whether we have an addiction problem or not. It is my conviction that if a person includes the principles taught throughout this text in a recovery program, the recipient of this teaching will have enough knowledge and understanding to make the decision to obey Christ instead of the flesh. This is true freedom from the bondage of sin, including the sin of addiction.

Other programs and materials may help a person be temporarily clean or sober, but they usually leave the person with an overwhelming sense of fear, guilt, and lack of hope, to be free from the addiction that enslaves them. It is my conviction that God has the answers for everything we encounter in our life. Addiction is no exception. This is the fundamental difference in a program with a secular viewpoint and one with a Biblical viewpoint.

The secular view of recovery is one in which the addict is cured through knowledge, and changes in his behavior and environment. These are only surface changes. The Christian view of recovery is one in which the addict is free from addiction by a change on the inside, or what we would call the "heart," through a supernatural change brought about by God, resulting in the addict's desire to please God rather than himself. Deuteronomy 8:1-3 explains this desire to us when it says,

> "All the commandments which I command thee this day shall ye observe to do, that ye may live, and multiply, and go in and possess the land which the LORD sware unto your

fathers. And thou shalt remember all the way which the LORD thy God led thee these forty years in the wilderness, to humble thee, and to prove thee, to know what was in thine heart, whether thou wouldest keep his commandments, or no. And he humbled thee, and suffered thee to hunger, and fed thee with manna, which thou knewest not, neither did thy fathers know; that he might make thee know that man doth not live by bread only, but by every word that proceedeth out of the mouth of the LORD doth man live."

In this passage of Scripture, God is revealing to us the nature of a man's heart, as it should be. He is telling us that our heart should compel us to follow His instruction and guidance in obedience to His commands because of what He has done for us. The Lord takes it even further by revealing to us the necessity of His Word for our very life. It is only through obeying the Word of God that we can truly live a happy and productive life.

> **Anything a person tries to do in the power of the flesh is humanism.**

When a person gives their heart and life to God, they are in essence submitting their will to God. The result of this obedience is a life that is meaningful and satisfying and one that is free from the bondage of sin. This can take place only through obedience to God's Word.

The secular position is, however, one in which a person relies upon the power of one's own will to free them from the bondage of addictions. This view results in a false hope and disappointing results. Anything a person tries to do in the power of the flesh is humanism. Memorizing 12 steps and hanging on to them for dear life is not freedom from bondage, this is only trading bondage for a different bondage.

Memorizing Bible verses is not humanism because the Word of God is alive and powerful; it has the power to change a person from the inside out. Hebrews 4:12 says,

"For the word of God is quick, and powerful, and sharper than any twoedged sword, piercing even to the dividing asunder of soul and spirit, and of the joints and marrow, and is a discerner of the thoughts and intents of the heart."

Because we believe in the power of the Word of God to change a person's life, we rely solely upon it. When the success of a program is dependent upon the participant memorizing a list of ideals, what that person can do for himself is all that is achieved. However, when we depend upon the power of the Word of God, we can expect much more than what man can accomplish, we can expect what God can accomplish in a person's life.

The Biblical view is one in which we believe that God gave us the answer to freedom from the bondage of addictions. This answer is in a relationship with Jesus Christ. God's Word helps us understand this principle. The addict must believe this by faith and act upon it to have deliverance from addictions.

While we must greatly emphasize the importance of a Biblical view of addiction recovery, it is not my intent to criticize any program that does not use a Biblical approach. I believe the Bible has all the answers to the problems men face in their lives. Although I do not believe a clinical approach to recovery is the correct approach, some people are helped physically through a clinical treatment process.

In this book, I choose to refrain from topics such as neurobiology and treatment models because our purpose is to deliver a purely Biblical solution. Understanding more in-depth medical and psychological topics have their place and are useful to a person desiring to further their understanding and education of addiction and recovery from a clinical standpoint, but may not have a tremendously useful place in the trenches of the addiction recovery ministry of the local church.

My desire is to stay away from the clinical and philosophical arguments and stay with the Word of God as the source of education and understanding for the addiction recovery ministry. I believe Christians have strayed too far away from the Word of God in too many areas of life. As a result, we have given too much emphasis to models, approaches, and treatments, as the answer to the sins of life-controlling behaviors. This in turn has produced a desensitization to sin as the culprit.

By placing more emphasis on disorders, assessments, and treatment protocols, instead of God's Word, we have inadvertently created an environment, even within the Christian community, where men are victims of their own behaviors, instead of the perpetrators of sinful acts. We have tried to "understand" rather than obey. We have brushed aside the sin and focused on the need to be esteemed through new and more intellectual competencies.

We have forgotten that men are sinners and need the Saviour. We have forgotten that true ministry is first to the lost and secondly to the edification of the body of Christ. We conjure up all sorts of new and fresh program ideas in attempts to be different from everyone else, all the while thinking we are progressive, and doing good things for people. We pat ourselves on the back and say how intellectual we are by developing new philosophies and protocols. Let us remember what Christ Himself told us in John 15:5 when He said,

"…for without me ye can do nothing."

Basic Principles
The following Basic Principles are the answers God gives us for a meaningful relationship with His Son, Jesus Christ. Knowing Him is true freedom from addictions.

God has always existed; in eternity past, present, and future. In other words, God always exists in eternal present. Past, present and future are for man's benefit only. (John 8:58, John 1:1)

God is the Creator of all life and all things that exist in the universe. (Psalm 19:1; 24:1, Colossians 1:17)

Because God chose to create man, man has a specific purpose in life. (Genesis 1:26, 2Timothy 1:9)

Man has a responsibility to the Creator and is accountable for what he does with his life. (Romans 14:12)

Man must fulfill the purpose for which he was created. (Romans 9:11; Ephesians 1:11; 2Timothy 1:9)

Because man is accountable to God, God has given man instructions in how to live a life that fulfills his purpose for being created. (Deuteronomy 8:3; Luke 4:4)

These instructions are in God's Word, the Bible. (2Timothy 3:16)

Man must be obedient to God's Word. (2Thessalonians 1:8)

Adam chose to disobey God's instructions in the Garden of Eden. (Genesis chapter 3)

Adam's disobedience brought sin upon the human race. (Romans 5:12, 19)

The penalty of sin is death. (Romans 6:23)

Jesus paid the penalty of sin for all mankind. (Romans 5:12)

Men must place their trust in Jesus Christ for salvation. (Romans 10:9-10; Acts 4:12)

Trusting Christ for salvation results in a changed life from the inside out. (2Corinthians 5:17)

The power to overcome addiction is found in having a time of daily communion with God. (Luke 9:23; Hebrews 3:13)

A daily, meaningful relationship with Jesus Christ gives our lives purpose. (Philippians 1:6)

Through studying God's Word, we find the truths by which we should live our lives. (2Timothy 2:15)

As we are obedient to God's Word God blesses us. (Psalm 24: 4-5)

Addiction is a continued worship of one's self rather than God. (Mark 4:19; Romans 13:14; Galatians 5:24; Ephesians 2:3)

Relapse is a result of obeying the flesh rather than Christ. (1Peter 1:14)

These principles are based upon the Word of God. They are also the foundation for the teaching found throughout this book. As you progress through this book, more detailed information that is helpful to ministering to addicts will unfold. By recognizing the need for ministering to the addict, a positive difference can be made in their lives, in the local church, and in our society as a whole.

> **The Church must move out of its "comfort zone" to reach addicts for Christ.**

By exposing Christians to this growing problem in our society and making available tools, insights and concepts for ministering to addicts, educated decisions can be made concerning reaching out to addicts through this neglected area of church ministry. It is my desire that those who engage in this type of ministry be prepared for what they are going to face concerning addictions and the problems addictions cause in the church and in our society. This is not an easy ministry. Often, there are few victories and many disappointments. As we have heard many times, and it is certainly true – One person coming to a saving knowledge of Jesus Christ is worth every effort.

The principles and concepts taught in this book give relevance and credibility to the need of ministering to the addict.

They will also give the ministry worker tools to develop a church ministry that reaches addicts for Christ through a process of systematically teaching them Biblical principles. It is also my desire that this book will give insight and conceptual ideas to those already working in this area of church ministry and that it will be an encouragement to them as well.

Addictions Have No Boundaries

Most everyone knows of someone who currently has, or has had in their past, a serious problem with some type of addiction. Therefore, it would not be presumptuous to say that most everyone will, at some point in their life, encounter the effects or consequences of a serious addiction problem, either directly or indirectly.

Many actors, entertainers, musicians, politicians, and other public figures, have had problems with addictions of various kinds. These popular personalities have lost public respect, endorsement contracts, and fan support, because of addiction problems that manifested in public outbursts. Many other very popular people from the above groups have even lost their lives because of alcohol and drug abuse.

The problem of addictions is much larger, even within the church body itself, than most church members recognize. There have been congregational leaders, Christian workers, and other people in high profile and influential ministry positions that have had addiction problems as well.

Life-controlling habits are not a respecter of persons. Anyone may become enslaved to any harmful behavior. Certainly, some behaviors produce less catastrophic results than others do, but the loss of freedom and sanity can result from any controlling activity.

Explanation of Terms

This book is an attempt to provide practical, down-to-earth, real-world, experience in the form of written material. Learning this material will result in a greater awareness in our Christian communities of the need to reach addicts through a viable and effective church ministry. The Church must move out of its "comfort zone" to reach addicts for Christ. It will be the task of this generation to make a difference in the lives of people caught in the bondage of addictions. This generation can only do this by ministering to addicts who are within our reach.

The subject of addiction is foreign to most people. It is one of the goals of this book to familiarize the Christian with common terms and phrases used in the addiction community. Many people have never been exposed to addictions even though addictions have touched almost every household in America. While it is not necessary to become a walking dictionary of terms relating to addiction and recovery, it is important to be familiar with the terminology currently used in treatment facilities and recovery programs.

Although we may use a particular word or phrase this does not mean we agree with its use in all applications. I offer these terms here because the majority of people in the addiction recovery community understand them. It is simply more expedient for us to use them. The reverse is true for secular programs as well. For example, as Christians, we use the word sin to define addictions; secular programs may use the word sickness or illness. We will try to define these differences as clearly as possible.

It would be wise to become as familiar as possible with all of the terms and phrases, to communicate effectively with certain secular and government institutions as is necessary. I have found, in working with addicts and their family members, many times it becomes necessary to communicate with courts, secular rehabilitation facilities, medical facilities, and certain government institutions. A thorough knowledge and understanding of these terms will help to equip a person in preparation for this communication process. Therefore, we use terms that have a different meaning to the Christian community.

This list of terms is certainly not exhaustive. There are many other good publications that can give many more terms and definitions. It is my hope to familiarize the Christian with only the most common terms. Once a person begins working in the ministry of helping addicts, their vocabulary and understanding of these and other terms will increase.

Common Terms

Addiction – (habit, compulsion, dependence, need, obsession, craving, infatuation) A state of physiological or psychological dependence. Addiction is more commonly referred to when a person is dependent upon a chemical substance. However, addiction also applies to any behavior that creates or evolves into a habit or dependency upon the particular behavior. My definition of addiction is any behavior that is the results of, or creates a dependency upon, the flesh rather than upon God.

Bargaining – (negotiate, exchange, agreement) To negotiate the terms of an agreement with somebody. To exchange one thing for another. Bargaining is a ploy, which is incorporated into the addict's behavior in an effort to manipulate many of their circumstances. This ploy is used to either gain illicit support for their addiction or is used during the addict's denial or grief process while going through a treatment program.

Chemical – (substance, element, compound) A substance used in or produced by the processes of chemistry. A chemical has a defined atomic or molecular structure that results from, or takes part in, reactions involving changes in its structure, composition, and properties. Reference is most commonly made for any drug being used by the addict.

Chemical Dependency – (drug abuse, drug addiction) An addiction to a chemical substance (Drug).

Chronic Illness - Describes an illness or medical condition that lasts over a long period and sometimes causes a long-term change in the body. For additional comments, refer to "Disease."

Codependency – (mutual need) The dependence of two people, groups, or organisms on each other, especially when this reinforces mutually harmful behavior patterns. Codependency is most often recognized in the relationship an addict has with their loved ones. In this scenario, the loved one carries guilt for some reason. This guilt causes the loved one to continue to support and provide the addict with money and services that perpetuate and enable the addiction behavior because they feel they must "fix" the problem with the person who has the addiction.

Destructive Behavior – Behavior that results in the destruction of relationships, one's physical body, the desire for others to help, or any other tangible or intangible service or treatment.

Detoxification (Detox) – The process of eliminating toxins or addictive substances, such as alcohol or drugs, from the body. I recommend that facilities that do not employ medical treatment processes have the participant, who is heavily using drugs or alcohol, enter into a medically supervised detoxification process prior to attending a residential program.

Disease - A condition that results in pathological symptoms and is not the direct result of physical injury. Many times the secular treatment facilities refer to addiction as a disease. While this may be the results of addictive behavior, it certainly is not the cause of the behavior itself.

"DT's" (Detoxify) - Street slang for effects of withdrawal. This withdrawal can be either voluntary or involuntary.

Functioning Addict – A person who is in bondage to a life-controlling habit, but is still able to perform his or her duties in the various roles as employee, family member, citizen, etc.

Intervention – (interference, involvement, intrusion, intercession) The act of intervening, especially a deliberate entry into a situation or dispute, in order to influence events or prevent undesirable consequences. This concept is used to convince the addict they need to change their behavior by taking away certain things on which the addict depends. This is normally relationships with family members who have provided either emotional or financial support in the past. This method of treatment is highly confrontational and can result in the addict withdrawing even further from the sources of positive influence that are much needed in their life.

Manipulation – (treatment, handling, exploitation, management,) To control or influence somebody or something in an ingenious or devious way. Many family members, friends, and other loved ones fall prey to manipulation by the addict. This is especially true when addicts are no longer able to financially provide for themselves.

Recovery – (revival, upturn, recuperation, mending, healing, improvement, resurgence, revitalization, renewal) A return to normal state. A gaining back of something lost. Recovery is most often referred to when defining the process of gaining freedom from a life-controlling circumstance or addiction. I use the term "recovery" in the same context that secular institutions use it. This is for their benefit only. The term "recovery" is also used throughout this book for the same reason. As Christians, we believe that a person who places their trust in Jesus Christ as their Saviour "recovers" by the daily cleansing of the Word of God in their life. We call this sanctification. Recovery is the by-product of a daily, meaningful relationship with Jesus Christ.

Reformation – (improvement, renovation, reorganization, restructuring, overhaul, restoration, rectification) A reformed state, especially a general improvement in somebody's behavior. Reformation takes place in an attempt of man to better his condition or situation through his own strength and ability. This is not the proper view for a Christian who is depending on God for change in their life.

Rehabilitation - ("Rehab", treatment, rehabilitation, healing, remedy, cure, analysis) To help someone return to good health or a normal life by providing training or therapy. Rehabilitation is the goal of treatment. This treatment process varies with the different rehab facilities around the country. Some facilities rely on medical practices alone for treatment. Others have a combination of medical treatment, therapy, and counseling to affect the desired change in the addict. Still other facilities rely on counseling alone in an attempt to facilitate change in the addict's behavior. No facility should be considered unsuccessful, if they are accomplishing their prescribed goals in the method of treatment they wish to employ. Christian facilities or ministries should have the transformation of the individual primarily at the heart of whatever program they choose to use. The soul of the individual is going to live forever either in Heaven or Hell. The first priority must be to give them a clear presentation of the gospel of Jesus Christ. Then, the Christian ministry should be able to disciple them by giving the addict the tools necessary to follow the Lord in a life that is yielded to Him

Relapse – (deterioration, decline, degeneration, reversion, waning, setback) The act of returning to a previous condition. Relapse is referred to in the rehabilitation process as a return to previously harmful habits and behaviors. Many times the effects of a particular addiction is greater upon the individual when relapse occurs. My definition of relapse is "A failure of consistent devotion to Christ." The only way anyone can keep from satisfying the desires of their flesh is to study the Word of God and to fill their mind with the Word of God through memorization and meditation upon the things of God.

Residential Treatment Facility - A term used to describe a rehabilitation facility where participants live on location for a determined period. The purpose of a residential program is to seclude the participant from their current environment.

Restitution – (giving back, paying back, restoration, compensation, recompense, reimbursement, amends, repayment, refund) The return of something to its rightful owner; Compensation for a loss, damage or injury; The return of something to a prior unchanged condition. In some cases, it is important for the addict to make an attempt at restitution to those who have been hurt by their behavior. Many times this is impossible due to the ties that have been permanently severed. If a person makes an honest attempt at restitution, and is prohibited from doing so because of the other individual's refusal, they are free from continued obligation.

Sanctification – (consecration, dedication, blessing) The process of achieving holiness. This process begins when a person places their trust in Jesus Christ for salvation and receives Him as their personal Saviour. Sanctification is a process, whereas, salvation is an event.

Substance Abuse - Substance abuse is the term used most often in discussions concerning drug and alcohol addiction by rehabilitation facilities and the medical community. This term is synonymous with drug abuse, alcohol abuse, drug and alcohol addiction, or any other chemical addiction.

> **My definition of addiction is any behavior that is the results of, or creates a dependency upon, the flesh rather than upon God.**

Therapy – (treatment, rehabilitation, healing, remedy, cure, analysis) Treatment of physical, mental, or behavioral problems that is meant to cure or rehabilitate somebody. There are many different types of therapy used for the treatment of addiction.

Transformation – (alteration, change, conversion, revolution, renovation) A complete change. Transformation is the change which occurs when a person places their trust in Jesus Christ and receives Him as their personal Saviour. Transformation can only be accomplished through the actions of God alone.

Twelve Steps – Synonymous with Alcoholics Anonymous (AA), or Narcotics Anonymous (NA) A method of gaining sobriety through group meetings and following a prescribed plan. As a Christian, we are dependent upon God alone to help us in times of need. To be dependent upon meetings or a prescribed plan may help a person be clean from drugs or sober from alcohol, but there are many other factors to consider, the main one being the eternal soul of the individual. Dependency upon a commitment to meetings or a "twelve-step" process is the equivalent of having another god in place of the one and only true and living God; a breaking of the very first commandment. God desires that we trust Him completely and be obedient to His Word. This takes commitment.

Withdrawal (Symptoms) – (removal, departure, alienation, retraction) A period during which somebody addicted to a drug or other substance stops taking it causing the person to experience painful or uncomfortable symptoms.

In summary, the difference in secular and Biblical based programs is the basis by which recovery is taught to the addict. The secular view does not usually achieve permanent and lasting recovery because it relies only on what man can do for himself. The Biblical view produces a lasting and permanent recovery because it is based upon the Word of God. God's Word teaches us that it is by God's power alone that we are able to live a life that is free from sin.

Life-controlling habits are sins. The sins of idolatry, lust, and pride, are at the root of all addictions. Having the correct understanding of this allows for teaching and instruction that can produce a lasting change in a person from the inside. This change takes place through knowledge of God that only the Bible can give. This knowledge may ultimately produce a new nature, given when a person is born again into the family of God and matures as a Christian. Consider the following verses found in the Bible in the book of 2Peter 1:2-10,

> "Grace and peace be multiplied unto you through the knowledge of God, and of Jesus our Lord, According as his divine power hath given unto all things that pertain unto life

and godliness, through the knowledge of him that hath called us to glory and virtue: Whereby are given unto us exceeding great and precious promises: that by these ye might be partakers of the divine nature, having escaped the corruption that is in the world through lust. And beside this, giving all diligence, add to your faith virtue; and to virtue knowledge; And to knowledge temperance; and to temperance patience; and to patience godliness; And to godliness brotherly kindness; and to brotherly kindness charity. For if these things be in you, and abound, they make you that ye shall neither be barren nor unfruitful in the knowledge of our Lord Jesus Christ. But he that lacketh these things is blind, and cannot see afar off, and hath forgotten that he was purged from his old sins. Wherefore the rather, brethren, give diligence to make your calling and election sure: for if ye do these things, ye shall never fall:"

In these verses, we are given the answer to how a person can live their life free from the sins that enslave them. ("purged from his old sins") This answer is the grace of God freely given to all who desire a new life in Christ. The life spoken of here is the life eternal for those who place their trust in Jesus Christ and thereby gain strength to resist the desires of the flesh as the person matures in the Lord.

> **Recovery is the by-product of a daily, meaningful relationship with Jesus Christ.**

This is necessary to begin living a productive life. In this new life, there are promises of God experienced beyond anything we could imagine beforehand. The life of the person addicted to some action or substance is not real life at all. It is only a very shallow substitute at best for the life God desires them to have. "There is no better living than a transformed life."

Once this new life is given, there is also given to the possessor of this new life a new nature. This new nature begins to desire to please the Person who gave the new life; this Person is God. Not only is this new life eternal in that the recipient will spend eternity with the Creator, but this is also the beginning of a new life on this earth.

This new life is filled with wonder and blessings that are new and exciting. These new experiences capture Christians in such a way that they reach the highest level of holiness possible in this life on earth. God commanded us to be holy as He is holy. He would not have commanded us to be something we could not attain. However, we must realize that obtaining the highest level of holiness is only possible through Christ living in and through us. God does this by adding to one's faith, virtue, knowledge, temperance, patience, godliness, brotherly kindness, and charity, as the person grows and matures spiritually.

The preceding Scripture first talks of faith because this is where it all must begin. It is on faith that all other characteristics rest. I believe this is essential in how we approach addiction problems in the lives of individuals. This is the most evident difference between secular and Biblical programs.

Faith must also have something upon which to rest. You cannot tell someone to have faith, and not give him or her something in which to have faith. We must tell people that their faith and trust must be in Jesus Christ. How do they attain faith? Romans 10:17 says,

"So then faith cometh by hearing, and hearing by the word of God."

We must first deal with the subject of Biblical salvation, then help them grow and mature in their faith. We can help the addict come to Christ through a process of planned systematic teaching of Biblical principles based upon the Gospel of Jesus Christ. This is the only hope for people in bondage to life-controlling habits. The next fourteen chapters convey these principles. Once a person has accepted Christ as their personal Saviour, they have the strength and power from God to live a life free from the sins that enslave them. ("for if ye do these things, ye shall never fall:")

Chapter 2

Addiction

Steve was the top sales rep in his division. He had a shelf in his office where he proudly displayed nine awards he had received over his twelve years with the company. He had a promising career and potential to go as far up the corporate ladder, as he desired. Everyone thought he would be the Vice President of his division in a few more years. They did not know all this was about to come crashing down around him. Because of his success and consequent income, he and his wife had become dependent upon the large salary and bonus checks he received each month.

They had become accustomed to living the lavish lifestyle his income provided them. They had a fine house on the lake with a three-car garage, a condominium at the beach, and a pleasure boat that was nothing short of a small yacht. Their debts were high, but his income always covered their debts with enough left over to support the entertaining she enjoyed providing for their friends.

Steve had a few hobbies of his own, one of which was a casual indulgence of betting on some of the races at the neighboring town's horse racing track. This was innocent enough. It was not as if he took it very serious or anything. The guys would get together every couple of weeks and play cards. Every year they would take a trip out to Las Vegas and blow a few thousand dollars at the casinos. It was all done in the spirit of having a good time.

Eventually, one of Steve's friends actually won big at the races and this peaked Steve's interest in the horses. He began to bet more money on the races. He started paying more attention to the breeding histories and bloodlines; trying to figure out how to beat the odds. He did pretty well too.

He made almost as much money at the races as he did all year from his job. He actually had thoughts of quitting his job. If he could win big one time, it would allow them to retire early and pursue some of their leisure interests full-time.

These thoughts led him down a slippery path as he started gambling more and more. He would even stop at a convenient store a couple times a week to buy lottery tickets. After all, fifty million dollars is a lot of money. Besides, someone was going to win it - It might as well be him. This continued a few more years.

Steve still made a very good income at his job, but he seemed to lose momentum for the position of Division Vice President. One evening Steve's wife received a phone call from his manager at the office. Steve had not been to work that day and had not called in sick. He had left home a little earlier than usual that morning, but she had no reason for alarm. He had been acting a little strange lately, but nothing terribly out of character.

That evening she began calling around to see if she could locate him, but she was unsuccessful. She called his cell phone, but it only went to voice mail. He had always been very good about letting her know if he was going to be late. She decided to wait a couple hours for him to show up. He never did.

When he did not come home that night, the next morning she called the police to file a report for a missing person. The next day was excruciating as she waited to hear from the authorities. Later in the evening on the second day of his disappearance, she received a visit from the police. They found Steve's body at their beach condominium.

He wrote a note to his wife apologizing for the pain she was about to endure and then took his own life. She fell to pieces. She could not believe this happened. How could this happen? According to the final police investigation, Steve had been gambling more and more over the past couple of years until he reached a point where everything they owned was in lien to the bank.

> **Addictions take a terrible toll on our communities and society.**

He even took out several large loans to cover his losses. Not only was he in debt to the bank, but there were also several people with questionable character to whom he owed a great deal of money. He made one last bet with borrowed money from a one of these shady characters in an attempt to get out from under this terrible financial trouble by making that one big score. He lost again.

The pressure of losing was more than he could bear. Until now, Steve's wife had no idea they were in financial ruin. She would have to start over, without a skill or husband, and with no money or assets with which to help. Her outlook on life was bleak at this point.

Consequences of Addictions

Addictions result in very serious, and many times terrible, consequences in the lives of addicts and their loved ones. Gambling is only one of many addictions. Drugs, alcohol, pornography, and tobacco are but a few addictions among many.

The consequences of these addictions can be, and many times are, as devastating as the portrayal at the end of the above story. Addictions take a terrible toll on our communities and society. Addictions remove from our society people who would otherwise be productive.

The problems resulting from addictions also cost citizens who are productive, by creating the need for more tax money necessary to fund research and treatment facilities in an effort to combat addictions in our society. It has become necessary for the government to research and treat addictions in state programs, as well as make it necessary to deal with the consequences of addictions many times in our court systems because the Church has not taken seriously the threat of addictions.

Sins of addiction are the results of choices men make that are in disobedience to the laws of God. All sin is disobedience to God's law and results in separation from the Creator. Sin prevents a person from achieving the intended purpose for which they were created. Separation from God began in the Garden of Eden and continues to this day. Only by Salvation through the shed blood of Jesus Christ applied to a person's heart and life can a person be reconciled to God. This is God's plan of redemption and the only way to freedom from life-controlling behaviors.

God desires that His creation have a meaningful relationship with Him. This relationship is only accomplished through a personal relationship with His Son, Jesus Christ. Sin drives man away from this fellowship and from the purpose for which he was created. This separation is accompanied by the damage caused by addictions, and makes the situation for the addict worse.

Emotional Damage
All addictions begin with the "first something," whether this "something" is the first experience with drugs, alcohol, gambling or other activity. These addictions ultimately create a shame or guilt that controls the mind of the addict. Many individuals continue to hide behind these sins of addiction because of this guilt and shame. As a person goes deeper into the addiction, the more guilt and shame they feel.

This vicious cycle will ultimately result in the destruction of the individual. Relationships are destroyed along the way. The most common relationships destroyed by addiction behavior are the relationships the addict has with friends and family. Other things often destroyed are jobs, financial independence, and even personal freedom in many cases.

The use of chemical substances, and other harmful behaviors are not only attempts to block out the feelings of guilt and shame later in the addiction, but are also an effort before the addiction to try and gain a feeling of acceptance. This desire to mask one's reality stems from feelings of inadequacy and disappointment.

These feelings of inadequacy are usually manifested in a person's life as the result of one of two things; either the parent or guardian's un-met expectations being blamed on the person, or the parent or guardian's lack of involvement in the person's life. The former creates an overwhelming sense of guilt in the mind of the addict. The latter causes deep feelings of insecurity, which allows opportunity for improper and unhealthy relationships of various types including worse addiction behaviors. The use of alcohol and drugs, or the harmful behaviors of voyeurism, gambling, as well as many other activities, become "relationships" in and of themselves and many times are a replacement, or type of substitute, for the right relationships that should be in the person's life.

The use of alcohol or other chemical substance gives a person a false sense of control over their circumstances. This control becomes a part of the addiction process and acts as a catalyst for the replacement of normal relationships. In other words, it becomes easier to build a relationship with the drug of choice, or the particular addiction of choice, than with people. As time passes, normal relationships with people become less important; until the only relationship an addict desires to have is with his addiction of choice.

The addict will try to spend as much time with the addiction as possible. He will spend all his money for it. He will even resort to stealing and committing other crimes in order to facilitate the continuation of this relationship. Ultimately, there are no boundaries the addict will not cross in order to continue the relationship they have cultivated with their particular addiction.

The addiction of smoking cigarettes is a powerful example of this truth. Most people view cigarettes as a harmless addiction, but any person held in the grasp of tobacco will disagree. As a side note, I have read that cigarettes are quite possibly the most traded commodity in the prison system of our country. Even though tobacco and cigarettes are not allowed in many facilities they are still smuggled in and used as bartering currency. This demonstrates the grip smoking tobaccos can have on any society.

The addiction of smoking cigarettes is perhaps one of the most difficult habits to break in the life of a person. Smoking also opens the door for other more damaging addictions as well. It is not difficult to progress from nicotine to marijuana to cocaine in a short period.

> **God desires that His creation have a meaningful relationship with Him.**

When an addict faces the prospect of losing this kind of relationship, they experience the same feelings as if they were losing a loved one or close friend. These feelings of grief include, but are not limited to anger, denial, bargaining, depression, and acceptance. Some stages may last longer than others may and can occur in a different order than what is given here. Other stages may not even take place at all, depending on the individual.

Physical Damage

The choice to engage in addictive activities often results in physical damage to the addict. Even though the addict knows right from wrong, they still make choices that bring about consequences that many times result in extreme physical damage to them. Physical damage includes organs of the body as well as the brain. This damage can be, and often is, permanent.

For example, in the case of alcohol use, organs are damaged by the absorption of the alcohol into the tissue of the organ. The most common organ damaged by alcohol is the liver.

"The liver breaks down alcohols into acetaldehyde by the enzyme alcohol dehydrogenase and then into acetic acid by the enzyme acetaldehyde dehydrogenase. Next, the acetate is converted into fats or carbon dioxide and water. Chronic drinkers, however, so tax this metabolic pathway that things go awry: fatty acids build up as plaques in the capillaries around liver cells and those cells begin to die, which leads to the liver disease cirrhosis. The liver is part of the body's filtration system, which, if damaged, allows certain toxins to build up leading to symptoms of jaundice. Some people's DNA code calls for a different acetaldehyde dehydrogenase, resulting in a more potent alcohol dehydrogenase. This leads to a buildup of acetaldehyde after alcohol consumption causing the alcohol flush reaction with hangover-like symptoms such as flushing, nausea, and dizziness." (1)

The prolonged use of any chemical substance can have a tremendous negative effect on organs of the body, the brain, and nervous system. A partial list of these substances is:

- Stimulants - cocaine, amphetamines, caffeine
- Hallucinogens - mescaline, LSD, PCP, marijuana
- Depressants - alcohol, barbiturates, sleeping pills, inhalants
- Opiates - morphine, codeine, heroin, methadone
- Psychotherapeutics - Xanax, Valium, Ativan

While it is not our desire to present a clinical approach to this issue, we do feel it is worthy to mention here the devastating affects chemical substances have on the body. There are many other good resources available today which give very detailed information concerning the effects of the misuse of certain chemical substances.

---

(1)(From Wikipedia, the free encyclopedia, article: "Alcohol Metabolism" and "Letters to the (almost) Doctor" located at: **http://endeavor.med.nyu.edu/~strone01/doctor.html**)

Drugs are certainly not the only addiction that has adverse effects on an individual. More information about the effects of chemical substances on the human body is available through other sources. Although physical and emotional damage often occur there is also psychological damage that often develops that may be undetected for long periods of time in some individuals especially in dealing with pornography and gambling addictions.

The sin of voyeurism, which includes the viewing of pornographic material, and gambling addictions, have just as devastating, if not more so, an effect on an individual as do drugs and alcohol use. Society as a whole does not recognize this because many people view gambling and pornography as innocent entertainment. What people do not realize is the devastating consequences of these addictions in the lives of those used up, kicked aside, and eventually destroyed, in the pornography industry, and the devastation of children or other family members of men and women caught in the clutches of a gambling addiction.

Once these types of activities are accepted into the lifestyle of an individual, the activities become very aggressive in nature by requiring of the individual all their time and resources. The force of the addiction then determines the resulting mind-set and thinking processes. As a result, the addict finds it very difficult to think or act in any manner not related in some way to the addiction.

When confronted with new experiences, the addict will even judge these new experiences according to the demands of the behaviors associated with the particular addiction. Over time, every behavior becomes an extension of the addiction because the brain responds instinctively to similar circumstances based upon previous experiences. This vicious cycle cannot be easily broken.

Addictions that pertain to pornography require much time to overcome because the behaviors and habits associated with them are multi-faceted to such a degree that they affect every aspect of the social life of the individual. Any social activity or interaction with the opposite sex simply becomes a source for more damaging behavior or even fantasy. Many times the addict cannot tell the difference between fantasy and reality in their conduct in these relationships.

Because it is so easy to hide pornography addiction, it is perhaps the most difficult of all addictions to recognize and treat. Pornography addiction is usually carried out in the privacy of one's home or office. Many people feel that the internet is the cause of this problem, but it is the end user to blame. The internet is only a media source, many times used for the wrong reasons.

> ...we live in a world laden with pornographic advertising and entertainment.

The internet is a wonderful tool to get the Gospel to the world, but it can also be a tremendous scourge on the world and body of Christ if not handled correctly. Many Christian workers and leaders find themselves entangled with the temptation to view pornographic material that is readily available on the internet. This is not the result of pornography being available, but rather the spiritual condition of the person. If their relationship with Christ were what it should be, then their response to the sin of pornography would be the same as Christ's response.

Pornography addiction holds a person in one of the strongest grips of any life-controlling behavior. Let us take an honest look at this terrible life-controlling habit. I have heard many people say that this problem in their life was the result of an outside influence. I have even heard preachers say that their pornography addiction was God bringing them to a place of humility and dependence upon Him. While I believe this can be the result if the person surrenders this sin to God, I do not believe God created the addiction. Pornography addiction is the result of a person's lust of the flesh. James 1:14 says,

> "But every man is tempted, when he is drawn away of his own lust, and enticed. Then when lust hath conceived, it bringeth forth sin: and sin, when it is finished, bringeth forth death."

God has clearly told us that He does not tempt man with evil. James 1:13 says,

> "Let no man say when he is tempted, I am tempted of God: for God cannot be tempted with evil, neither tempteth he any man:"

We understand that we create the temptations in our life by our own activities, and that God has nothing to do with sinful temptations. However, God is merciful to us and gives us a way to resist the temptations we produce by the lusts of the flesh. 1Corinthians 10:13 says,

> "There hath no temptation taken you but such as is common to man: but God is faithful, who will not suffer you to be tempted above that ye are able; but will with the temptation also make a way to escape, that ye may be able to bear it."

What is this "way" that God has created that will enable us to escape these temptations? Galatians 5:16 says,

> "This I say then, Walk in the Spirit, and ye shall not fulfill the lust of the flesh."

This brings us full circle, to where we understand that pornography addiction is nothing more than a person lusting after that, which does not belong to them. Jesus said in Matthew 5:28,

> "But I say unto you, That whosoever looketh on a woman to lust after her hath committed adultery with her already in his heart."

Jesus deals with four topics in this passage of Scripture. All of them reveal a single condition. The first subject is a man looking. This speaks of a man who is seeking to gratify his flesh. We understand that those who are lost naturally live this way and do not see the consequences of this activity. Unfortunately, this activity has found its way into the life of many Christians as well.

Many local church leaders have fallen prey to this devastating habit. This activity in the life of a Christian is the result of disobedience to the Word of God. The Christian who takes part in this behavior is forgetting several things; that Christ died for them at Calvary, paying the penalty of their sin; that the Holy Spirit lives in them and therefore present when they involve themselves in this addiction behavior; and if they are married, they are defrauding their spouse.

The second aspect Jesus deals with in this passage of Scripture is lust. The person Jesus is talking about here already has a problem. The lust he has for looking on the flesh of a woman who does not belong to him reveals this problem. Prolong viewing of pornographic material creates an image in the mind of the participant that prevents them from being satisfied when they are with their spouse. A spouse cannot possibly meet the unreasonable expectations of a person addicted to pornography.

This brings us to the third subject with which Jesus deals: the subject of adultery. Again, God is dealing with the heart on this issue. If a man looks at another woman in a way that allows him to desire that woman in a physical way, God is saying that because it is already in his heart to do so, he has committed adultery. Many times pornography addiction results in infidelity and divorce, which carries many more repercussions for children and other family members. The results of an addiction to pornography can grow far beyond adultery and divorce; it can lead to a perverse lifestyle that destroys all semblance of normality.

When a person is heavily engaged in pornography addiction behaviors, their mind is drawn into an unrealistic realm of fantasy and expectation. When these fantasies are acted upon, they result in unmet expectations that further draw the addict into behaviors that are more perverted in an attempt to gain the same level of excitement. This pattern is called: "The law of diminishing returns."

The last subject Jesus deals with in the passage is the heart of the person he is describing. The Bible speaks much about the heart of man. Scripture tells us how the heart both effects and reveals at the same time. This is because the heart is the seat of the emotion and will. Consider the following passages of Scripture:

> Jeremiah 17:9 – "The heart is deceitful above all things, and desperately wicked: who can know it?"
>
> Proverbs 4:23 – "Keep thy heart with all diligence; for out of it are the issues of life."
>
> Luke 6:45 – "A good man out of the abundance of his heart bringeth forth that which is good; and an evil man out of the evil treasure of his heart bringeth forth that which is evil; for of the abundance of the heart his mouth speaketh."
>
> Proverbs 23:7a – "For as he thinketh in his heart, so is he:"

Another reason pornography addiction is hard to recognize is that we live in a world laden with pornographic advertising and entertainment. We are bombarded daily with some form of pornography. This includes partial, and in some cases, full nudity in television programs and movies. Even advertisements use many forms of so-called soft pornography to sell products. Therefore, recognition of pornography addiction may be masked by our senses because we have accepted the use of pornography as normal in our society. This is a very dangerous state of mind, as it can result in acceptance of this devastating addiction.

The Bible is very specific about sins that are the result of lust and sexual deviancy. These sins are against the flesh and result in harsh consequences. God does not look lightly on sins against the body, especially for those individuals that are in the family of God because our bodies do not belong to us. We are the temple of the Holy Ghost. As the temple of the Holy Ghost, we are to remain pure and free from sinful behaviors of fleshly indulgence.

As Christians, we should not allow ourselves to be influenced by the overwhelming amount of pornographic material displayed every day by the mainstream media. We have a responsibility to God to live holy lives as He has commanded. We also have a responsibility to protect our children and grandchildren from the ravages of this terrible industry.

Sin

Drug and alcohol use, pornography, gambling, tobacco use, as well as many other indulgences, are only outward manifestations of an inner condition of a person's heart. The manifestation of addictions is the result of a root problem the Bible calls sin.

Sin, put in its simplest term, is disobedience to God's laws. When a person is right with God there is a desire within that person to please God and to live in a manner that is obedient to the laws of God; this desire is present even when, at times, they fall short of this goal. This desire is the result of the quickening of or making alive the inner man or soul of a person who has accepted Jesus Christ as their personal Saviour. This desire will grow to be stronger than the desire to satisfy one's self.

> **God gives us the desire to please Him when we trust Jesus Christ for salvation.**

God gives us the desire to please Him when we trust Jesus Christ for salvation. A person who is not right with God will do almost anything to try to suppress the natural working of the conscience, which lets the person know that they are in contradiction or disobedience to God's laws. This person will try to hide or cover up the convicting work of the conscience that God created as a natural part of every human being.

A person who lives in disobedience to God will make every effort to fill their waking hours with things that distract them from the reminder that they are not right with God. Alcohol, drugs, gambling, and pornography, are among the top distractions used to accomplish this aim. Even excessive sports participation, television and other seemingly harmless activities, may accomplish the same purpose.

I must make it clear that our conscience is not our guide. God's Word is our guide. Our conscience can be, and most often is, influenced greatly by the activities we allow into our life. Our conscience responds mainly to what it is taught. Therefore, it will only guide us according to what it has learned through experience. This is why it is critical that a person begin following Christ in obedience to God's Word early in life.

There is a part of the conscience that God has created to give all human beings a natural awareness of His existence. Over time, this natural awareness can be reduced to nearly nothing through constant sinful activities. However, this awareness of God is very real in a person.

For example, Helen Keller was born in 1880. She became a blind, deaf, mute having acquired these handicaps before the age of two years old due to an illness. As a young child, she would have fits of anger, smashing dishes and breaking things with a terrible temper. Her relatives considered her a monster. Helen met Anne Sullivan at the age of six. For nearly sixty years, Helen Keller and Anne Sullivan would become inseparable.

There was a bond created between the two of them that would only be broken at Anne's death in 1936. Anne opened the world of language to the blind and deaf Helen. Anne, also being blind, taught Helen to understand language through finger spelling. This was the first time anyone could communicate with Helen and there came a time when Anne wished to tell Helen about God.

As Anne began to talk to Helen through the finger spelling, telling her about God, Helen replied to Anne, "Good, I have been thinking about Him for a long time." How was this possible? How could a young girl, who had never seen or heard, know about the Creator, except it be placed in her conscience by the Creator Himself?

God has commanded us in Exodus, chapter 20, to have no other gods before Him. Anything that takes the place of God in our life is an idol. Idolatry is the worship of the creature rather than the Creator. Addictions are simply idolatry; idols are things that we allow to dominate our time and energy leaving God only what is left over, if anything. Adam and Eve tried to hide themselves from God after they sinned. People today do the same thing by blocking out the convicting nature and consciences, making them believe they can hide from God.

> **God's terms for coming to Him are that we must have our sin dealt with first.**

We understand that when a person finds themself living contrary to God's Word, or laws, it inevitably leads to a diminished standing with God, other men, and even one's own self. When we act contrary to God's law by committing sins of addiction, many consequences follow.

Addictions affect our relationship with God

When a Believer in Christ commits sins of addiction, or any sin for that matter, fellowship with God is broken because of this disobedience. This does not mean the Believer is no longer a child of God. Only the fellowship is broken, not the relationship.

For example, if my son were to disobey me, even though our fellowship may be broken for a brief period, he is still my son. He does not cease from being my son just because he disobeyed me. He is not my son because he obeys me; he is my son because he was born into my family. He will always be my son regardless of what he does - No matter how horrible a thing he might do.

When a non-Believer, someone who is not a member of God's family, commits a sin, the judgment and penalty for that sin has already been established. Because that person has broken God's laws, a judgment is made of "guilty." This is the result of a person *not* being born again into the family of God. (John 3:3-8) Man has the choice of whether or not to accept God's plan for eternal life, however, man must come to God on God's terms rather than on man's terms. The Bible also says in Romans 6:23,

"For the wages of sin is death; but the gift of God is eternal life through Jesus Christ our Lord."

We see in this verse a very clear picture of the purpose for Jesus coming to this earth. This purpose was to pay the sin debt for all humanity and therefore pay the penalty for sin that God demanded. The Bible says in Romans 3:23,

"For all have sinned, and come short of the glory of God."

The judgment of guilty is not only made, but the sentence is also passed. This sentence is death. This death is ultimately man's separation from God in Hell. All a person must do to avoid this separation is to, by faith, trust in Jesus Christ for salvation and they will be born into the family of God.

When we accept the truth that Jesus already paid our penalty for sin, which was His death on the cross of Calvary, we do not have to pay this penalty ourselves. This, according to the preceding verse, was the gift that God gave to us. The great thing about this gift is that it is free to anyone who will receive it!

God's terms for coming to Him are that we must have our sin dealt with first. Man's terms are that he wants to go to Heaven so he will try to live a good life or even pray a prayer to have the chance. Everyone wants to go to Heaven, but wanting to go there and living a "good" life is not what God requires.

God requires that our sins be forgiven. Our sins are forgiven through believing that Jesus Christ is God's Son and that He died on the cross to satisfy God's requirement for the payment of our sin. By placing our faith and trust in Jesus Christ alone for the forgiveness of our sin, and accepting Him as our personal Lord and Saviour, God births us into His family.

Natural Law

Even though a person may be in the family of God, there are still consequences for sin committed in the flesh. These consequences are Natural Laws. Natural Laws are laws that God established that are given to us for instruction, and pertain to the actions of any person, regardless of race, religion, or gender.

> **A literal burning hell awaits all those who reject Jesus Christ as their Saviour.**

The Unbeliever and Believer alike are accountable to these natural laws. The type of law that is local, state, and national, is not a natural law. The punishment for breaking these laws is carried out through means such as receiving a ticket, citation, or time in jail. The type of natural law created by God has the same consequence for both the Believer and Non-Believer alike, and is attached to a particular action. This is the "Law of sewing and reaping." This law is given to man in the Word of God for the benefit of man. We find this law in Galatians 6:7. It says,

> "Be not deceived; God is not mocked: for whatsoever a man soweth, that shall he also reap."

This is where men get the saying, "What goes around, comes around." Consider the following verse of the Bible John 3:17 & 18,

> "For God sent not his Son into the world to condemn the world; but that the world through him might be saved. He that believeth on him is not condemned: but he that believeth not is condemned already, because he hath not believed in the name of the only begotten Son of God."

There is also another effect of sin in the life of a "lost" person. When a person who is not born again into the family of God sins, that person wounds their own conscience each time they commit sin. This person, over time, may wound their conscience so much that they become hardened to the gospel message of Christ. This person may then begin to commit terrible sins merely for the fun of it, reducing themselves to such a low state that they try to get others to become as they are. The Bible speaks of this condition as "having their conscience seared with a hot iron;" Make no mistake about it; there is no fun in the consequences of this condition. A literal burning hell awaits all those who reject Jesus Christ as their Saviour. Romans 1:28 says,

> "And even as they did not like to retain God in their knowledge, God gave them over to a reprobate mind, to do those things which are not convenient;"

God tells us in Romans 1:29-32 that He will also give men over to their sinful ways. Any time a person, acts in dependence upon anything accept God it displeases Him. This includes dependency upon a one's self or a 12-step list of ideals. Proverbs 3:5-7 says,

> "Trust in the LORD with all thine heart; and lean not unto thine own understanding. In all thy ways acknowledge him, and he shall direct thy paths. Be not wise in thine own eyes: fear the LORD, and depart from evil."

When a person places their dependency upon a chemical substance, they are saying either there is no God, or they are simply rejecting the knowledge of God. Having a dependency on anyone or anything other than God, is a false dependency, therefore, a false hope. This type of thinking creates, or gives place to, addiction behavior that results in the consequences of the natural law associated with that behavior or habit.

Addictions affect our standing with others

In the beginning, the addict hopes to gain a feeling of euphoria or some other physical sensation or "high" by using chemical substances, gratification of their flesh, or participation in some other illicit activity. They want to feel good. They do not think about what it may be doing to their body or their mind. This is where idolatry begins.

Men worship themselves (the creature) through self-gratification, and continue to disbelieve anything negative will happen to them. The addict does not believe, at first, this pattern of behavior will change anything in their life; especially with the relationships they have with their family, friends, and coworkers. They are convinced that they can continue this self-gratifying activity and control the addiction rather than the addiction controlling them. This is never the case when it comes to addictions. Ultimately, the addiction will control every aspect of the addict's life.

At later stages in the addiction, and after all relationships have been destroyed, just trying to reach a feeling of normalcy is a terrible struggle for the addict. They must continue the destructive behavior just to feel normal. The result of this is a greater emptiness and greater alienation from people that love them.

It has been said that, "Sin will take you farther than you are willing to go, keep you longer than you are willing to stay, and cost you more than you are willing to pay." How true this is, certainly in the life of the addict. The results of addictions are devastating on the relationships of the addict. However, the saddest part of this is the separation and loss of those relationships that could be truly meaningful in their life - The most important one being the relationship they could have with God.

Society
Sins of addiction diminish one's standing with their fellow man by failing to meet the expectations society has of its citizens. A person who is controlled by sins of addiction rarely, if ever, contribute to the socioeconomic development of the community that surrounds them, or in the general society of the country in which they live. Instead, these individuals are a drain on society and its resources.

They are a burden to society because the resources needed to deal with the negative side effects of their addiction are kept from other social programs that are useful to the community as a whole. There are many other detrimental effects addiction behaviors have on so many different facets and functions of the community of which the addict is a part.

Many times addicts are also on the wrong side of the law simply because of the illegal use of controlled substances. They often find themselves on the wrong side of the law because the money required to support the addiction is so great, many times the addict resorts to illegal activities such as theft, fraud, illegal manufacturing, etc., to continue their behavior. Sins of addiction, therefore, alter, in a profound negative way, the addict's relationship with society in general.

Family and Friends

Addicts are rarely able to maintain a consistent healthy relationship with even their closest family members; whether this be their spouse, parents, children, siblings, or close relatives. This includes the close friend and co-worker as well. The reason for this is that the relationship the addict has with the addiction is stronger than all other relationships.

> **The most common reason for drinking is social acceptance.**

When we consider the amount of money, time, and energy spent by the addict to propagate the addiction, this becomes clearly understandable. The addiction requires so much interaction and attention there is no room left for other relationships. Therefore, friends and family take a back seat to the relationship the addict has with the addiction. All other relationships become what could be considered a threat to the addiction activities.

This threat, along with the shame and guilt that accompanies addiction, is more than the addict can consciously handle. It is much easier, and emotionally safer, to just seclude one's self from friends and family and continue the addiction. Addictions may only appear to affect a small percentage of our society, but in truth have very far-reaching consequences.

There has been much damage to the moral infrastructure of our society because of addictions. This infrastructure consists of values and principles that have been in place for centuries. These values and principles are ignored when addictions have control in the life of a person. The resulting consequence is a tearing down of social stability.

When there is no foundation or objective standard by which people make decisions for their life, they make decisions based solely on the emotional desire of the moment. This is a good definition of addiction in and of itself. When pre-established and proven principles of truth and right are not upheld in society, chaos and a sense that any behavior is OK, whether it harms someone or not, is the result.

The Functioning Addict
There is a stage where the addict does not believe they are an addict. This denial stage is actually earlier than most people want to recognize. The reason for this is that many people are what we call "social" users, whether it is drug or alcohol use.

For example, a person may begin drinking a glass of wine with his meal, either from personal desire, pressure at an evening dinner with coworkers, or may even begin at home with their spouse. This activity seems harmless at first. In fact, many people state that this is the only time they drink. This may be the case, but when we consider that it is more common that a person not like the taste of alcohol the first time they try it, and therefore it must be an acquired taste, such a statement does not make sense.

Very few people actually like the taste of alcohol on their first drink. Therefore, they must force themselves to drink the alcohol. There are many reasons a person chooses to drink alcohol even though they may not like the taste. The most common reason for drinking is social acceptance. This brings out a very important point.

Many people do not have the internal or emotional strength to refuse social drinking because they feel it will alienate them from their boss, or make them look as if they are not a team player. Many good people have fallen into this terrible trap. The pressure from coworkers and managers can be unrelenting, but principled people must never trade their principles for acceptance, no matter what the cost to their position or status as an employee.

Another reason given is - "It calms me from the long day of working at the office." This is in itself a dependency on the alcohol to calm their nerves rather than some other non-chemical method. Is it not much better to allow the Lord to calm us than to use some chemical that is dangerously harmful to our bodies and carries with it such a great risk of addiction?

This person eventually moves from the stage of "forcing themselves to drink alcohol" to a person who is now over the dislike phase and has progressed to the, I am use to it, stage. Keep in mind that they had to force themselves to get to this phase. Most people will say at this point, "I didn't have to force myself." This is a natural response and expected. This is the classic statement of denial, which makes them feel better about their condition.

From here, the addiction grows stronger. The person will continue with denial until they convince themselves they are not addicted, and they just choose to drink. When they are shown the progression of the addiction, by pointing out the time they reached the stage of drunkenness for the first time, they may even respond with anger. This drunken state is how the body naturally rejects harmful chemicals. They still do not accept the idea that they are now well on their way to destroyed relationships and a destroyed life. At this stage, they are what we call a "functioning addict."

At this point, they will reject even the notion that they are controlled in any way by the alcohol. They will attest that they are in control and they can stop any time they want. Then why do they not? The answer is, because they cannot. Even though they may say they like drinking and can function reasonably well with their role in society, there is still the "need" to drink some kind of alcoholic beverage.

The stage of "functioning addict" is a precursor to the "non-functioning addict." It is very difficult to stop using a chemical substance once begun. Alcohol is a drug. As a drug, it has terrible side effects on the human body when ingested into the system.

There is an affection with addictions that is stronger, in most cases, than the natural relationships one may have with other people. Just as with human relationships, the addict will spend an enormous amount of time with their addiction. They care about it, think about, plan schedules around it, and feel pain when separated from the object of their addiction.

> **God's laws do not change and they are non-negotiable; we do not bargain with God.**

As an example, because alcohol is accepted in our society, and is legal to both sell and possess, there is a deception surrounding alcohol addiction. The deception is, because it is legal, it must be OK. This is very dangerous especially in the life of a Christian. The use of alcohol as a beverage can, not only result in an addiction in the life of a Christian, but it can also be an obstacle for a weaker Christian. If a person is honest enough to admit they have a problem with an addiction, they are in a place to receive help; however, there is a battle that will be fought in their life throughout the process of recovery.

Those who commit themselves to a rehab or recovery program are faced with the same emotional battle as one who has lost a loved one might face. This is because when a relationship is severed, there is a natural process of grief that takes place. There are usually five stages to this grieving process. These stages are well known in the health and rehab community. They are as follows: Denial, Bargaining, Anger, Grief or Depression, and Acceptance. These stages do not necessarily take place in this order, nor do they each necessarily take place in every individual.

Denial:
Denial is a self-preservation mechanism triggered in an attempt to resist or avoid the truth. This is particularly true in the life of an addict. Most people, who are chemically dependent, will experience denial, even at the expense and hurt of themselves and those closest to them. It is necessary for the addict to recognize this stage early and to admit honestly their guilt to God, who is the only source of help and hope for them. This opens the door for true healing to begin and reduces the likelihood for continued decline. Admitting they are guilty will allow the "recovery" process to begin.

Bargaining:
Bargaining is typically a reaction by a person who is at a stage where they do not realize the reality of their condition. At this phase, or stage, they may think they can maintain or control the decline by determining for themselves the level of treatment they require. They may feel they are still in control and want to bargain their way through the process by, once again, determining for themselves where they are in the stage of addiction recovery. They do not realize their condition. They may feel no need of making progress toward recovery whatsoever. Many times this process of bargaining takes place with a person who does understand the condition they are in, but still desires to have the benefits, as they perceive them, of the addiction.

In other very practical terms, bargaining is attempted when a person who is hiding their addiction is caught, whether by a family member or a law enforcement officer. At this point, they are willing to do just about anything to keep from paying the penalty of their actions. Any level of bargaining results in the erosion of any positive movement toward recovery. We are reminded that obedience to God and His law cannot be bargained.

God's laws do not change and they are non-negotiable; we do not bargain with God. His laws, principles, and precepts are absolute and do not change. God loves and is compassionate toward His creation, but we must not mistake His compassion for something it is not. God still demands and deserves holy living in the lives of His creation. This bargaining attitude should always be avoided; humility is the key attitude in obtaining God's help and mercy.

Bargaining is also another way of justifying a person's own actions. The "bargaining" takes place internally when they make themselves believe they are not as bad as someone else in their condition is. Therefore, they bargain with themselves to only do activities that are "not as bad" as someone else's activities.

Anger:
Anger is one of the basic of all human emotions. The Bible says, "Be angry and sin not." It is not wrong to be angry. It is what we do with the emotion of anger that can become sinful. Many times a person will allow the emotion of anger to dictate an improper behavior toward oneself and to others. This improper behavior is sinful, and must be guarded against. It is possible to use the emotion of anger to change a behavior that needs correcting. This is the proper response. If, however, anger is not turned loose of, then additional problems occur.

A person should never hold on to the emotion of anger because it can very quickly turn into bitterness. It has been said, "Bitterness destroys the vessel that contains it." Anger is a natural emotional response by a person who feels a fear of loss when there has been an injustice or offense carried out against them, even when the perpetrator is themselves.

The right response is forgiveness. It is extremely difficult for those who are struggling with sins of addiction to forgive themselves much less someone else. Such lack of forgiveness yields bitterness in the life of the addict. Therefore, we must recognize the need for God's grace to overcome this bitterness and anger.

God's grace, in the form of humility, enables us to, instead of focusing on the offense, focus on the needs of others. This same grace also gives us self-control when faced with temptations and wrong desires. Anger can be a helpful emotion, if responded to correctly.

Grief/Depression:
Grief is an emotion that most people only associate with the loss of a loved one or close friend. Many times, people view grief as a weakness. This is because they do not understand the reason or purpose for this natural emotion. Grief can be a powerful tool in the process of recovery from addiction. By allowing one's self to grieve properly, a cleansing process takes place in a person that may not be accomplished by any other means.

> **When a person's values rest in their achievements or acceptance by others this value may easily be destroyed.**

The grieving process is important to the progression toward the acceptance stage. It starts the addict down the road toward the acceptance stage through cleansing, and paves the way for accepting the truth about their condition. There is no shame in grief. Grief should be embraced and appreciated for its purpose in our lives.

Many times this step is considered a state of depression. Depression is viewed as a time when the person has the attitude of not caring what happens to them. This is not the same as clinical depression. Clinical depression is the result of physical imbalances. What we are talking about is an emotional phase. This emotional phase of grief or depression is normal.

Acceptance:
Acceptance is perhaps one of the more critical elements in this five-step process. Acceptance is also necessary to understand God's truth about recovery. A person who is struggling with addictions should accept the Word of God as the source for true recovery. By also accepting one's condition, there is a realization of the need for help to change. There are many things in the life of the addict that can bring them to a place where they accept their need to

change. This realization opens the door for lasting change in the addict's life.

Addictions affect confidence

Most every person desires to achieve some level of acceptance in society. Most people desire to achieve some level of success and achievement in the eyes of their peers. Some people spend more time and energy on this than others do perhaps, but most everyone has this desire nonetheless. When these expectations are not met time after time, and they remain un-met for a prolonged period, there is an overwhelming sense of failure, which many times opens the door to substance abuse.

When a person's values rest in their achievements or acceptance by others, this value may be easily destroyed. This type of value system may also become, in and of itself, a type of addiction. The need to attain a certain "position" or level of success in the eyes of society is a state of mind that inevitably leads to disappointment in one self.

This may also lead to a desire to withdraw from society or even one's responsibilities as well. A loss of job position can lead to an overwhelming feeling of rejection and failure that can produce a domino effect of downward progression toward addiction. This is one of the reasons why God did not intend for our value and worth as a person to reside in our achievements or accomplishments. The roles we play in life are not what make us who we are. These roles may be: father, mother, brother, sister, employee, employer, etc.

It is important to accept the truth that all things were created for God and for His glory. As part of His creation, we have the responsibility to be obedient to the purpose for which we were created. Sins of addiction hinder and destroy the ability to fulfill this purpose. Only Jesus Christ can give us the strength to overcome this. Sins of addiction are sins that must be confessed, just as any other sin. Through this confession, there is hope. Our hope rests in the person of Jesus Christ.

Some people may be more prone to addiction than others may, but all have a will to choose whether they will participate in addiction forming activities. There is so much warning about addictions today that anyone who falls prey to them is without excuse. Man is responsible for his actions and behaviors. Choosing to drink alcohol, gamble, take drugs, or look at pornography, is a decision that has grave consequences, both on the individual and their family.

As horrible as addictions and the consequences that go along with them are, as ministers of the Gospel of Jesus Christ, we must always convey a reflection of God's love for the addict. We love Him because He first loved us. For the addict to love God enough to change his behavior, the addict must first see the love of God. The addict will see the love of Christ manifested in our lives first.

This truth is essential in teaching addiction recovery. The love of Christ should be a natural part of any person's life that desires to help other people overcome life-controlling habits. It is easy for us to become callused or desensitized to addicts because of the kind of behaviors that are inherent in their activities. When we have a close relationship with the Lord, He reminds us of our own frailties and need for humility. We must recognize that all of human nature is fallen, including our own.

Chapter 3

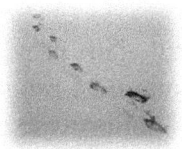

Recovery and Relapse

The most difficult task of an addiction recovery program is to give the addict tools that will permanently deliver them from the clutches of an addiction. It would be wonderful if addiction recovery were possible through changes in a person's environment, this would be an easy fix. Simply move the person to another area and the job is done. We all know this is not the answer.

We know instinctively that changing a person's environment only changes the place from which the addict will carry out his addiction. It would be equally wonderful if we could give the addict a medication prescription that would cure them of their addiction. Besides making the pharmaceutical owners very wealthy, this would do away with much anguish and grief on the part of all parties involved with the addiction. Again, this simply is not the answer.

Most Directors of rehab centers, if they are honest, know that we must deal with addiction and the addict from a different viewpoint. They are not sure what this viewpoint should be, but they know it needs to be one that produces permanent behavior modification to achieve complete recovery. There are support groups, therapy sessions, ongoing counseling, and a myriad of other post-rehab activities that have developed over the years, all for one reason - The problem of relapse. There must be a solution to this problem if we are to effectively stem the raging tide of addictions in our society. The solution can only be found in changing the person from the inside out. Let us take a look at the basics.

Why do people still fall prey to addictions even after attending rehab and other treatment programs? What is the purpose of rehab, if the programs do not provide permanent recovery? These questions reveal a very important aspect that many people, in the field of addiction recovery, fail to acknowledge or simply do not understand.

> We must recognize that every form of addiction begins with the individual, not from an outside influence on the person.

In order to offer a real solution to the dilemma of relapse, we must first understand the true nature of the problems that we are attempting to combat. We must recognize that every form of addiction begins with the individual, not from an outside influence on the person. Why is this important to understand? If we are to know the real solution to addiction problems, there must first be a clear understanding of the addiction and recovery process.

What is the addiction and recovery process? Addiction and recovery are one in the same, once you understand the complete picture. Most addiction recovery programs, both secular and faith-based alike, deal with the aftermath of the addiction, not the root cause of the addiction; It is much like doctors who treat the symptoms of an illness rather than the cause.

As it will be stated more in depth in the next chapter, addictions are simply destructive habits formed over time. Habits are behaviors that take place automatically due to prolonged and duplicated activities and feelings. There can be negative, destructive habits as well as positive, constructive habits.

The only way a Special Forces Operator in the military can perform his duties with accuracy, is through muscle memory training on a daily basis, resulting in disciplined control of his thinking and muscle movements, which in turn become habits of movement. This does not mean that it is necessary for the operator to conduct literal operations daily, it is only necessary to train daily. When it comes time to carry out a covert military operation, the soldier is able to carry out his duties successfully because he is in the habit of doing so through the regimen of daily training.

There are many good habits that people perform on a daily basis that we would say are beneficial. Good personal hygiene, being at work on time, good eating habits, etc., are all behaviors of a person that we would say has good discipline. Yet, these activities are simply habits formed over a period in the life of a person. Recovery is no different.

Once understood that addictions and the solution to addiction behavior is the same process of what we call recovery, it is much easier to develop a program that enables a person to find lasting freedom from the addiction. This is why addiction and relapse are truly not separate issues. Recovery is not the goal. Recovery is the by-product of non-addiction behavior.

The goal of most all Addiction Recovery Programs is for an addict to "recover" from his or her addiction. In fact, when you speak to most individuals who have participated in or are currently participating in AA (Alcoholics Anonymous) or some other similar program they will actually say, "I am a recovering alcoholic" or "I am a recovering drug addict" or "I am recovering" from some other addiction. They are always recovering, never recovered.

It is my belief that this idea of recovery is misguided at best. So, how do we define addiction and recovery? By what criteria do we make a judgment as to whether or not a person has "recovered" from the addiction of alcohol, drugs, or any other addiction?

Many people define recovery in a vague way so they can use this definition to their benefit. This becomes the gauge as to whether or not their particular "program" is effective. This does no one any good, much less the addict. Most rehab facilities have a "track record" that they like to advertise to draw people to their program. This record of accomplishment is promoted as being the number, or percentage, of people that have been successfully treated.

If we are going to change the marginal results of our programs, whether secular or faith-based, we must change our approach to addictions and recovery alltogether. Remember, recovery from addictions is not the goal. Recovery is the by-product of something much more important in a person's life. Recovery is the result of a life surrendered to God. When a person yields their will to the will of God, they place themselves in the wonderful position of receiving help from the Creator.

When a person seeks to have a meaningful relationship with the Creator, they are submitting themselves to the only power available to man to resist the devil and deliver him from the temptations that cause him to behave contrary to God's laws. We must understand that the addict should not pursue recovery as if it were a prize. They must pursue a right relationship with Christ.

When a person pursues a right relationship with Christ, the goals change. The addict no longer looks at addiction as behavior problems; they see addictions as God sees them - As sins. Only then, can a person deal with addictions the way God desires that they deal with them; to repent of the sin and ask for His forgiveness. This is the difference between "Reformation" and "Transformation."

When a person is reformed, they only attain as much recovery as they can muster in and of themselves. (Please see the definition of Reformation in the first chapter) The only thing changed is the surface behaviors. This alone is not sufficient to produce a lasting recovery. When something is broken, it cannot "fix" itself without outside intervention. The very best man can do, with regard to healing himself, is very inadequate to produce a permanent change in his life. My Pastor (Dr. Clarence Sexton) has said often, "God gives His best to those who leave the decisions to Him."

Transformation is completely of God. It is not something that man does. It is what God does in the life of the individual. Transformation is complete; it is permanent, it changes the heart. Transformation is what takes place in the life of a person who trusts in Jesus Christ for salvation. Once this transformation has taken place, the process of "Sanctification" begins.

> **Recovery is the result of a life surrendered to God.**

Before a person can experience freedom from life-controlling habits through the process of transformation and sanctification, they must first have a desire to receive help. If a person does not want to change, it does not matter how many rehab or recovery programs they attend, they will not receive the help they need to break free from the life-controlling habit. Many addicts want a different life, but are not willing to give up the addiction to have it.

Some addicts desire to change, but do not know how to break free from the addiction cycle. Honesty with God and self is the first challenge to overcome. Once a person is honest with God and themselves, they can move forward toward recovery.

Christ-likeness

Sanctification is the process God uses to produce Christ-likeness in the daily life of a person transformed by the power of God. This sanctification takes place over time. For some people there are things changed immediately after becoming a child of God. For others there is a period where God replaces the wrong things that once controlled a person's life with things that are pleasing to Him.

Sanctification is not accomplished in a set period, but in a lifetime. The method God uses to accomplish this is reading, studying, memorizing, and meditating upon His Word, the Bible.

Every person is different; therefore, God deals with each person differently although not apart from His Word. The same power that created the universe and all that is in it, is the same power contained in the Word of God we hold in our hands. This power changes the life of the person controlled by addictions, and nothing else. Such change places the addict on the right path to recovery.

The Right Path

Looking at addictions the way God looks at them is essential in freeing the addict from the bondage that holds them firmly in its grip. The greatest "recovery" that has ever taken place, is given to us in Luke 19:10,

> "For the Son of man is come to seek and to save that which was lost."

Once our "vision" is corrected, we can see the right path to right actions. Once addictions are seen as the sins that they are, they can be dealt with according to how God commands the addict to deal with them. God's way of dealing with sin in our life is for us to repent of our sin and confess our sin to Him. This confession is a humble acknowledgment that we are sinners who have offended a Holy and Righteous God, and that our sins have separated us from Him. In addition, we repent or turn away from, that sin because we know it offends our Saviour who has given Himself for us. ("Repenting" simply means that we honestly agree with God about our sinful condition and change our minds about sin, which leads to a change of behavior and actions.).

We also acknowledge that this repentance is the only way we can have a right relationship with God. This humility brings God's grace to our life. "Grace" is God's unmerited favor. In other words, we do not deserve God's grace, but He extends it to us because of who He is, not because of who we are. The Bible says in Romans 5:20,

> "But where sin abounded, grace did much more abound:"

This obedience of humility results in God's grace bestowed upon our lives. In 1Peter 5:5, the Bible says,

> "for God resisteth the proud, and giveth grace to the humble."

The Right Process

The addict can only come to this place of repentance and understanding through a process of a Systematic Teaching of Biblical Principles. Once the addict's mind is changed, and he is convinced that the path he is currently on is the wrong path, he must go in a different direction. This does not mean that there is never a failure or a mistake made. This gives people peace. They do not "fall off the wagon" as some say. Recovery can then be understood as, a process of sanctification, which takes place over time. Sanctification is not an event; it is a process.

> **Sanctification is the process of God making us Holy.**

When a person stumbles and falls, they get up again, ask God for forgiveness, and move on with their life. However, there is a warning necessary. The Bible warns us against making an occasion to sin. Addicts should not place themselves in the position that encourages them to disobey God further. If drug use is the addiction, the addict must not go to places where he can easily acquire them. If alcohol is the problem, the addict does not need to be around people who are drinking or go in places of business that serve alcohol as a beverage.

If pornography is the problem, the addict needs to avoid the magazine racks and unsupervised Internet usage. Recognizing these truths will help the addict. This is simple, but many fail to take these simple steps. This is why we said previously that addiction and recovery are one in the same. They are the two sides of the same coin, so to speak.

On the one side, there are behaviors that are destructive to the person, and on the other side are the behaviors that are constructive in the person's life. The addict will either flip a coin every day, leaving it to chance whether or not he will live life free from life-controlling habits, or he will decide to spend time in God's Word and in prayer each day, gaining the strength to live free from bondage. Just running out into the world every day without spending time with God is the formula for even the strongest Christian to fail at some point, and many do fail because of a lack of personal time with the Lord.

We must also remember, just because God forgives our sin, does not give us a license to sin. We all must keep ourselves clean from the world, the flesh, and the devil. It is a daily challenge for all of us. If the addict will live according to the Word of God, recovery will take care of itself. If we understand that recovery is the natural result of living according to God's Word, it relieves the addict of the pressure to "do" or "be" something in the eyes of men. What a person does, in the eyes of God, is the most important way to view their actions.

It is a mistake for any program, either secular or faith-based, to expect a person to show results of permanent changes in their life by attending a 30 day recovery program, or by coming to meetings once a week for a few months. The right view of recovery is that we see the need for people to follow Christ in obedience to God's Word each day. This is the true biblical view of addiction recovery.

The Right Person
Sanctification is the process of God making us Holy. God uses this process in our life to bring us closer to Him and to help us "walk in the Spirit." It takes time for the addict to reach a place where they are strong enough to resist the things that have controlled just about every aspect of their life for such a long period. These strongholds are not easily broken down. They can be broken of course, but it is not going to happen overnight.

The addict will not always win these battles, but thank God, He has already won the war! Christians who are strong in the faith also have the same battles everyone else has. The difference is in allowing the Holy Spirit of God to have complete control of one's thoughts, desires, and actions.

The right process is following the right person, Jesus Christ. When we study the Word of God and memorize verses of Scripture, we find they enable a process of cleansing never experienced before by the addict. The addict will eventually "see" the things they were unable to see before. God reveals to the addict the things that are necessary to change their life. He desires that we all be more like His Son, Jesus Christ.

Relapse

If we understand recovery to mean living a life that is obedient to God's Word, we can also understand that relapse is simply a failure to live in obedience to God's Word (the two-sided coin). We must pause here and take a closer look at the meaning of this. We do not want to use a term that will lay an undue burden on someone who is trying to do right.

Some would say recovery is a goal or achievement reached as the result of treatment. If this were the case, we could also say that relapse is the result of a lack of treatment. Treatment, then, becomes the focus. We must look at Recovery and Relapse from a Biblical perspective in order to understand what is necessary to achieve lasting results.

We refer to someone who has relapsed as having "fallen off the wagon." The goal of most programs, both secular and non-secular, is this elusive place on the "wagon." Why do we do this? Whose wagon is it anyway? Where is this wagon going? Who is driving the wagon? Maybe the wagon is going too fast! Maybe there is no one driving and the horses are running wherever they want. In this case, I would want off the wagon myself. On and on we could go. You get the point!

Recovery is talked about as if it is the point at which we can all put down our books and pencils and say, "they've arrived." We can pat each other on the back and say, "see, it did work." Then if they "relapse," we can say, "whew, I guess I'm still needed." This kind of thinking is more prevalent in recovery programs than most people want to admit, and could not be more wrong.

Many people who offer recovery services and are in the "business" of working with addicts need some instrument to validate their existence. Relapse can be easily used as this instrument. Again, I am not saying that an addict should not participate financially in their recovery process, but that the motive of the program provider should be pure.

When the addict goes into relapse, the addict can always be pointed to as being the cause. After all, it is their problem, is it not? Many facilities use relapse as a tool to lure addicts into their program. They claim to have a certain level of success, which refers to the percentage of individuals who have not relapsed after leaving their program.

> **Relapse is an unrealistic measure of the success or failure of recovery programs.**

The problem with this kind of claim is the impossibility of a measurement that can cover the wide variation of results. Who determines the standardization of results? If we are going to use relapse as the criteria of success, there should be clear definitions of the terms used to define success.

Think about the massive amount of labor and resources needed to follow up on the number of addicts who participate in even the smallest of programs. Can we measure the effectiveness of a program? Yes, we can, but not how most are doing it today. There needs to be a total change of this mind set when it comes to defining the success criteria by which we gauge the effectiveness of a program.

What they are really saying is - "We really don't care why they fell off the wagon or that they even fell off the wagon, we just want them to last a certain length of time after completing our program. Moreover, when they finally do relapse we are glad to be here to pick them up again. Oh, and by the way, don't tell anyone, but the money isn't too bad either."

Not all recovery programs that charge for their services have this attitude. Although it is more prevalent than most are willing to admit. I believe an addict should shoulder the financial responsibility for their recovery process, but the program provider should be responsible to give the addict the truth. When the addict participates in the cost of their recovery, this is taking responsibility for their own actions. This attitude is a good start toward the recovery process. If they are willing to invest money in their own recovery they are more likely to be serious about the program in which they choose to participate.

Many ministry programs are also using secular methods, thinking they are helping people be clean or sober. They may even do so, for a period, whether short term or long term. However, the real problem is not being addressed. The real problem is sin - Disobedience to God's laws. Relapse is an unrealistic measure of the success or failure of recovery programs. The Bible tells us in Proverbs 24:16,

"For a just man falleth seven times, and riseth up again:"

God used the number seven as an example of an unspecified number in this passage. In other words, it makes no difference how many times we stumble or fall due to the frailties of the flesh. A person who is trusting in Christ will rise up and continue through the power of God's forgiveness. He tells us in 1John 1:9 that we have the opportunity for complete recovery when He says,

"If we confess our sins, he is faithful and just to forgive us our sins, and to cleanse us from all unrighteousness."

It is unrealistic to think that a person will never stumble once they attend a recovery program. This is placing an unfair expectation and an undue burden on the addict. The Bible also tells us in Ecclesiastes 7:20,

> "For there is not a just man upon the earth, that doeth good, and sinneth not."

If God is telling us that, we are going to stumble, why should recovery programs expect something different? It is my belief that a realistic goal of a recovery program is one in which the addict is discipled by telling them the truth about sin and God's forgiveness of sin through repentance and trusting in His Son, Jesus Christ. Then, they can be given the tools by which they can live a different life. There must be a strong emphasis placed on Scripture memorization, prayer time with God, and the study of God's Word on a daily basis. These are the foundations for a life free from addiction.

> **The correct approach to presenting the gospel to the addict is by starting where God starts in His Word.**

Once this is accomplished, we can look at the life of the addict over a longer period to discover whether they were serious. We will be able to see plainly whether they have applied the lessons taught and the tools given to them during the recovery program. The success of a program should be determined by the measure of character visible in the life of the addict over a period. This is perhaps the best, if not the only, realistic measurement of the success of a recovery program.

The measure of character developed in the life of the addict is revealed by their response to circumstances they encounter. In other words, it is not circumstances that make people what they are; it is circumstances that reveal the character of the person.

The main factors that determine the success of any particular program are the principles and tools given to the addict during the term of the program, and the seriousness of the participant. When we view relapse in light of these factors we understand that relapse is not to be feared or used as a standard to gauge the effectiveness of a program.

The Inner Man

It is the heart of a person that causes him to either obey or disobey the laws of God and man. The inner man needs changing, not the outer environment, for there to be lasting, positive, constructive, behavior in the life of a person. Why would we spend so much time, money, and effort to continue traditional programs that have historically proven to be so marginally effective or outright ineffective? An obvious reason, which we eluded to a couple paragraphs back, is the money gained through operating such a program.

We know some people will be offended by this, and they should be, but it is the truth. Recovery programs are a "growth industry." Their numbers, under the guise of good intentions, are silently and steadily growing. Some of the better-known facilities around the country charge outrageous amounts of money for a single thirty-day program. These amounts reach into the tens of thousands of dollars or more.

There are over 125 registered drug or alcohol treatment programs within a one hundred mile radius of the city in which I live. This number does not include all of the programs that are a part of church organizations and outreach ministries. We know this is duplicated all across the country.

Ministry-based programs have a great opportunity to make a difference in our society now. We recognize that there are many churches that already have a ministry outreach to the addict. We thank the Lord for all of them and want to be an encouragement to each one. There is a tremendous need for many more church ministries in this field. Now is the time for churches and Christians to get involved in this ministry. Addictions are at an all-time high. It will be the Church that makes a lasting difference in this problem.

Some people have the "lock'em in a room with a Bible and God will do the rest" type mentality - Until it is one of their own family members or church members. Then they realize how foolish this idea is. Oh yes, it is the power of the Word of God that transforms a life. However, how we approach this is critical. We must use Biblical methods. There must be understanding and wisdom used in how we present the truths of God's Word to the addict.

Just as our Lord tells us that not all Christians are able to eat meat, the addict is unable to digest anything spiritually until they have been born again, and then only milk to start. There must be a gentleness yet toughness at the same time in this process. There needs to be gentleness concerning Biblical truths: knowing what to present to them when, and toughness in the discipline and routines of administering the program. Finding a balance between the two will come through experience. Addicts are not as tough as some might think. They are actually the opposite. Most are selfish and have a low tolerance for pain.

There are those who have lived a hardened life that are addicted to drugs and alcohol of course, but most of these individuals are incarcerated long term. It is my experience that the majority of addicts simply need salvation. They will come to know God better as they turn their life over to Him, but only as we have given them the tools to accomplish this. As the person grows spiritually, we move on to doctrines and deeper truths of the Scripture.

This process must begin in their hearts and flow out in their lives as they "work out" their own salvation, by working and teaching others what they have learned. It will take time for the addict's body to rid itself of the toxins and effects of the chemicals built up in their system. This could take 36 months or even longer depending on the level of drug or alcohol use, or the severity of the mental disruption.

The addict's mental state can also make it very difficult for them to perform even normal logical thought processes. This hinders the addict from understanding even the simplest concept. Therefore, it is important how we present the gospel to them. The gospel must be presented to them in a different manner than we would to a healthy person who does not have an addiction problem. The same gospel that speaks to the hearts of everyone is the gospel the Holy Spirit will use in the life of the addict to bring them to Christ. The difference is in how we deliver this message of the gospel.

The correct approach to presenting the gospel to the addict is by starting where God starts in His Word: In the beginning (Genesis 1:1). Most addicts have had very little, if any, teaching concerning spiritual matters. The majority of addicts have had few good role models to pattern their life after. Because of the combination of the lack of knowledge of spiritual things and the damage caused by drug and alcohol use, the thinking and reasoning of the addict are much different from ours. Therefore, it is necessary to lay a foundation on which to present the gospel.

Experience has proven that when a clear foundation of basic truths is laid prior to presenting the gospel, there is more responsiveness and openness to the gospel on the part of the addict. This is not always the case, but in the majority of cases, this is the right method. Since it is more beneficial, in most cases, to lay this foundation first, it is to the advantage of the teacher and ultimately the addict to follow this guideline.

It is important to recognize that whatever curriculum the teacher employs in teaching addiction recovery, that addiction recovery is not as much about the program curriculum as it is about the addict giving God His rightful place in their life. Chapters seven through twelve give basic principles that cover this concept in the proper manner. Following the order given in these chapters will enable the Director of the addiction recovery ministry to present these truths to the addict in a way they can build upon to receive the Gospel into their heart at the time God appoints. When this model is followed, the addict comes to understand the principles necessary to make a choice concerning following Christ. I have successfully used this process model in addiction recovery programs.

Recovery and Relapse do not have to be a mystery to anyone, especially the local church ministry. Using these terms interchangeably, and understanding that they are really two sides of the same coin, will help the recovery ministry educator to approach their own ministry from a Biblical viewpoint. Having this viewpoint is necessary for an effective program.

Chapter 4

Recognizing Addictions

As soon as Bill and Nancy walked up the steps and into the church foyer they noticed an unusual silence around the auditorium. Theirs was an average size church with around 300 people regular in Sunday school. The morning service was a special time at their church. The singing, preaching, and fellowship afterwards were such a wonderful time for Bill and his wife. He and his wife Nancy were usually one of the last families to leave the property after the services. They enjoyed talking with other families, the Pastor, and Music Director, after the service was over. They would always let them know what a blessing the service was. They also enjoyed talking to the friends they have made since joining the church more than five years ago.

Everyone in the church seemed to be very close. Many families had grown children with families of their own who were also members. There were many children and young people in their church. This was quite unusual for the churches in their area and they were glad their church had a good youth program. Bill and Nancy were serving in several different ministries of the church and he was currently serving as a Deacon. He had served as the assistant to the Music Director at their previous church and had filled in from time to time here when the full-time Director was not present. There was usually a good bit of activity before the services.

This time things were different. Small groups of people formed all around the auditorium. Bill knew instinctively that something was wrong. This was very unusual. Before he could set his Bible down on his pew, one of the Pastor's staff approached him. "Bill can we go somewhere private and talk for a minute?" the staff member asked. "Sure" Bill replied. Now his mind was racing even more than before. What could be going on that has caused such a stir around the church this morning. This church was not the gossipy kind of church that they had experienced before. This was a very spiritual and loving church. The people had a genuine love for one another.

What could possibly be the reason for all the commotion? As Bill stepped into the side office of the church with the staff member, a very uneasy feeling came over him. The staff member started the conversation by telling Bill that the Pastor was going to make an announcement this morning at the beginning of the service. He proceeded to tell Bill what all the stir was about.

The Pastor had contacted the staff member early that morning to inform him of a phone call that he had received just minutes before. It was very difficult for the Pastor to convey the information and struggled to hold back emotions as he spoke. The Pastor told how the Music Director's wife had called him to let him know that her husband was placed in jail the previous night for driving under the influence of alcohol. It seems that the Music director had been eating dinner with clients at a restaurant and had partaken in alcohol as the beverage for the evening dinner. Evidently, when he left the eating establishment it was late in the evening and he had been drinking enough for it to affect his driving.

The local police officer knew who he was, but had no choice but to take him to jail. The Pastor directed the staff member to ask Bill if he would lead the music for the next few weeks until they could make a decision about the next step to take. Bill gladly agreed to do whatever was needed. He was stunned and could hardly speak. How could this happen?

No one even knew the Music Director was having a problem with something like this. Bill knew that this could have a terrible effect on the congregation. As they prayed, before leaving the office, Bill asked the Lord silently to give him the grace to lead the music in a way that would help people get through this trial. Bill and Nancy found out later that one of the Police Officers at the jail was a brother-in-law to one of the family members in the church.

The Pastor did make the announcement at the beginning of the service. He said that the Music Director was having a struggle with something about which the church body needed to pray earnestly. He even called a special time of prayer before the service, having all the men of the church come forward to the altar to pray.

What Bill did not realize at first was that some of the church members had formed up in small groups before the service to pray for the Music Director and his wife. This made Bill and Nancy even more grateful to be a part of this church. The Pastor called a Deacon's meeting directly after the morning service. At this meeting, the Pastor told the Deacons all the details given to him by the wife of the Music Director. The Pastor was visibly shaken by this event.

He told the Deacons that the hardest thing for him to deal with personally was the fact that he never knew the Music Director, and long-time friend, was even having a problem with alcohol. This man had always seemed to be very spiritual. He was a dynamic Director of Music and did a wonderful job with the music program. He had the respect of the entire congregation as well as the Pastor. How could this happen to such a person?

During the following weeks, the Pastor learned more information until a complete picture came clear. It seems that the Music Director had some back trouble early the previous year that required some surgery, but was not severe enough to knock him out of his duties at the church. With the medication he was given, he actually did very well during the recovery from the surgery.

His recovery took a little longer than usual and before he knew it, he needed the medication more and more. He should have had very little pain at this point, but one thing led to another until he found it necessary to get the medication from sources other than his doctor. An addiction had formed for the medication and when he could not get the medication, he would drink in secret as a substitute to the pills. This led to the night, almost two years later, when he decided to risk not drinking in secret. He had met his clients at a restaurant that had a dimly lit interior so he would not be easily recognized. He had lost control.

The music director never gained control of the addiction. He eventually lost everything; his wife, his home, the fellowship of the Church, his testimony, and eventually, his life. He died several years later because of his alcohol abuse.

> Most of us do not recognize addictions in the lives of others.

This story is based on true events. Unfortunately, stories like this one are common in many communities across our country. How many people do you know have a struggle with some form of addiction? How did you become aware of the addiction problem in these people's lives? Most people learn of the addiction problem of others through word of mouth.

Most of us do not recognize addictions in the lives of others. Even very close family members have a difficult time seeing addictions in the lives of loved ones. In the Church, we usually know of someone having an addiction problem through prayer requests. Why are addictions so hard to recognize?

One would think family members and fellow employees, because they spend so much time together, would be able to recognize signs of addiction problems in another person. Unfortunately, this is not the case. There are several reasons why most people do not recognize signs and symptoms of addictions in others. One very common reason is simply that they have never been exposed to people with addictions. This is especially true in our local churches. This does not mean addictions do not exist in churches. It simply means that many times they are not recognized.

Another common reason addictions are not recognized is that addicts do a very good job of removing themselves, as much as possible, from those who they perceive as a threat to their activities. They may also feel shame and embarrassment over having a problem with addictions, or fear that if the right people find out about their problem, they may be forced to give up the addiction. This is because, in many cases, addictions are "relationships" that demand complete loyalty and much attention.

These relationships, fostered over time, become entrenched in the addict's every-day life. Addicts become so incredibly deceptive in their behavior they themselves become fooled by the addiction. The addict reaches a point in the addiction where almost every moment is spent devising ways to spend more time with this relationship. The prospect of losing this relationship results in overwhelming fear and dread.

An addict would rather give up a good paying job, a relationship with another person, or even self-respect, before giving up the addiction. This is one reason why addictions are so devastating in a person's life. This is also why addictions are so difficult to spot in others. They are covered up, and dressed up, to resemble something they are not. Many addicts try very hard to give the impression that their addictions are "discrepancies" or just character flaws or personality differences. The addiction reaches a point where it controls every aspect of the addict's life.

Many people are so involved with their own life anyway that they do not have the time or concern to know whether or not someone is struggling with life-controlling habits. Sometimes even Christians in the Church seem to have this view. Addictions can be very difficult to recognize in someone who does not want their addiction exposed. How do we look through this veil of deceit and see addictions in a person's life? There are several attributes necessary for a person to recognize addictions in the life of other individuals. These attributes are a desire to see, discernment, and knowledge. The following three sections give a good overview of these attributes.

Desire to see

The first attribute is simply we must want to see. There is no point in looking if we are not willing to see. What do we mean by this? People see what they want to see. For instance, when three people look at a forest, one may see the beauty of creation; another may see the resources available in the wood, while a third may only see the forest blocking them from going in a straight line from point A to point B. The same is true concerning people who have addiction problems.

> **How we see addiction, is a reflection of our spiritual understanding.**

Some Christians see addicts as people who have caused their own problems and need to get themselves out of trouble. Others see them as helpless and suffering and feel compelled to try and help them in some physical way, but have no compassion whatsoever for the condition of their soul. Still others do not even recognize there is an addiction problem in our society and therefore are oblivious to any need of helping the addict.

Finally, there are those who understand that we all have a fallen nature and that the addict is simply satisfying the desires of their flesh, and therefore they need the Saviour who can make a lasting change in their life. How we see addiction, is a reflection of our spiritual understanding. When we have the right view of God and our responsibility to Him, we have the right view of life-controlling habits as well. When we see sin as God sees it, we understand that addictions are just "controlling sins" in a person's life.

We are only able to do this through personal knowledge of the Word of God. Allowing God to teach us from His Word produces greater obedience in our life toward Him. As our obedience to Him increases, so does our understanding of the Scriptures increase, and therefore our knowledge and discernment will increase as well.

Discernment
The second, and most important, attribute a person must possess is the ability to discern. The ability to discern is necessary when dealing with people who have life-controlling habits. Many addicts become great con artists. The addict has learned through much trial and error how to, not only hide the addiction from those they perceive as a threat, but to obtain resources by which they can perpetuate their addiction.

From where do we obtain discernment? Discernment comes from God. We increase in discernment as we study the Word of God and the Holy Spirit makes application of God's Word to our lives. In other words, discernment is one of the most important by-products of our understanding of the Word of God. As our knowledge and understanding of the Scriptures increase, so does our ability to discern.

The person possessing discernment can be very lonely at times because they see things others do not see. People who are uncomfortable being "seen through" avoid people of discernment many times. This is because not everyone chooses to be transparent. If a person is not transparent, they become uncomfortable when another person can see things about them and their life, that are hidden from the view of the average person. Even though having discernment can be lonely, it is necessary for three reasons:

- To perceive danger
- For intercessory prayer
- To know truth from error

Discernment will first enable us to perceive when danger is present. Knowing of such danger is vital in not only our physical life, but our spiritual life as well. Discernment given to us by God will equip us to perceive danger present in the life of the addict, allowing those dangers to be exposed.

As the Holy Spirit makes us aware of unhealthy attributes or problems in the life of the addict, we will be motivated toward intercession for the addict. In other words, as we perceive that something is not as it should be in the life of an individual, we can take the actions necessary to help the individual overcome these struggles. Such action should never be that of gossip or condemnation.

One of the most important actions we can take is to pray for the individual. We are to use discernment in the ways in which God intended us to use it. Intercessory prayer is one of these ways. We must pray for God to work in the life of the addict, and to guide us in our ministry to the one addicted.

Thirdly, discernment enables us to know truth from error. While this is necessary in our daily walk with Christ, it is vital in our ministry to the addict who hides his addiction and cons his way through life. Knowing truth from error is not only important in our understanding of how to teach addiction recovery, but will ultimately enable us to help restore the life and relationships of the addict.

In Galatians 6:1, God's Word teaches us that we should restore the person overtaken in a fault. As we restore the addict, we must also have an attitude of meekness (Meekness is simply strength under control). Failure to have an attitude of meekness could result in gossip, condemnation, and even pride.

Pride results in our feeling that we are better than others are. This feeling many times is directed toward those who have addiction problems because we are not struggling with their addiction. God is not pleased with pride in our life. The Lord says in Proverbs 16:18,

"Pride goeth before destruction, and an haughty spirit before a fall."

People called to minister to and work with addicts must have and maintain a humble spirit. If we truly have compassion for those suffering with addictions, we will have this attitude of restoration in our hearts.

Knowledge

The third attribute or quality a person must possess is knowledge. Knowledge can be gained in a number of different ways. While personal experience is perhaps the best teacher, second best is learning from those who are experienced. This can be accomplished through, this course, courses offered through your church ministry, or courses available from other trusted sources.

A good way to gain knowledge is through self-study and by reading books that deal with the subject of addictions. Secular books have a lot of technical information and are good resources for knowing how the secular world views addictions of various forms. There are also many other resources available to help a person to better understand the problems inherent in particular chemical substances that are abused by addicts today.

> **We increase in discernment as we study the Word of God and the Holy Spirit makes application of God's Word to our lives.**

You must be careful when selecting secular material. While certain books are a valuable source of clinical information, it is necessary to understand that many books convey a philosophy on the cause and cure of addiction derived from a very secular, humanistic point of view. God's Word is the final authority on the subject and contains everything necessary to deal with addictions effectively. Written material that is doctrinally sound and Biblically correct is not only beneficial, but is crucial to this learning process.

There are men to whom God has given insight on this subject just as He has given such for commentaries and other books written on the Scriptures. Addiction is a very difficult subject to deal with in a person's life. The experience of a person who has worked with addicts is valuable in the sense that the knowledge gained from those experiences can be passed on to others who may not have had those same experiences.

Take this book for instance; it does not contain all the information a person would need in order to deal with every situation in an addict's life, but what this book does convey is the knowledge from personal experience, which this author has learned and gained through circumstances and situations working with addicts over the years.

Your own personal experiences may, and will, vary somewhat. Given the opportunity, you should pass on your experiences as well. There are Biblical reasons why we teach others what we know. The Lord gives us the command in 2Timothy 2:2 to pass our knowledge on to others. I believe He is pleased with this as long as what we pass on is truth grounded in the Word of God, as we seek to teach others.

Characteristics of Addictions
As you may now know, recognizing addictions in someone's life can be a very difficult thing. However, there are some very common characteristics present in most every addict. Some of these characteristics manifest themselves at various stages in the life of the addiction. We will not try to cover each specific addiction in this chapter. However, a more detailed overview is explained in the following chapter under "Effects of Addictions."

In the following few sections we will deal with several general characteristics of how addictions are exhibited in the life of the addict. The following chapter will deal with various segments of our society affected by addictions.

Understand that there are many very subtle characteristics that may not be readily seen. Each individual has a unique set of personality characteristics, which may either accentuate or subdue certain addiction characteristics. Experience will be the best teacher for learning these nuances.

Once certain basics of human character are learned and a person starts applying addiction characteristics to these personalities, it is much easier for them to "spot" addiction characteristics in an individual. Keep in mind the main purpose of recognizing addictions is to be in a position to help the individual as the Lord gives the opportunity.

Addiction Behavior
Addiction behaviors are generated over the life cycle of the addiction. Some behaviors are created through repetitive actions, while others are generated as a non-voluntary response to the substance abuse or destructive activity in which the person is engaged. The more prolonged the exposure to certain substances and activities, the more severe the resulting behavior.

The behaviors caused by addictions are different from one addict to another. However, there are significant similarities in the behaviors of addicts that allow us to distinguish or recognize these behaviors as being a result of the addiction rather than personality. It is also important to recognize that some people do have personality traits that closely resemble addiction behaviors. Take caution when making a judgment in this area. As mentioned before, experience and discernment will help a person be able to recognize addiction behaviors for what they are.

When we recognize addictions in the lives of others, this places the addict in the position of receiving help, even if he is not aware that others recognize his condition. Many times, the addict's process of finding help is started by someone other than himself. Take care not to push the addict away, by confronting them at the wrong time or in the wrong manner. Always show the addict respect. If the addict feels that a person trying to help them looks down on them in some way, the person trying to help loses the ability to accomplish the very thing he desires.

I have found that having a policy of not approaching a person with addictions, works best even if someone else feels they need help and asks me to talk with them. The reason for this is that many times a person is uncomfortable or ashamed to admit their addiction problem to someone they do not know or to someone they respect. Approaching a person about an addiction problem, without an invitation, can cause them to respond with a strong defensive posture. In cases like this, it is much better to wait until they seek help on their own. Until the addict wants help, they will not receive help anyway.

> ...the main purpose of recognizing addictions is to be in a position to help the individual as the Lord gives the opportunity.

The key is to allow the Lord to open the door for the right time. I believe this policy is necessary even for someone who has a severe case and may possibly need to participate in a residential program. If there has been an invitation extended by the addict through the Pastor or other person in the church, then I will have a meeting with the addict, but still only if it is at the addict's request.

Different addictions produce different behaviors in the addict. For example, drug addiction will have a different set of behaviors than those of the gambling addict. Addiction to pornography or voyeurism will have different effects on the person's behavior than that of drugs and alcohol.

Even different still are the behaviors of seemingly harmless addictions to sports, eating disorders, and other indulgences. All of these areas can result in a specific addiction. This is one of the places, at which we differ with a secular approach to addictions. It is our conviction that addictions are simply idolatry resulting from indulgences of the flesh. We commit idolatry when we give anything else the place in our life that God should have. Colossians 1:18 says about Jesus Christ,

"...that in all things he might have the preeminence."

This means that Jesus Christ is "the one and only," not "one of."

While some addictions have, what we would consider to be, less severe consequences, they are nonetheless addictions. Addiction to a sport like football or auto racing has few negative side effects that are visible to the outsider. There certainly can be consequences for family members though, who may be neglected because of this type of addiction, not to mention the spiritual neglect of all concerned. Addiction to foods and other food related disorders do have visible consequences. Whether or not the addiction has visible effects, the root cause of such behavior is the desire to over indulge.

My position on all these forms of addictions is a simple one. Man indulges himself on things that are desirable to the flesh or even harmful to the flesh because he does not have the discipline from God to suppress his fleshly desires. The view that these things are manifestations of idolatry is not a common view.

Webster's dictionary defines idolatry as, "Excessive attachment or veneration on anything, or that which borders on adoration." Addictions certainly fit this definition. This has been true since the Garden of Eden. Every aspect of the fruit of which Adam and Eve ate was very desirable to the flesh. It was pleasant to look upon. It was desirable to make one wise. I am sure it had a very good flavor as well.

The problem was not with the qualities or properties of the fruit. The problem was with Adam and Eve's disobedient response concerning eating the fruit God commanded them not to eat. Adam and Eve made a decision that having what they wanted and what appealed to the flesh was more important than being obedient to the commandment God gave them to, not eat of the fruit.

Self-gratification is the fundamental basis for every sin that man commits. Every sin committed by man can be categorized in one of three ways: Lust of the Flesh, Lust of the Eyes or the Pride of Life. The motivation for all three is idolatry. This Biblical foundation is necessary for there to be hope for the addict's recovery. The addict must also recognize they have made decisions; some of these have been poor.

Addictions are Habits
The idea that addictions are habits is not a popular view among some circles of addiction rehabilitation. This is because the real definition of addiction is far too simplistic to warrant the financial support needed and enjoyed for continuation of their programs. This may be a controversial statement, but it reveals what I believe to be the truth about many addiction recovery programs. We know that addictions are habits because they are learned behaviors.

"Let's get right down to the bare metal" as they say. Everything we do, every action and every behavior, is learned. These behaviors are taught to us and therefore, we learn the majority of our behaviors during our formative years. In other words, we act out the things we see our parents and siblings do, and we repeat vocally what we here others say. The reason we act out what we see and repeat what we hear is that they are repeated often enough that we learn to mimic them. This is why a young child can learn to speak a foreign language much easier than an adult does. This holds true even though our actions are influenced to a degree by our personality.

The mental health community has adopted a viewpoint of addictions derived from a report from the American Psychiatric Association called DSM-5 (Fifth edition of the Diagnostic and Statistical Manual of Mental Disorders). The DSM-5 report says that certain individuals are predisposed to addictive behavior based upon three factors: biological factors, psychological factors, and social factors. To simplify this for the reader, what they are saying is, if a person becomes an addict, that person's genetic structure, their thoughts and emotions, and their social environment dictates the illness of addiction.

While we agree that these factors may influence behavior to a degree, there comes a point, or an age, in the person's life when their environment no longer dictates to them. When a person reaches a certain age, they have the ability to choose whether their behaviors are good or bad. Unfortunately, and in most cases, they choose the bad behaviors instead of the good behaviors. If you have had the privilege of rearing children, teenagers especially, you know this truth to be all too real. The problem of not being reared in a Christian home only compound this problem because there is no basis or foundation for making good choices.

While exposure to negative behavior during the formative years, or even after, may influence greatly a person's actions in a given circumstance, it is in no way proof that the individual cannot control these impulses or behaviors after they reach a certain age. This age is different for all, but is always reached prior to adulthood. In the Christian community, we call this the age of accountability. This is the age when a person knows their actions have consequences, and they know the difference between right and wrong behaviors.

This truth seems to be ignored by many of the "professionals" in the mental health field. Given the choice, most people would, rather not be held accountable for their actions. This is part of man's nature. This allows for any behavior to be accepted and for the opportunity to circumvent the naturally resulting consequences. Many addicts find themselves in this condition.

Man learns from his mistakes, and when he is not held accountable for his mistakes, he either learns nothing at all, or learns to justify his actions. When those in authority consider certain behaviors as illnesses, man learns to place the blame for his actions onto someone or something other than himself. This mind-set also creates the need to rationalize addiction behavior, thereby making it necessary to create agencies and bureaucracies for funding research and treatment. The result is a political environment in which the government-ran rehabilitation facilities are filled with addicts that take no responsibility for their actions, and the financial burden of treatment is spread across the taxpayer base in the form of entitlements.

If all society lived in this way, there would be utter chaos across the globe. This indeed is why there is so much chaos even now. Man has learned that if everyone could just ignore the consequences of their actions, no one can be held accountable for the actions that destroy. It is interesting how people want recognition for the actions that result in good, but want to hide from the consequences of decisions that are destructive.

Furthermore, it is my belief that addictions are not illnesses. Certain addictions may create an illness in the individual, either mentally or physically, but they are the results of addictive behavior, not the cause of them. What makes the difference in the DSM-5 model and our belief is that man has a will to choose, regardless of what they have been exposed to early in life, and that these choices become more and more ingrained or subconscious the longer they are acted upon.

Habits are formed when a person repeatedly performs any behavior, whether good or bad (positive or negative), over a long period. As the behavior is repeated in the same context or environment, there is an incremental increase over time in the mental link between the action and the context, thereby creating the habit.

Over time, and with prolonged action-to-context connection, there is a subconscious and automatic response to any stimulus, resulting in behavior that takes place without thought or choice. We call these behaviors habit. If the stimulus can be removed, so can the habit. It is therefore necessary to allow the natural consequences of addictions to take place to allow the learning process to take root. At the same time, it is very important to teach the truth about why man acts in these ways and how to prevent future destructive actions.

Since bad habits form through this process of prolonged action-to-context connection, we can conclude that good habits can be formed the exact way. Therefore, with Biblical knowledge and training, a person can slowly replace the bad habits with ones that are pleasing to God and that are for the good of the person. The remaining piece of the puzzle is the motivation necessary to make such a change. Having laid some groundwork for recognizing addiction behaviors, let us look at some of the more common traits found in the behaviors of the addict that can be seen by an observer.

Common Traits

First, we will look at the more easily seen traits. These include behaviors such as:

1. Unexplained anger at insignificant occurrences
2. Withdrawal from social activities
3. Needing to borrow money for unexplainable reasons
4. A change to a different group of friends
5. Unkempt appearance
6. Unexplained nervousness or hyperactivity
7. Bursts of energy followed by long periods of sleep
8. Significant drop in school grades
9. A decline in work performance on the job
10. Mood swings
11. Poor judgments or decisions
12. Irrational behavior
13. Secrecy
14. Paranoia
15. Significant weight change (Loss or gain)
16. Seclusion, (Periods of withdrawal from usual activities)
17. Decline in spiritual involvements
18. Drug or alcohol paraphernalia observed (Scraps of foil-backed paper, unknown substances wrapped in foil, short straws, small clear bags, spoons, syringes, matches or lighters, small brown bags, paper for rolling cigarettes, pipes, hollow cigar casings, etc.)

In the following sections we will comment on a few of the signs mentioned in the above list. Keep in mind that this list is not conclusive. These are common behaviors seen in most addicts. This list primarily deals with the addictions of drugs and alcohol. Other addictions such as gambling and pornography have a different set of behaviors characteristic of those addictions.

For example, the gambling addict may come home later than usual from work because he is stopping by to play the poker machine in the local quick-mart. There may also be torn lottery tickets or receipts found in the floor or compartments of the car. The bank account is always a sure place to find signs of the gambling addiction.

If the addict has a good paying job, and there seems to never be enough money for expenses, this could be a sign that the money is being used in gambling activities. One other sign could be unknown people, usually males, calling on the phone. This could be a "bookie" or someone working in their behalf.

> ...addictions are simply idolatry resulting from indulgences of the flesh.

As for the pornography addict, there are signs of secrecy that can reveal this kind of addiction. Excessive amounts of time spent on the computer, bookstore receipts for magazines, or a change in temperament can all be signs of the pornography addict. This addiction affects the thinking processes of the addict. I am reminded of the verse in Titus 1:15 that says,

> "Unto the pure all things are pure: but unto them that are defiled and unbelieving is nothing pure; but even their mind and conscience is defiled."

The addiction to voyeurism, which includes the viewing of pornographic material, leads to this defilement. Our society has winked at this and other forms of gratification as being innocent because they appeal to the strong fleshly desires of human nature.

However, this type of addiction has a very devastating effect on our society as a whole and on individuals in particular. We will now deal with several characteristics or behaviors found in the above list.

Unexplained anger

Many times a person who is struggling to keep their addiction hid will have a hard time keeping their emotions in check. Human beings can only endure a certain amount of stress before they break under the pressure. Having an addiction and wanting to hide it usually results in a breakdown somewhere in the defensive armor of the addict. They cannot keep up a front all the time. Sudden fits of anger is one of those telltale signs of addictions, especially drug and alcohol addiction.

Withdrawal from social activities

The last thing the addict wants to do is place themselves unnecessarily in a position of vulnerability with others. The addict knows instinctively that when they are in the presence of others, especially those who have known them for some time, they are in danger of being found out. Withdrawing from group activities is a safe way to keep their addiction hid. In some cases, the addict will do just the opposite of this in an attempt to throw off suspecting persons. This may last for a while, but cannot be sustained over a long period.

Borrowing money

A lot of money is needed to sustain certain addictions. Addiction to drugs and gambling can be the most expensive habits to maintain. However, there are those people who only spend a certain amount each week, usually at the end of the week when they get their paycheck. This type of addiction activity is called "binging." The addict waits for the weekend when they have the most money and binge on either the drug of choice or alcohol or both.

Binging is a very dangerous practice that can result in overdose or poisoning. Binging can take place at any time, but most often happens on the weekends. This binging behavior actually deceives the addict into thinking they are rewarding themselves for the times they are not drinking or using.

More times than not, when the addiction has progressed to later stages, the addict does not have sufficient funds to cover the expense of maintaining the addiction. The addict will then resort to coercion of family members to lend them money, selling personal items, theft, or other illegal activities to pay for the habit. Money and material things are not the only costs associated with addictions.

Sin of any kind will result in the taking away of one's resources and eventually freedom itself. The Bible says, "The wages of sin is death" This is spiritual and physical death, the ultimate loss of freedom. There are other types of death also: Death of friendships; Death of business; Death of trust. We must let the sinner know that Jesus Christ came to give life and to give life more abundantly.

Change of friends
One of the more noticeable changes in the life of the addict is the type of friends with which the addict is associated. (Perhaps the choice of the word "friend" here may not be the best word.) There are many different clichés that are used in reference to people associating with others: "Birds of a feather flock together"; "Guilt by association"; "Misery loves company"; and others. It is accurate to say that we identify with those whom we associate. If someone you know suddenly has, a different group of friends that may appear to be the wrong crowd, this could be an indicator that they are struggling with some form of addiction.

We like to "second guess" ourselves at this point because we do not want to believe that there is something sinister going on so we overlook this sign. Most of the time, it is not innocent. There is a reason addicts like to be around one another. Seeing others with an addiction problem makes them feel better about their own condition. This is why an addict feels that it is necessary for someone helping him to have been an addict also. This knowledge makes the addict feel better about having an addiction problem. "Misery loves company."

The truth is if the only person that can help the addict were someone who has also been addicts themselves, then all the teachings of Christ would have to be ignored. The Scripture says that Christ was tempted in all points as we are yet without sin. Christ did not commit any sin much less a sin of addiction. Christ is the only answer as the addict seeks deliverance.

> **Sin of any kind will result in the taking away of one's resources and eventually freedom itself.**

Addicts also spend time with each other because the resources of other addicts much easier support the object of their addiction. If the addiction is to drugs or alcohol, then they can very easily get their hands on either. This is why it is important that the addict, who has a desire to give up their addiction, remove themselves from the sources of supply for their particular addiction. Many times this means relocating to a different town or city. This is a small price to pay for sanity, health, and life itself.

Unkempt appearance

Just as people are identified by the friends they have, so are people identified by the way they look and the clothes they wear. If you see someone who is wearing a blue uniform with a badge on his shirt, you would assume that he is a police officer. If a person is wearing a hard hat and a tool belt, you would think that they are a construction worker. If a woman wears a white uniform you would automatically think she is a nurse. This is common in our society. We identify with a certain group of people by the clothing we wear. This also goes for the addict.

While an unkempt appearance may not mean that a person has an addiction, it can be a strong indicator nonetheless. Many people who have addiction problems are wealthy and lack few material possessions. Yet they seem to loose pride in their appearance and manners when they are in the clutches of an addiction. Addictions do not discriminate. They will easily kill the wealthy and poor alike. We have seen this several times in the lives of certain, well-publicized celebrities in months and years past.

Why does this happen? It is because the addict loses all inhibitions. This includes the absence of modesty in appearance. When the addicts no longer have respect for themselves, they no longer have respect for anyone or anything else. This lack of self-respect allows the addict to accept a lower standard of conduct and appearance. Not all addictions cause a downturn in appearance, but the potential is certainly there in every addiction.

Nervousness or hyperactivity, Bursts of energy, Paranoia
These three signs can be grouped together because many times they are evident in the behavior of the addict at the same time, in various combinations. A burst of energy is usually caused by drug use and is commonly followed by a long period of sleep. There is a scientific reason for this behavior.

In non-technical language, it is much like the effects of eating foods loaded with sugar. There is a short period when the body uses the energy potential and then drops to a low once the sugar has worn off. The effects of a long-term cycle of drug and alcohol use produce physical effects that are progressively destructive to the brain. This results in diminished reasoning abilities.

Damage caused by a long-term cycle of drug and alcohol use results in the addict developing a strong sense of paranoia. This decline of normal thinking can cause the addict to make irrational decisions resulting in injury to oneself and others, or worse. Many times the addict thinks everyone is "out to get them."

Addicts have told me in counseling sessions that they actually thought the police were just outside their door waiting for them to come outside. There are people who may possess some of these traits who do not have an addiction problem. Discernment is needed in recognizing the difference.

However, learning these traits can be a useful tool in helping Christians minister to addicts. As said before there are certain vague nuances that, when combined with other behaviors, give a strong indication that there is undesirable activity taking place in a person's life. The ability to recognize these nuances is gained through experience. Recognizing addictions is not necessarily a science. It is more like an art or a skill, requiring much discernment.

Other Traits

We have seen some of the more common traits of addiction problems that are recognizable by an observer. There are also traits that are not so easily recognized. These traits are randomly present in the behaviors of the addict. They could also be categorized as "ticks" or oddities in a person's behavior.

There are also several traits or nuances that give some indication of possible addiction problems. These could include a change in speech patterns, a slowed response, uncommon alertness, subtle repetitive foot or hand motions, reasoning inabilities, subtle eye movements, cravings for specific foods and drinks, or even certain words used in conversation. The Bible refers to this very thing in Matthew 12:34 where it says,

> "...for out of the abundance of the heart the mouth speaketh."

The sort of activities in which a person is involved, is reflected in the content of the person's speech. No matter how hard they try to cover up their involvement with a sinful activity, the discerning person will be able to see through the attempted cover-up.

> **Damage caused by a long-term cycle of drug and alcohol use results in the addict developing a strong sense of paranoia.**

These and other nuances or traits, in conjunction with the more common behaviors mentioned earlier, can be a revelation of addiction activities present in the life of a person. As also stated before, these are not definitive behaviors. Many people exhibit odd or erratic behavior that are not symptoms of addiction. Care must be taken not to accuse or judge someone mistakenly.

Experience will enable the counselor or ministry worker to distinguish between the two. Once these skills have been developed they become useful in understanding what each person needs in their life. The Lord can use this knowledge to help the counselor develop a plan of correction for the particular addict.

Everyone is different. Therefore, addicts must be approached differently concerning their particular addiction. While all addictions do have some common characteristics, it is important to recognize the differences that exist with each individual. This recognition is necessary to reach them with the gospel.

This is also why we have developed an on-line addiction Recovery program called "Discovery of Hope – Biblical Pathways to addiction Recovery" This on-line program is self-paced to allow the participant the opportunity to complete the course in the privacy of their home or office. Many people who need help with addictions do not get that help because they cannot leave their job or home to attend a residential program. Transformed Life has developed this course based on the idea that each individual is at a different place in his or her life. To find out more about the "Discovery of Hope" program, go to www.nomoreaddictions.com.

Characteristics of Addiction: Summary
Characteristics of addiction vary with each person. Recognizing these characteristics is not always easy because there are different characteristics for each addiction. It is important to be able to see through the veneer of the addict. Although these traits are common, learning these characteristics can assist the recovery teacher in dealing with each individual separately. The addict will many times:

1. Deny their addiction
2. Sacrifice relationships for the addiction
3. Involve others in the addiction

4. Practice secrecy until others accept their addiction
5. Defend their addiction
6. React in anger to those who disagree with the addiction
7. Go to unusual lengths to continue or feed the addiction
8. Engage in the addiction at any time
9. Use whatever is needed to continue the addiction
10. Never be satisfied by the addiction

These characteristics are true in any type of addiction. They are not limited to any one particular addiction. Knowing these characteristics can greatly help the recovery teacher in recognizing addictions in someone who may not be known to have an addiction. However, much caution should be taken in approaching someone thought to have addiction problems.

If someone is suspected of having difficulties with addictions, it is appropriate to convey those concerns with the person only if the conversation is preceded with genuine concern for the individual. Most people can tell if someone else is genuinely concerned about them.

Recognizing addictions in others is not typically an easy burden to bear, but it can be a useful tool in developing relationships with the purpose of helping others. The Lord gives grace to those whose motives remain pure. People who work in recovery ministries find that recognizing addiction behaviors becomes a necessary skill of effectively ministering to the addict.

Chapter 5

Effects of Addictions

Drugs, alcohol, pornography, gambling, and other addictions all have very devastating consequences in the life of the addict. These effects are not limited to the individual addict. The effects of addictions have reached into just about every home in America. There is hardly a family anywhere who has not been affected by an addiction of some kind in the life of someone they know, whether this is a family member or a friend of the family. The Church is not exempt from this either. Christians everywhere have faced addiction problems and their effects either directly or indirectly.

Addictions have a very devastating effect on our society as a whole, and are a growing problem. Our government spends millions of dollars each year combating the problem of addictions in our society. While the government may cite data regarding the decline in certain addictions to a particular drug of choice, overall, addiction problems are steadily increasing. As Christians, we also see areas of addiction that the government or medical community may not recognize. In addition to this, the Christian's approach to the cure for addictions is also different.

The world's approach to addiction is to send the addict to the medical clinic or rehabilitation facility where the person "dries out" or is "detached" from the addiction for a period. They are sent on their way, only to relapse into a much greater bondage than before. The Christian approach to addiction is to tell the truth in love. Addictions are sins. The problem in the life of the addict is a sin problem. The problem in our society is a sin problem.

The right view of the effects of addiction in the individual, and in society, is the view that sin is the root cause of addiction problems. Once we understand the cause, we can also understand the cure. The cure for addictions lies in the fact that God forgives sin.

> **The Christian approach to addiction is to tell the truth in love.**

Sin is conquered by faith and trust in Jesus Christ for salvation, and a daily relationship with Him. Man does not have the ability to conquer his own sin problem. God alone has the power to free man from the bondage of sin. Man must recognize this truth in order to experience deliverance from addictions. We will look at the effects addictions have on the individual, the Church, and society.

The Individual

The numbers of different physical effects addictions have on the individual are as vast as the number of individuals who have addiction problems. Everyone is different. The physical effects of addictions are different for each person. The same addiction can have a wide variety of effects depending on the person's physical condition or health, and their personality characteristics or emotional condition. The physical effects mentioned in this segment are commonly felt effects that are recognized in the majority of addicts we have worked with over the years. With sufficient study and experience, these effects should become obvious to those working in the addiction ministry outreach.

It is not our intention to focus on just one particular kind of addiction when looking at these effects. As stated before, addictions come in various forms. There are many different kinds of addictions. Even though there are many different physical effects addictions have on a person, there is a far more serious effect addictions have on a person than just physical affects.

The mental and emotional effects addictions have on individuals are much more devastating because they last much longer than do the physical effects. The typical period for certain chemicals to be cleansed from the body, ranges from months to several years. However, the mental and emotional effects can last a lifetime and have residual effects on others.

> **Sin is conquered by faith and trust in Jesus Christ for salvation, and a daily relationship with Him.**

Addictions are not something new to man. Since God created Adam and Eve in the Garden of Eden, there has been the desire in man to fulfill the lusts of his flesh. This lust is the basic root of all addiction. It is the desire for pleasure and for self-gratification, which drives this lust. This behavior is idolatry, as mentioned in the previous chapter. Satan deceived Eve into thinking she could satisfy her flesh, ignore the command of God, and not suffer the consequences of that decision.

Adam was not deceived, but rather made a conscious choice to disobey the command of God. This decision had terrible consequences. The effect of this choice was to plunge the human race into darkness, caused by sin and separation from God. This is the ultimate effect of sin. The Bible says this ultimate effect is death. This physical death is also the result of many addictions. The most devastating effect addiction has on the individual is not the physical death; it is the spiritual death of separation from God.

There are various stages of pain and suffering between the first drink, the first hit, or the first high, and the result of physical death. However, separation from God is an eternal effect that cannot be reversed once a person dies. There is no cure available when a person dies without knowing Jesus Christ as their personal Saviour.

When a person dies without knowing Jesus Christ, the resulting separation from God is permanent. The Bible speaks of this when it says in Mark 8:36, 37,

> "For what shall it profit a man if he shall gain the whole world, and lose his own soul? Or what shall a man give in exchange for his soul?"

Drug and alcohol addicts know they are playing with a loaded gun. They are playing "Russian Roulette" with their lives when they use alcohol and drugs. However, what they may not be aware of, is that they are separated from their Creator.

Separation from God has much greater consequences. This consequence is eternal. Satan's number one lie is that there is time to make things right with God. In other words, Satan tells people that they have plenty of time to get things right with God because they have their whole life ahead of them and there is no hurry. The Bible says in James 4:14,

> "Whereas ye know not what shall be on the morrow. For what is your life? It is even a vapour, that appeareth for a little time, and then vanisheth away."

There is no time other than the present to make things right with God. The Bible says in 2Corinthians 6:2,

> "behold, now is the accepted time; behold, now is the day of salvation."

It is in knowing God, and through His power alone, that cures the addict from the bondage of addiction. Even though the spiritual consequences of addictions are far more devastating than physical consequences we cannot ignore the physical affects addictions have on a person.

Many times, it is necessary to deal with the physical effects of addictions before the addict can understand spiritual things. Many times, the side effects of the addiction must subside before the addict is responsive to the gospel. This can be a very long process. Physical effects can last for years after someone has stopped their addiction activities. This is especially true with certain types of drugs.

Helping a person overcome these physical effects is not an easy task. The addict must be willing to help with their process of recovery. Proper diet and exercise, willingness to follow instructions from God's Word, and courage to recognize addictions as sins, are also essential to this process.

It is uncommon for someone who is currently under the influence of drugs or alcohol to respond to the gospel message. However, with God all things are possible. Therefore, we should give the gospel to every person whether sober and clean or not. We do not know what is going on in the heart and mind of an individual; neither do we know to what extent their understanding may be impaired. Therefore, we should not refuse to tell anyone about the Lord Jesus Christ.

> **There is no time other than the present to make things right with God.**

When dealing with certain types of addictions, such as alcohol and chemical substances, many factors hinder a person's thinking and reasoning ability. This hindrance is due to the body's response to the chemical's presence in the body and the brain. Mental and emotional changes often occur from a constant involvement in the viewing of pornography or the continual participation in gambling activities. These forms of addiction have a terrible effect on the individual that may not be seen in their outward appearance. Even so, there are certain telltale signs of these addictions.

As stated previously, experience in working with people who have addiction problems in these areas will sharpen your skills in recognizing these signs more clearly. As with chemical or substance abuse, addiction to pornography, and gambling affect the mind in recognizable ways. There is a sense of humiliation or shame that a person who is addicted to voyeurism or gambling carries with them. It is not something they can generally recognize in themselves and therefore they cannot mask it very easily.

People who are addicted to pornography and gambling may recognize that there is some kind of change in them and therefore will try to change something about their person in an attempt to throw others off. Therefore, these addictions affect how these individuals respond and react to others. As for the married person, continued involvement in pornography will result in a situation where the addict can never be satisfied with their spouse, many times resulting in separation and divorce.

> **Abuse of alcohol and other chemical substances can cause premature death even in a healthy person.**

The psychological change that takes place with people engaged in prolonged addiction activities and exposure to chemical substances is what I call a false logic or disrupted thinking. This disrupted thinking allows the addict to make sense of what they are doing to their mind and body, even though the activity is destroying them physically. Any addiction is harmful to a person, but becomes significantly more dangerous if not realized.

Abuse of alcohol and other chemical substances can cause premature death even in a healthy person. Alcohol is a drug. Therefore, the effects of alcohol and other chemical substances can be classified in a similar manner. Many pills have the same effect on the body from an outward appearance, as does alcohol.

While some drugs have the same result as others concerning behavior, there is a difference, however, in the response of the human body to a particular chemical substance. Illegal drugs have very negative effects on the body, not because they are illegal, but because they destroy critical tissue of the brain and organs.

Effects from slowed response times, loss of memory, even a total vegetative state are possible with only small quantities of certain chemicals. Use of chemical substances can also result in danger to the lives of innocent citizens in circumstances where the user is operating public transportation vehicles or heavy machinery. Alcohol and substance abuse can also increase the risk of cancer, heart disease, kidney or liver failure, obesity, and other disorders. The most common side effect of alcohol abuse is cirrhosis of the liver.

Even though some people believe alcohol may have a small health benefit, the risks of abuse are too great when compared to any benefits this substance may have for it to be considered useful. Therefore, alcohol should be avoided completely. Christians should avoid the use of alcohol as a beverage. Alcohol consumption not only destroys the body, which is the temple of the Holy Spirit, but it also can be an obstacle to a weaker Christian.

God warns us in His Word against allowing our behaviors to become "stumbling blocks" to the weaker Christian. The Bible tells us in 1Corinthians 8:9,

> "But take heed lest by any means this liberty of yours become a stumbling block to them that are weak."

In addition, verses twelve and thirteen,

> "But when ye sin so against the brethren, and wound their weak conscience, ye sin against Christ. Wherefore, if meat make my brother to offend, I will eat no flesh while the world standeth, lest I make my brother to offend."

Realizing this is a point of debate for many people, I am not trying to be divisive in this. I do believe, however, that we should live as closely to the Lord as possible. We must decide that our conduct is going to be Biblical, not just acceptable to others.

Because a particular practice is accepted in certain religious circles or a religious denomination, it does not mean that drinking alcohol is God's best for His people. Each person must answer to God for himself in this. I leave this subject with this final thought: There are many more reasons, both physical and spiritual, why a Christian should abstain from using alcohol as a beverage, than there are for its use.

The Church

Many church members do not readily see the fact that addictions have an effect on the Church. While addictions do have a very devastating effect on the individual, they also have a tremendous negative consequence on the Church as a whole. Most people see addictions as an individual problem that affects only the addict and a small circle of people around the addict. This could not be further from the truth.

This kind of thinking must change before the Church will be effective in ministering to the addict. When church members have life controlling habits that are destructive, there is the potential for the addict to influence weaker Christians and even young people. The Scripture says in 1Corinthians 15:33,

> "Be not deceived: evil communications corrupt good manners."

It is not the other way around. As long as there are sinful people on the earth, there will be addiction problems. I hope that there will also be people who care enough for the addict to point them to Christ. Our methods of helping the addict must be purely Biblical. No other way will be lastingly effective. God has given everything we need, in His Word, to reach the addict for Christ. What man can do for himself is not sufficient. The reason most Christians do not see the need for a recovery ministry is, first, they do not see the addict as a soul in need of the Saviour. Secondly, they do not see the effect addictions have on the local church.

Do not misunderstand why there is a need to reach the addict. It is not simply because they need help or because addictions have a negative effect on the church body. This would be a noble cause, but it is not the primary motive. The primary reason for having a ministry outreach to addicts is to give them the gospel. The motive for this is to glorify God. The mission outreach to addicts is no different from the mission outreach to any other unreached people group in the world. Providing an addiction recovery program by way of a church ministry is simply a soul-winning endeavor.

The effect addictions have on our churches range from the secret to the very public. Many times over, we have known of those who were in a position of leadership in the church who were caught in some lewd act or other scandalous behavior. It is not my intent to bring up the specifics of these for discussion because the Church has suffered quite enough because of Christians who have allowed their flesh to rule their behavior.

What makes this even more shameful is the position of influence many of these people have had over a large number of other church members. The Lord will hold them more accountable than those who have not been in such highly visible positions. Yet, the devastation is just as real.

> **"Behind every tragedy in human character lies a process of wicked thinking."**

Many churches have suffered because the Pastor or Music Director ran off with the Pianist or Secretary. There are even those who have engaged in some lewd or sinful act in public. The Bible says in Luke 12:2

> "For there is nothing covered, that shall not be revealed; neither hid, that shall not be known."

We can conclude that those who "get caught" in a public sin have a much larger private problem with addiction to the kind of activity in which they were caught.

Bob Jones Sr., the founder of Bob Jones University, once said, "Behind every tragedy in human character lies a process of wicked thinking." This wicked thinking is exactly what the Scripture talks about in Proverbs 23:7 where it says,

"For as he thinketh in his heart, so is he:"

The Scripture also says in Matthew 12:34,

"for out of the abundance of the heart the mouth speaketh."

Scripture declares that speaking and conversation is a reflection of what is occurring on the inside of man. In Scripture, conversation many times is synonymous with conduct. In other words, the actions of a person reveal what is in their heart. What is in the heart of a person is what they dwell on in their thoughts. What they dwell on in their thoughts is the result of what they allow in through the eye gate and ear gate.

How does this affect the church? This kind of behavior, which is the results of addiction, weakens the church body by being an obstacle to those who are not strong spiritually and by sending the wrong message to the lost.

Most people would agree that there is a large percentage of church members that are not as spiritually mature as they should be. This is a very difficult thing to measure in terms of effect, but we all know this to be true. When someone in the church is found to have a moral failure in their life, this effect ripples through the church body like a silent, destructive shock wave. Time will reveal the real devastation caused by the behaviors of church leaders who have been of notable reputation who have allowed their flesh to control their behavior.

There is a larger number of church members who are not in these more visible positions of influence who still have caused much damage to the individual local church body. No one is exempt from having a measure of influence on others. While younger and less mature Christians are influenced more by the damaging failures of other church members, even older and more mature Christians are also affected.

Immoral behavior in the lives of God's people brings a reproach on the name of the Lord. This kind of behavior sends a message to the lost that Christians are hypocrites. The lost will not want to become Christians if we are no different from them in how we live. This applies to any activity or behavior.

As we have discussed before, everyone does not readily see addiction problems. In other words, addictions are not always manifested by obvious outward behaviors. Many behaviors are subtle and reveal an addiction only in very subtle mannerisms and nuances. When the addiction does reveal itself, it is usually to everyone's surprise and dismay.

> **Satan, at minimum, desires to prevent us from being effective in spiritual warfare and to render us ineffective as soldiers for Christ.**

Christians even say from time to time, the individual "fell into sin." No one "falls" into sin. As described a moment ago, a person found to have a moral failure, did so after much thinking over time and by giving in to the lusts of their flesh. This response can only be after a prolonged period of allowing their flesh to rule their thoughts and culminates in the destructive act. This prolonged period of allowing their flesh to rule their thoughts, many times results in or produces an addiction.

The same process takes place when a drug addict takes their first hit or experiences their first high. The feeling is exhilarating and they want to continue even though they know the dangers. So does a church member who is allowing their flesh to rule them. Human beings, saved or lost, have the potential to accommodate any desire of their flesh if not restrained by the power of God. A Christian who succumbs to the flesh will destroy their own testimony as well as affect the spiritual growth of other Christians.

This is more common in our churches than most people will admit. Many times a Pastor has difficulty because there is a member in the church that has an addiction to control or power. They work against the Pastor instead of with him. God is not pleased with this. The Church is the center of all outreach and ministry to the world. Without strong Christians, the Church is weak and unproductive. This weakness is due to a lack of Biblical knowledge and obedience in the lives of God's people.

Addictions to football, baseball, fishing, hunting, racing, and many other sports activities, in addition to one's career and job, have distracted many Christian fathers from the importance of instilling God's Word into the hearts and lives of their family members. These types of addictions seem harmless enough, but still have the same effect on the Church, as do drugs and alcohol. Allowing sports or a career to rule the life of an individual opens the door for other addictions as well. These activities remove people from attending Church services, where strength is gained, or from laboring in the fields that are white unto harvest and in need of laborers.

Some people may think this is an unreasonable stance against sports or other recreational activities, and is too strong. My point is not to suggest that sports or recreational activities are wrong, but rather to point out the fact that anything, not given its proper place, can distract the Christian from their main purpose. This purpose is to worship and glorify God, and to be a witness for Christ so the lost can see the way to salvation in Christ. We must remember that Satan, at minimum, desires to prevent us from being effective in spiritual warfare and to render us ineffective as soldiers for Christ.

Because of addictions, families suffer from the lack of leadership in the home, which spills over into the Church. Consequently, the Church also suffers for lack of leadership and role models. Christian men must understand their God-given responsibilities for leading their families in a godly manner so the Church and our Society will be strong as well. "God-given responsibilities never conflict." (Clarence Sexton)

What is the answer to the problems in the church? It is the same answer to the problems in the life of an individual. The Holy Spirit of God must have free reign in the hearts and lives of Church members individually. The Holy Spirit must control a person rather than their desires of the flesh. Without this controlling of the Holy Spirit, families will splinter and churches will split or cease to exist.

The influence the church now has on our society pales in comparison to the influence it once had. This is a result of people following the desires of their flesh instead of following the revealed will of God in their lives. Addictions come in many different forms. Some are more devastating than others are. All addictions have a profound effect on the Church as a whole. This effect has weakened the influence of the Church in our society. Therefore, our society has suffered because of the weakening of the Church.

Our Society
We have seen how addictions have had a terrible effect on individuals and on the Church as a whole. There has been a terrific price paid by our society both in terms of financial and moral instability. Many families have been affected by addictions and their consequences. This price cannot be easily measured.

There are still consequences that have not been realized, that will be manifested in years to come. At the time of this writing, there are many news stories of popular celebrities who have had terrible battles with drug and alcohol addictions. Some have even died because of drug overdose. Drug and alcohol addictions have been the cause of many premature deaths of singers and actors over the years.

As society continues to search for the answer to addictions, Christians must continue to tell them the truth in love. Society will never find a cure for addiction while they look to man for the answer. A desensitizing of our culture and society has taken place toward the things that were once unacceptable in public. Because addictions have had so much media coverage and so many celebrities have addictions problems, there is a sense that having an addiction is almost a rite of passage for celebrities. This is tragic.

Many young people idolize these celebrities and follow their activities so closely they want to imitate the behaviors of these celebrities. What they see in this celebrity culture is, being strung out on drugs is "cool;" it is "faddish" to be "blasted" out of your mind; getting drunk in public is "fun;" acting like a fool is the "hip" thing to do.

> **Society will never find a cure for addiction while they look to man for the answer.**

What is not seen, are the lives of those who have been destroyed because of addictions. There are even television shows based on the attempt at recovery of these celebrities. What these television shows may not show is the result of devastation in the lives of these same celebrities.

Poverty

I have personally seen many families who have suffered financially because the husband and father were in bondage to an addiction. Families in this situation have had to sell personal items in order to sustain the cost of the family's living necessities while the husband and father were in rehabilitation. Many times divorces and separations occur because of addictions. We have witnessed the breakup of a multitude of families because of the problems related to drug, alcohol, and other life-controlling habits.

Addicts find themselves unable to sustain funding for their addictions, especially in the later stages. In many cases, the addict becomes dependent upon other family members or close friends to maintain the addiction. If the family members or friends allow this, it can cause a real financial hardship for them. Many families have sacrificed time and money to find treatment for their loved one in bondage to addiction.

There is also a phenomenon related to these circumstances of giving that we call Codependency. Codependency is, when a person feels they are responsible for fixing the addict's condition. The codependent can be a family member or just a friend. In either case, many times the codependent person will spend huge amounts of money and resources in order to fix the problems of the addict. They do this, often at the risk of personal financial instability in their own life. Poverty is a reality for individuals and families caught in this horrific life of addictions.

Violence

Addictions are also one of the primary causes of violence in many cultures and societies. Addictions and violence go hand in hand. Not only do addictions create a culture within themselves, they also alter many aspects of normal cultures within a society. Violence has always been a by-product of drug and alcohol addiction in particular. However, other addictions also create an environment where violence can take place.

When a person does not have the ability to control their desires because of addiction, they also do not have the ability to control their emotions. Because anger is a basic human emotion, the addict is powerless to control the emotion of anger. At times, this anger results in extreme violence.

Many times the addict will commit violent crimes in order to fund their addictions. Through robbery, extortion, illegal gambling, or other types of criminal activity, the addict cultivates in themselves a predisposition for criminal and, sometimes, violent behaviors. Crime in our society would be reduced greatly if it were not for the effects of addictions.

Addiction behaviors relate strongly to the amount of crime present in our society. There has been much news recently concerning the violence on our southern border because of the activities surrounding drug trafficking. This traffic is due to the insatiable appetite our society has for illegal drugs, namely cocaine and marijuana. If we stop the demand for the drugs, we will effectively stop the supply of them.

Not only is the violence that surrounds addiction activity a major problem in our society, but the casual use of drugs has filled our jails and prisons with mandated sentencing. Although necessary, the establishment of mandated sentencing has cost our society both in terms of judicial overload and in a drain on law enforcement services. I believe stiff penalties for drug use can be a deterrent, but the system is broken when it cannot provide a solution to curb the demand for the drugs, while posing those stiff penalties. This is where the Church's addiction recovery ministry can make a huge difference in our society.

Apart from helping the addict receive Christ as their Saviour, one of the greatest things Christians can do for the addict is to help them gain freedom from their addiction so they, their spouses, and their children, will live a much safer and happier life. Our society will be a better place because of it. The freedom found in Christ and the freedom from all forms and impacts of addiction will make a profound effect upon the individual, the Church, and our Society.

Chapter 6

Biblical Approach

There are many different approaches to the treatment of addictions. The government's approach is to spend millions of dollars in an effort to educate and combat the ever-increasing problems in our society that are a result of addictions. Addictions and addiction related crimes are on an increase in our society. Many times local police and other law enforcement agencies are overwhelmed with crimes that result from illegal activity generated by addiction behavior in our society.

The historical - secular view has been to pour as much money as possible into researching addiction problems. This is done in hopes of finding a cure. This is a noble cause, but misguided. In reality, this is a small bandage on a very large open wound.

It does not matter how much money they spend on research and how much they want their research to be meaningful, this approach will never remedy addiction problems. This is not because the information gained from this research is valueless; it is because they cannot change human behavior with research and government programs.

We must deal with human nature by responding Biblically to sinful desires. God's Word gives us the tools to deal with human nature correctly. The Christian approach is much more effective, and costs far less money to operate than do government intervention programs. The Biblical approach is the only program that has the ability to transform a person from the inside out. Without the internal change happening within a person, there will not be a permanent recovery.

We who know the truth are under obligation to tell the truth in love. The information contained in the following chapters is very basic to the Christian life. These chapters are the foundation to helping people with addictions. The student of these chapters must learn the information well so they can teach the principles to others. This is the starting point in teaching addiction recovery. The principles given in the following chapters were developed in hands-on, real-life programs and were used successfully to help transform many lives that were in bondage to addictions.

> **We must deal with human nature by responding Biblically to sinful desires.**

A humanistic approach to addiction recovery is to offer an environment where the addict is removed from society for a determined period, with the hope that through psychological therapy, medical treatments, and social reprogramming, the addict will be convinced that his or her behavior is inappropriate for society. While it may be true that addiction behavior is inappropriate, it does not deal effectively with the root problem. The root problem of addiction is the fallen nature of all human beings.

The mistake many Christians often make is in accepting the world's view of the remedy to addictions by copying their methods. God's Word is the only real remedy to the problem of addictions in a person's life. God's Word must be the source we use for teaching addiction recovery, not some man's philosophy, or list of ideals.

A thorough understanding of the following six chapters will enable the teacher to develop a program that is suitable to their particular circumstances and ministry. It will also be helpful to understand how very closely these chapters are connected with one another. These chapters are the basic principles I believe are essential for laying a solid foundation to reaching the addict with the gospel.

If we do not understand what God says in the principles conveyed in the following six chapters, it may be difficult to establish groundwork for presenting the gospel to the addict. The addict must understand who God is and our responsibility to Him, what truth is and from where it comes, where man came from and the accountability we have to others and to God, the importance of instruction and obedience in our lives, the purpose for which we are created, and the importance of obedience to God's laws.

The answers to these things do not lie in research programs, extended counseling sessions, and psychotherapy. The answer lies in a decision the addict makes about the person of Jesus Christ. I present these topics in this book because, along with the gospel message, they need to be the core teaching in any addiction recovery program.

There are already too many programs that exist today, which supposedly have the cure for addiction. I would say the world is making a valiant effort to help reduce the problems of addiction. It is a misguided effort however.

There are programs and facilities all around the country that are very sincere in their efforts. Many of these programs are helping people reach a level of sobriety. This is good, but not best. I have said before, anything that helps a person be productive in society has value to that society, but we should be more concerned about eternity. The problem with these programs is we live beyond this life.

If there were no life after death, I would say do all you can to help a person be happy and productive in this life. The truth is there is life after death, and there is a Living God to whom we all will have to give an answer. The real question is "What are we doing to help men be right with God now?" Being right with God means a person can live in the fullness of God's blessings, both in this life and in the life hereafter.

By helping people prepare for eternity, we are also helping them have a peaceful and productive life now. There are even so-called "Christian" facilities that are using the Bible to lure people into their program, but do not actually help the person experience true recovery. This is not because their means are wrong. It is because their message is wrong.

Many facilities offer a wide range of services that are nothing more than a "drying out" program. Many of these facilities exist only to make money. It takes more than programs, facilities, and "drying" a person out, to effectively help them obtain lasting victory from the bondage of addictions.

There must be a daily commitment to a relationship with Jesus Christ. Recovery takes place as the participant reads, studies, and memorizes Scripture. The goal of developing a meaningful relationship with Christ, through prayer and the study of God's Word, is at the heart of addiction recovery.

Facilities that offer services to help addicts must recognize what is truly necessary to have effective results. Parents, spouses, teachers, employers, Pastors, ministry leaders, and physicians, can all play an important role in addiction recovery by leading the addict to the right kind of program. These people should also understand what God says about addictions.

The correct approach to addiction recovery is in developing a program based upon the Word of God. We have already learned that true recovery is the by-product of a relationship with the Creator. There is no other way to understand the requirements of this relationship apart from the Word of God. It is in the Bible that God teaches us how this relationship works.

In chapters seven through twelve, I give what I believe to be essential elements of a foundation for permanent recovery from life-controlling habits. These chapters are necessary because they present truths found in God's Word about the basic requirements God gives human beings for living a life that is pleasing to Him.

There are more truths, other than these basic elements, that are necessary for the Christian life. These are only the foundation on which to begin. Understanding these basic truths will bring a person to a deeper level of spiritual maturity in their life. It has been my experience that most people who have participated in a recovery program have never learned these principles. It has also been my experience that when a person is presented with the truth, they recognize it for what it is. This gives them the opportunity to make the decision of whether they will be obedient to the things God shows them about their own life.

> **The root problem of addiction is the fallen nature of all human beings.**

The other impact these truths can make is to correct a person's thinking processes. In other words, by learning the principles given in these next chapters, a person will have a true picture of the purpose and meaning of life. The individual must still make a choice of whether or not they will accept or reject Jesus Christ as Saviour. The knowledge of God and God's will for man will assist in helping him respond to the Gospel of Jesus Christ.

The recovery program educator must also have a thorough understanding of these truths in order to teach these principles effectively. Remember, the object of any recovery program is discipleship after salvation. Truth, God, Belief Systems, Man and Creation, Accountability and Relationships, Instruction and Obedience, and Purpose, are each foundational elements of any truly effective addiction recovery program.

These principles are the core elements of Transformed Life's addiction recovery program, "Discovery of Hope – Biblical Pathways to Addiction Recovery" and are available as an online course at www.tluonline.com.

Core Principles

> "...in the house of God,
> which is the
> church of the living God,
> the pillar and ground
> of the truth."
> I Timothy 3:15

Chapter 7

Truth

God gives us everything we need to know about how to help a person gain lasting freedom from the bondage of addiction. The best knowledge we can have about anything is to know the truth of the matter. Truth is necessary for man to know how to make right decisions. The truth about addiction and recovery is vital to creating a lasting and viable solution that enables the addict to gain permanent freedom from the addiction.

The Bible says, "Ye shall know the truth, and the truth shall make you free." Because the Bible is the final authority, we must allow the Word of God to do the work in the life of the addict. This is the only method that will have lasting results. This is the correct Biblical response to addiction recovery.

Not only do we need to use the Word of God as the source of truth for our programs, we must also recognize the need to teach these truths in a systematic way. A Systematic Teaching of Biblical Principles (Truths) is the only way to lay a proper foundation on which to present the answer to life-controlling habits.

For us to understand how to deal with addiction behavior, we must first understand and address the truth about addiction. We must also answer the question why sins of addiction are wrong. To do this we must understand the difference in truth and error, the existence of God, the nature of man, and our responsibility to God. These are fundamental to understanding addiction behavior, and are the foundations for a life free from the oppression and bondage of addictions.

Truth

What is truth? There are many different beliefs concerning the meaning of truth. There is only one real definition of truth. Truth must be an objective standard that cannot change. If it could change, it cannot be truth. Truth then must be a universal constant that does not change by some external force. Webster's 1828 dictionary defines truth as:

> 1. Conformity to fact or reality; exact accordance with that which is, or has been, or shall be.
>
> 2. Conformity of words to thoughts, which is called moral truth.

Having conformity to fact or reality means there must first be fact and reality. In other words, before we can conform to fact or reality, they must exist. From where do fact and reality come? Who determines what is fact and reality?

For us to understand what truth is and from where it comes, we must look to the only source of truth. This source is God. God is unchanging. He has always been and will always be. He said of Himself that He is the same yesterday, today, and forever. Therefore, God is truth.

I do not pretend to understand this completely, but I accept it by faith because God tells it to us in His Word, the Bible. The real question is whether man believes this or not. You see, there can only be one source of truth: man or God, and we must choose which one we believe. Man has made a mess of this world, but all God's ways are perfect. Deuteronomy 32:4 says,

"He is the rock, his work is perfect: for all his ways are judgment: a God of truth and without iniquity, just and right is he."

Many people believe truth is relative to a person's experiences. Subjectivity in such "truth" cannot be constant. This cannot be objective since it is subject to the experiences of each individual. If there is an objective standard we are to follow, we must understand what this objective standard is and from where it came.

Webster's defines objective as:

1. Belonging to the object (emphasis added); contained in the object. "Objective certainty is when the proposition is certainly true in itself; and subjective, when we are certain of the truth of it. The one is in things, the other in our minds." - Watts

Law

Enter the truth by means of the "law." The law states that green means "go" yellow means "caution" or "slow" and red means "stop." Disobedience to this law can result in physical death. The same is true with God's laws. The Bible says the law is a taskmaster that brings us to Christ. We know we sin because God's law is present to show us our sin.

Without order, there is chaos. God gives truth to us to maintain order and unity in our lives. Let us look at the story of Adam and Eve. Because man broke God's law, which was, do not eat of the tree of the knowledge of good and evil, he died physically and spiritually just as God said he would.

> **Because the Bible is the final authority, we must allow the Word of God to do the work in the life of the addict.**

The Bible says God is a Spirit and they that worship Him must worship Him in spirit and in truth. To die spiritually means to be separated from God. This has already occurred. God banished (separated) Adam and Eve from the Garden of Eden, and from His presence, because they were no longer pure and holy. They broke God's law. Without obedience to the objective standard of God's laws or "truth," there are terrible consequences and chaos.

The next logical question would be, "Who makes the law?" Our society gives the authority to make our laws, to people we have chosen to represent our interests and us; we call these people Senators and Representatives. Therefore, we have a "representative republic" form of government. These individuals make the laws of our land (Nation) by listening to us, then creating laws that fairly represent our interests. Many times these laws are subjective to the experiences of men.

Man should be careful not to create laws that are in conflict with God's laws. When the laws of man conflict with the laws of God, we must defer to, or obey, the laws of God first. God has given man the authority to create laws. However, this authority is limited to the civil affairs of man and should be made in strict accordance with the laws of God. These laws should reflect the holy and righteous nature of God.

> **Man should be careful not to create laws that are in conflict with God's laws.**

There is another objective form of government that existed before man. It is not altered, determined, or controlled, by man in any way. This government belongs to the Creator and is a heavenly form of government. In this form of government, God is the supreme authority. He determines the laws, and these laws supersede man's laws. Because we are His creation, we must obey His laws before man's laws.

The authority by which God determines these laws exists in and of Him. He is God; therefore, He makes the rules. He is sovereign; therefore, everything He does is right. Man was a part of God's government before he sinned against God. This sin resulted in God allowing man to develop an earthly government. Man developed his form of government initially on the principles that reflected God's laws. God determines what is truth and right because He is sovereign. This means He answers to no other.

The objective standards we have in the world, come from the laws of God, and not from the laws of man. The laws of man are, and can only be, a reflection of the laws of God. Disobedience to man's law results in punishment equal to the offence. The same is true with God's laws. The Bible says the wages (or payment) of sin (which is disobedience to God's law) is death or separation from God. This is referring to both physical and spiritual death as mentioned previously. God's laws are to guide the development of man's laws. Without the laws of man, our society would be in turmoil.

Without God's guidance in the lawmaking process, our society would be in chaos. We actually see more and more of this chaos happening because man's laws increasingly do not reflect the nature of God. Without recognizing the importance of following God's laws in our life, our life has no real meaning or purpose. Many people try to live their life the way they want. They think they are making themselves happy by doing so. This is the very reason why so many people are empty and struggling to make sense of their life.

A Lie in Eden
Even though God created man a perfect being and placed him in a perfect environment, man still chose to violate God's law. God gave to Adam and Eve everything necessary to make them happy. The Bible gives us the record of how Adam and Eve disobeyed God's law.

In Genesis 3, we see how God commanded them not to eat the fruit of the tree of the knowledge of good and evil. God told them that if they did eat the fruit of this tree, they would surely die. Satan convinced Eve that she would not die, contrary to what God had told her. She then ate of the fruit and gave to Adam to eat also. Because Adam willingly and knowingly ate of the fruit in disobedience, God's law was broken. The punishment for breaking God's law had to be satisfied.

Adam and Eve died both physically and spiritually. They died at once spiritually. God cast them out of the Garden of Eden and most tragically, from His presence. They also started dying physically and eventually passed away. God was right and Satan was wrong.

> **God determines what is truth and right because He is sovereign.**

Every time a person dies, it reminds us that Satan is a liar. God gave them everything and Satan took it from them. This is the same today. God has given us everything we need to trust Him by believing on His Son Jesus Christ for salvation. He has also given us the ability to be free from life-controlling habits, but Satan prevents this many times by telling people "there's no punishment for sin," "there's no reason to fear anything, just have fun while you can." These are Satan's most effective lies, and many people follow after these lies by drinking, partying, as well as living loose and immoral lives, but there is a day of payment coming for all people who forget God. The Bible says in 2Corinthians 4:3-4,

> "But if our gospel be hid, it is hid to them that are lost: In whom the god of this world hath blinded the minds of them which believe not, lest the light of the glorious gospel of Christ, who is the image of God, should shine unto them."

Adam and Eve chose to disobey God's law. This disobedience plunged the human race into sin. From that day forward every person born is born a sinner. The Bible says in Romans 5:12,

> "Wherefore, as by one man sin entered into the world, and death by sin; and so death passed upon all men, for that all have sinned:"

Romans 3:23 says,

> "For all have sinned, and come short of the glory of God;"

These verses tell us we all have a sinful nature, and we do sin, not because of our environment or circumstances. God has also created a plan whereby we can have forgiveness of sins and once again dwell in the presence of God. By this plan, we can deal with the sin in our life. This is where we find real hope.

Sin

The truth is, God created man to love and to have fellowship with Him. Because of man's disobedience to God's law in the Garden of Eden, man committed sin against God, which resulted in permanent separation of man from God. Man continues, even today, to disobey God's laws.

Because God is pure, holy, and righteous, man cannot fellowship or even be in the presence of God because of sin. This again is spiritual death. Addictions are simply disobedience manifested through the desire to please self instead of pleasing God.

The Bible tells us sin, which began with Adam, continues today in us. We find this again in Romans 5:12. Therefore, we see that not only did the sin nature pass to us as well, but the penalty of our sin was also passed on to us. Every human being owes the payment for the punishment of sin.

Because man is sinful, every deed that man does in the flesh is also sinful. The very best that we can do in the flesh still falls short of the holiness of God. How then can we ever hope to have forgiveness of sin and be in the presence of God? God provided a way for the penalty of sin to be paid. It is the only way; there is no other way but this way. Acts 4:12 says,

> "Neither is there salvation in any other: for there is none other name under heaven given among men, whereby we must be saved."

This name is Jesus Christ, the Son of God.

The Gift of Salvation

Jesus died in our place on the cross. Jesus paid the entire penalty for sin that God demanded. Jesus said in John 14:6,

> "I am the way, the truth, and the life: no man cometh unto the Father, but by me."

Because Jesus paid the price of death for us, we must accept this gift in order to see God. We accept this gift of God's salvation by personally placing our faith and trust in Jesus Christ, God's Son, as our Saviour. We do this through prayer by admitting that we are a sinner and asking God for forgiveness for sin and asking Him to accept us into His family. This is God's plan for our salvation from the penalty of sin. It is His law and His truth. We must obey Him.

The following points are a simple explanation of true Bible salvation:

> All men are sinners
> Sin must be paid for
> Death is the penalty
> Every man-made attempt to pay for sin is insufficient
> God provided a payment
> Jesus Christ, God's Son, paid our debt as us on Calvary
> Man must repent and trust in Jesus Christ for salvation

For the believer in Christ there are many evidences of salvation. The most obvious is when God speaks to the heart of a believer. Over time, as God answers our prayers and our faith in God grows, a relationship is built. This relationship results in a process called "Sanctification." Sanctification is the result of living in obedience to God's Word. Sanctification is a process where God sets believers apart as holy servants for His purposes.

The by-product of living in obedience to God's Word is, not fulfilling the lusts of the flesh. The desire of the flesh to partake in things that are harmful, diminish as we become more obedient to God. This is the true meaning of "recovery." The process of sanctification, which is a process of God making man holy, results in what the world calls "recovery." In this sense, we are all in recovery.

God and Man

Because God is truth and all truth comes from God, we must begin with God. How do we know God exists? People have told me they did not believe in God. A man told me once he knew nothing about God. Therefore, he had no reason to believe God existed. The Bible says in its very first verse,

"In the beginning God..."

The Bible does not try to prove the existence of God. It declares it. The Bible also says that no one has seen God at any time. Have you ever seen God? No one has. How then do we know of His existence?

We must believe He exists by faith and in evidences manifested through a personal relationship with Him. God gives us several ways in the Bible that help us understand the truth of His existence: Conscience, Nature, and The Word of God.

Jesus paid the entire penalty for sin that God demanded.

Conscience
Romans 1: 19-20 says,

> "Because that which may be known of God is manifest in them; for God hath shewed it unto them. For the invisible things of him from the creation of the world are clearly seen, being understood by the things that are made, even his eternal power and Godhead; so that they are without excuse:"

In this example, the Lord clearly tells us that it is a natural part of man to know of the existence of the Creator. This is inherent in the conscience of man. In other words, it is already a part of man's nature to know of God because God has instilled it, or revealed it, to every man in his conscience.

Nature

Man knows there is a God because nature reveals this fact to him. The world, in which we live, reveals the presence of a Creator God. The Bible says in Psalm 19:1,

> "The heavens declare the glory of God; and the firmament sheweth his handywork."

Psalm 24:1-2 says,

> "The earth is the LORD's and the fullness thereof; the world, and they that dwell therein. For he hath founded it upon the seas, and established it upon the floods."

These verses tell us nature itself reveals the presence and power of the Creator God. When we consider the human body in all its wonderful complexities, we see what the scientists are now calling "intelligent design." Of course, we know this intelligence to be none other than God, but the scientist must acknowledge that the human body could not exist from a random act in space or even some far out theory of man evolving from a lower form of life.

There are mechanisms and processes in the human body that are programmed with the exact sequences needed to generate cells specific to a particular purpose. This type of programming cannot come from random mutations. Israel's king David said in Psalm 139:14,

> "I will praise thee; for I am fearfully and wonderfully made: marvelous are thy works; and that my soul knoweth right well."

The Word of God

The Word of God also reveals the existence of God and His creation of the world. In Hebrews 1:1-2, the Bible says,

> "God, who at sundry times and in divers manners spake in time past unto the fathers by the prophets, Hath in these last days spoken unto us by his Son, whom he hath appointed heir of all things, by whom also he made the worlds;"

John 1:1-4 says,

> "In the beginning was the Word, and the Word was with God, and the Word was God. The same was in the beginning with God. All things were made by him; and without him was not any thing made that was made. In him was life; and the life was the light of men."

These examples contain sufficient information to make us realize the truth about the existence of God. There is no denying this truth. To deny the existence of God is to deny our own existence. To refuse to believe in God, is a refusal to acknowledge the accountability we have toward God and His laws. The Bible also says in Psalm 14:1,

> "The fool hath said in his heart, There is no God."

The person who refuses to acknowledge these truths must work very hard to deny them. He must choose, contrary to what he knows instinctively in his heart and what he sees in nature, to betray the truth. It is actually much easier to believe in God by faith than to deny Him. Even though this is true, man still has the ability to continue to deny the existence of God, and many do. Having the will to choose is the most distinct characteristic given to man by God. This is one of the characteristics that make us different from plants and animals. However, to deny the existence of God does not remove the fact that all people will someday be held accountable for their actions, which are dictated by their beliefs.

The Nature of Man

All the things God created have a nature of their own. The different animal species have differing natures, which correspond to the purpose for which they were created. Plants and animals have their function in the world. People are not an exception to this.

Many people teach that man is a product of his environment. Many government programs try to change the environment in which some segments of our society live. It is their belief that if a person's environment is conducive to good behavior, that person will behave properly. The problem they fail to realize is, these environments are exactly what man created. Therefore, they are already a product of man's behavior. In other words, man creates the environment; his environment does not create him. Granted, this is a very simple analysis.

> **The by-product of living in obedience to God's Word is, not fulfilling the lusts of the flesh.**

Man continues trying to change who he is by changing his surroundings. Yet, we still have an increase overall each year in crimes and deaths around the world. Why? Is it because we have failed to produce enough "good" environments? No! It is because man can change everything in a person's environment, but the man is still the same.

A pig is a good example of this truth. The pig wallows in mud because it is a pig, not because it is in a muddy pin. It is in the nature of the pig to wallow in the mud. You can give a man, who does not care about himself, wealth, place him in a nice home, give him a good job, clothe him with the finest clothing available, give him the best education possible, and if nothing changes on the inside, within a few years he will be broke, homeless, jobless, and destitute.

You can take the pig out of the mud, wash it thoroughly, put clothes on it, put perfume on the pig, turn it loose and it will go as straight as it can to a mud hole; Why? Because it is a pig, it is in its nature to do so. Cats do not wallow in the mud because it is not in their nature. They are just the opposite; they are constantly cleaning themselves as a part of their nature.

There are more government programs today to help the environment of man than ever before in history. Why, then, is man not getting better? It is because man is not naturally "good" as the secular humanists will have you believe.

If man were naturally good it would not have taken long after his creation to discover what was necessary for him to learn how to get along with one another. Instead, man continues to have more and more conflicts with others. We see this in the wars of the past and present. This fact is not due to the environment in which men live; it is because of his fallen nature. Man's actions and environments are simply a reflection of what he is on the inside. Several influences reveal what men are on the inside. They are:

- Money or Wealth
- Recognition or Popularity
- Authority or Power
- Pressure or Conflict

Many people believe these circumstances change a person from what they were. It is my belief that these changes in their station in life only reveal what they already are in their character. If a person is kind and giving, having wealth only magnifies this characteristic and they give more generously. If they are cruel and mean to others, having authority or power only gives them the opportunity to be cruel to even more people.

We must understand that a sinner is not a sinner because of what he does. He does what he does because he is a sinner. This truth must be recognized in order to understand the true nature of addictions. It is the inside of man that makes him do what he does. If he has a character flaw or moral failure or some other characteristic which is not what it should be, he will act upon these flaws. The only way to change our actions is to change what creates those actions. There must be change on the inside before anything on the outside will be different.

The Bible says man's heart is deceitfully wicked. We can tell this just by looking around at our own society. Man is definitely not a product of his environment. His environment is a reflection of his sinful nature. At one point in my life, I was involved with a local government's housing project. I was in charge of a team of people who would clean up and remodel housing provided by this particular city. It was always interesting to me how that in just a few short years those houses looked the same as they did before we remodeled them. This was because the people who lived in them did not change.

> **Man's actions and environments are simply a reflection of what he is on the inside.**

If a person is to have any understanding of truth, they must accept the fact that all objects must have been created by design rather than the belief that things simply appeared through a big explosion in space. The complexities and intricacies of the world in which we exist scream out the truth that all things were created with a definite design and purpose.

Created beings have a purpose!

The meaning of this statement is explained best by examining the nature of any object. That is, what role does a particular object have in creation? Take a tree for instance. A tree is an object. It exists because we can experience it with all five of our senses if we choose to do so.

One of the roles the tree plays in our world is to give off oxygen for us to breathe. Through a God-designed feature of the tree, and plants in general, trees absorb carbon dioxide, which is exhaled from the lungs of human beings and animals, and through a complex process called photosynthesis, is used to produce oxygen, which is needed for human beings and animals to breathe and live.

Therefore, we can say all processes taking place within the tree are in and of itself. This makes it an object.

Trees and plants do not have the ability to change the purpose for which they were created. If they could, and did, we would die. Therefore, we can also say trees are fulfilling the purpose for which they were created. We can say that a tree is an example of an objective standard because it does not change in its purpose and function.

This means objects cannot choose to change the purpose for which they were created. The difference between objects and man is, man had a mind and a will. Humans can change their circumstances through the process of changing their mind. We change our mind about many things. This ability is called "will." Our will is revealed by the choices we make in life, regardless of whether those choices are good or bad.

Responsibility

No one would argue that we all have responsibilities. We have the responsibility to pay our bills. We have the responsibility to be good citizens of our country. We also have a responsibility to support our government through the payment of taxes. We have the responsibility to work hard for our employer.

Those who are married have the responsibility to be faithful to their spouse. Those who have children have the responsibility to rear their children in a proper manner. We all have certain responsibilities that go along with the privileges we enjoy as free citizens. If duty calls, we have the responsibility to serve our country in the military.

There are many other responsibilities we could mention, but the point is, we all have responsibilities. These responsibilities have a way of defining who we are. Because we are created in the image and likeness of God, our basic responsibility is to reflect the characteristics of the Creator.

For example, we know a watchmaker by the timepiece he creates. In other words, when you look at the artisanship of a watch, you automatically know what kind of watchmaker made the watch. You know if he was a meticulous artisan or not. You know if he takes pride in the work, he does. You also know how much effort he put into making the watch.

The watch tells us how important it is to the watchmaker. The materials used, the precision of the mechanisms, the quality of the assembly, all tell a story about the watchmaker. The watch could not create itself. It did not come into existence through a random violent act. It had to be carefully and meticulously created. It was also created for a specific purpose; to tell time.

The watch reflects the workmanship of the watchmaker. It cannot do this in and of itself. The watch must behave according to the manner in which it was created. This is the only way we can know the watchmaker. You might even say the watch is accountable to the watchmaker.

As created beings, the most important responsibility we have is to be obedient to God, the Creator. Our purpose in life is clouded by our willful disobedience to God. The first disobedience of Adam created a sinful nature for all humankind. This sinful nature has become worse over time. It has not become better. We see this in the events of the world today. Many believe the world is becoming a better place to live. I must say, they show extreme optimism, because things are not getting better, they are getting worse.

Our primary responsibility toward God is to reflect His nature and to fulfill the purpose for which we are created. We can only do this by having a daily meaningful relationship with God. This relationship gives us purpose and direction in this world. It creates in us an understanding of our place in the will of the Creator God.

A New Nature

Once we understand that we are born with a sinful nature this helps us understand that it is natural for us to choose things that are not good for us; things that God never intended for us. It is our nature to do wrong and make bad choices, but it is also God's desire that we do right.

When we are born, we have one nature. This is the flesh. This is the part of us that is still alive even though we are dead spiritually, just as Adam and Eve were. We will also die physically just as Adam and Eve did. Hebrews 9:27 says,

> "And as it is appointed unto men once to die, but after this the judgment:"

God had to make Adam and Eve alive again spiritually. He must make us spiritually alive again also. This spiritual change takes place when we accept and follow the plan God created for our salvation.

If God desires that we do right, and our nature is to do wrong, how can we ever hope to do the opposite of what our nature dictates? How can we live right when our nature will not let us do right? The answer is, God will give us a new nature when we repent of our sin and trust in His Son Jesus Christ for salvation. Jesus said in John 3:3,

> "Verily, verily, I say unto thee, Except a man be born again, he cannot see the kingdom of God."

Being "born again" is another way to express having a "new birth." This new birth makes us a part of the family of God. In fact, we become the very children of God. We cannot do right in our flesh, but we can do right living in the new life that Christ gives. God's Spirit dwells in us and gives us the strength we need to live right and make good choices. The Bible says in 2Corinthians 5:17,

"Therefore if any man be in Christ, he is a new creature: old things are passed away; behold, all things are become new."

Romans 6:4 says,

"Therefore we are buried with him by baptism into death: that like as Christ was raised up from the dead by the glory of the Father, even so we also should walk in newness of life."

Because we are now the children of God we have all the benefits that being children of God brings; eternal life, God's blessings, inheritance of Heaven, and the Holy Spirit of God, who now dwells in us. 1John 4:4 says,

"Ye are of God, little children, and have overcome them; because greater is he that is in you, than he that is in the world."

His riches become our riches. His strength becomes our strength. We do not deserve any of these things. By reading God's Word we gain knowledge of the things we should and should not be doing. We then have a responsibility to be obedient to those things we learn are right. James 4:17 says,

> **God will give us a new nature when we repent of our sin and trust in His Son Jesus.**

"Therefore to him that knoweth to do good, and doeth it not, to him it is sin."

Because we are children of God we are to submit our will to His. He is worthy of our love and obedience. This is one of our responsibilities toward Him. We are the ones who broke His law. We are guilty. We must recognize this and surrender our lives to Him. When we try to take things into our own hands and do things our way instead of God's way, we make many mistakes. Some mistakes follow us the rest of our life.

When we follow God in obedience, we receive His blessings on our life. Once a person has accepted Jesus Christ as Saviour, the Holy Spirit comes and takes up residence in that person. It is through the power of the Holy Spirit that we are able to obey God. The new nature God has given us desires to please Him.

This nature is what Adam and Eve possessed before they disobeyed God in the Garden. The flesh still wants to have its own way. There is a struggle between the flesh and spirit. Only when we follow the things of the Spirit, in obedience, do we have the strength to do right.

The Holy Spirit reveals the truths of God's Word to us, and the understanding of God's Word enables us to know what is right. We can then act upon what we learn in obedience. We still must choose to do right, but now, we have the help of the Lord to accomplish this. Without this new nature, it would be impossible to please God.

This is why a new nature is such an important topic. By choosing to make the decision to accept Jesus Christ as Saviour, we are acknowledging the following things:

1. We are a sinner who deserves separation from God.
2. Sin is a terrible offense to God and we need to repent (change our mind about) of sin.
3. We must ask God to forgive our sin and take control of our life.
4. We place our trust in Jesus Christ, alone, for salvation.

When we accept Jesus Christ, God's Son, as our Saviour, God then takes the spotless record of His Son Jesus and applies it to our record as though we were never a sinner. This is the only way God's demand for the payment of sin can be satisfied. It is a choice that each of us must make as an individual. No one can make this decision for us.

Application

The main emphasis of this chapter is to help people understand from where truth comes, to be honest with themselves, and determine that they will act upon the truths learned by being obedient to God. We must also understand that addictions are sin against God. However, just knowing the truth cannot be sufficient to produce change in a person's life.

There must be a conscious decision to take what is learned and apply it to one's life in obedience to God. God desires to help us in every area of our life. We need only to be obedient to His Word and trust Him for this help. The Bible says in Proverbs 3: 5, 6,

> "Trust in the LORD with all thine heart; and lean not unto thine own understanding. In all thy ways acknowledge Him, and he shall direct thy paths."

This is God's way for us to live our life. He does not want us to go through life not knowing what to do or where to turn. He already knows what path we should take. When we follow Christ, we do not need to worry about the path we will take because He is always with us and He knows the way. He wants us to trust Him for everything. After all, He knows the future for each one of us.

He knows exactly what we need and what we do not need. He knows what will be harmful to us and what will help us be the people we should be for His glory. Why would we not want to follow Him and trust Him for direction in our life?

I wonder how many people would turn down directions to the nearest hospital emergency room in the event a loved one needed immediate medical care. Why do so many people turn down God's instructions for having a happy and fulfilled life? It is because they fail to understand the truth of what fulfilling our responsibility to God brings to our life, simply as a by-product of our obedience to God.

When we live according to the commands given to us in God's Word, we are in a position to receive the blessings of the Lord. The reason most people do not follow God's Word is because they do not truly believe God is who He says He is. They want to live their own life and go their own way. They do not believe there is a judgment day approaching. They believe they can live any way they want to and not be accountable to anyone for how they live. They are sadly deceived.

If God is who He says He is, we must place our trust in Him and be obedient to what He commands. We must not only place our trust in Him to guide us in our daily walk, but we must believe that we will answer to Him one day for how we live our lives. He loves us and He wants to bless us more than we know. We must follow His commands in order to be happy and not be cast away or ashamed at the Day of Judgment.

We clearly understand that truth comes from God. God has given us every truth we need to live in obedience to Him, which enables us to live free from the bondage of addictions. He has given us the Bible as the source of truth and the Church as the instrument of declaring His truths.

If we are going to know the truth about who God is, what our responsibilities toward Him are, and how to serve Him, we must get it from the Bible and in the Church. This is why it is so very important that churches have a vision of winning lost people to Christ. It is the Church's responsibility to ensure the Gospel message goes out to every people group in the world, not just those of a foreign language or nationality.

Chapter 8

God - Belief System

Before we can understand how addictions take such a strong hold on someone's life, we must understand why people make good and bad decisions. There is one core reason a person makes the decisions they do, whether those decisions are constructive or destructive in nature. These decisions are simply an act of the will. We discussed in an earlier chapter the thought of addictions being habits. Addiction habits are a reflection of the will of a person early in the addiction cycle.

While habits are simply learned behaviors, there are reasons why a person chooses a particular behavior over another. We must step backward from the behavior and ask what causes a particular behavior in the first place. The answer to this question is also a simple one. We act or behave in response to what we believe about ourselves in relation to God. In other words, our beliefs govern our will. This is why it is so important that we understand how God views a person.

Understanding how God views us and what we believe about God in return, dictates our actions in any given circumstance. In other words, our beliefs form our experiences. What we believe about God is another reflection of what we were taught in our formative years as a child. It is necessary, for a productive and fulfilled life, to be taught the truth early in life about who God is and what He reveals about Himself to man. This is perhaps the most important chapter in the book. We must first understand who God is before we can understand what it is He wants us to do and how we are to live. Hebrews 11:6 says,

> "But without faith it is impossible to please him: for he that cometh to God must believe that he is, and that he is a rewarder of them that diligently seek him"

The Bible assumes the existence of God
As mentioned in the previous chapter it is not our intent to try to prove the existence of God. God makes no such attempt and neither will we. The Scripture always assumes the existence of God and never seeks to prove it. Instead of trying to prove the existence of God, the Bible presents His existence as a truth. The Bible declares in Psalm 14:1,

> "The fool hath said in his heart, There is no God."

We understand from this verse of Scripture that not only does the Bible assume the existence of God, but it also refers to a person who says they do not believe in God as a fool. Since the Scripture assumes the existence of God, does God give us evidences of this fact or does He simply make a statement we are expected to believe. Because God is entirely sovereign, He has the right to do either.

However, because He also loves us, He gives us a revelation of Himself. God reveals Himself to us in three different ways. These are nature, conscience, and His Word, the Bible. The reason it is important to review how God reveals Himself to us is that we must establish a foundation of why and how our belief systems shape our thought processes. To do this we must start in the beginning and move forward in a logical manner.

God reveals Himself to us in nature

There are evidences we find in nature that reveal the creative power of God. A person could not possibly consider the wonderful complexities and structures that exist in our physical world and declare the absence of this creation power. To believe that the world, with all its complexities and order, came into existence through some cosmic explosion in space is as ludicrous and absurd as believing that the many vehicles that are driven on our highways around the country came into existence through an explosion at a nearby automobile factory.

> **We act or behave in response to what we believe about ourselves in relation to God.**

Order does not and cannot result from disorder. Complexity cannot result from simplicity. Neither can unity be the results of chaos. There must be a divine intervention for complexity to happen. The secular humanists of our day want us to believe the opposite. They want us to believe the absence of a Creator God. They want us to believe this because if we recognize the true origin of nature, which includes humanity, then we must also be accountable to the Creator of this nature. There must be a divine designer for our complex world to exist.

Satan does not want us to believe in the existence of the Creator God. Satan has worked very hard to create substitutes for many things given to us by God - creation, music, love, etc. Satan wants to deceive people into thinking that man is not accountable to God. Therefore, Satan has used certain men to develop another explanation to how the earth got here. They call it evolution. Even though Satan has been very successful at this substitute, it does not change the reality that man is still accountable to the Creator God and will someday stand before Him in judgment.

God reveals Himself to us in conscience

When man honestly examines his heart, he can only conclude that there is a Deity, to whom he must answer. This Deity is none other than God the Creator. Have you ever asked yourself why the world is so "religious?" The world is so very religious because man is aware of the fact that there is more to come after this life is over.

Man is seeking to substitute the truth that God gave us about himself and our responsibilities toward Him. What we believe about this will affect our life in every way possible, including where we will spend eternity. We do not just exist in the "here and now." Religion attempts to fill the longing a person has for the truth, with a substitute for worshiping the one and only true and living God.

Unfortunately, religion only satisfies the conscience. There can only be one truth; we saw this in a preceding chapter. Man must choose to believe this one truth or deny it. Most people in the world today choose to satisfy their conscience rather than obey what the Creator of all things has commanded.

God reveals Himself to us in His Word
God cannot lie. In Titus 1:2 He says,

"In hope of eternal life, which God, that cannot lie, promised before the world began;"

Everything He says in His Word, the Bible, is true and we can have complete confidence in this. Truth is only one way to describe God's nature. He is more than truthful and He is more than trustworthy. He is both trustworthy and truthful because He is truth.

We describe God using other words, but none of these "make" God who He is. He is the one who makes these qualities what they are. The word love is another example of this. The Bible says in 1John 4:8

"God is love"

Because God loves, this does not mean that being loving is what makes God who He is. It is just the opposite. God loves because He is love. He is not only loving and trustworthy, but He is kind and compassionate. He is omnipotent or all-powerful. He is omnipresent or everywhere at once. He is omniscient or all knowing. He is immutable or never changing. He is everlasting-to-everlasting or eternal. Many books have been written about the revealed character of God. It is important for us to know and remember that whatever may be our present concept of God, we must seek to know the truth about God, that we may understand what our responsibilities are toward Him.

> **Most people in the world today choose to satisfy their own conscience rather than obey what the Creator of all things has commanded.**

The Bible gives us a clear presentation of what our concept of God should be. It is our responsibility to search for this proper concept. When we find the proper concept, it is our duty to accept it as our own. The following verses of the Bible will help us to have the correct concept of God:

John 4:24 "God is a Spirit: and they that worship him must worship him in spirit and in truth."

Romans 11:33 "O the depth of the riches both of the wisdom and knowledge of God! how unsearchable are his judgments, and his ways past finding out!"

Psalm 90:2 "Before the mountains were brought forth, or ever thou hadst formed the earth and the world, even from everlasting to everlasting, thou art God."

1Timothy 1:17 "Now unto the King eternal, immortal, invisible, the only wise God, be honour and glory for ever and ever. Amen."

1Timothy 6:16 "Who only hath immortality, dwelling in the light which no man can approach unto; whom no man hath seen, nor can see: to whom be honour and power everlasting. Amen."

Exodus 6:3 "And I appeared unto Abraham, unto Isaac, and unto Jacob, by the name of God Almighty, but by my name JEHOVAH was I not known to them."

James 1:17 "Every good gift and every perfect gift is from above, and cometh down from the Father of lights, with whom is no variableness, neither shadow of turning."

Deuteronomy 4:35 "Unto thee it was shewed, that thou mightest know that the LORD he is God; there is none else beside him."

Isaiah 43:10 "Ye are my witnesses, saith the LORD, and my servant whom I have chosen: that ye may know and believe me, and understand that I am he: before me there was no God formed, neither shall there be after me."

Exodus 9:14 "For I will at this time send all my plagues upon thine heart, and upon thy servants, and upon thy people; that thou mayest know that there is none like me in all the earth."

Matthew 19:17 "And he said unto him, Why callest thou me good? there is none good but one, that is, God: but if thou wilt enter into life, keep the commandments."

Belief systems
Now that we have established that addictions are simply habits that are learned behaviors, that our behaviors are generated from our will, that our will is governed by our beliefs, and that these beliefs form our experiences, it is helpful to understand from where our beliefs come. If our beliefs form our experiences, what exactly are beliefs?

> Belief – A persuasion of truth on the grounds of evidence distinct from personal knowledge.

System – Regular union of principles or parts forming one entire thing; regular method or order.

Way of life – Behavior based upon patterns of thought; routine actions based upon a series of accepted principles or theories.

What is a belief system? If we take the definitions above and form them into one statement that describes what a belief system is and how it affects our life it would be something like the following:

A Belief System is a conviction of principles that determine our response to any circumstance we face in life.

The belief system to which we adhere determines the decisions we make. For instance, if a person's belief system does not include believing they are accountable to God, they will ignore the laws of God and make decisions that are based only upon the person's desire of the moment. This kind of decision has obvious consequences, as history has taught us.

If a person's belief system does not include believing they will answer to the laws of our country, they will do things that have no regard for the laws of this country. Because man has allowed Satan to deceive him there are many wrong beliefs about the role man plays in this world. Having the wrong belief system allows a person to make decisions that are contrary to the laws and commands of God.

> **Having the wrong belief system allows a person to make decisions that are contrary to the laws and commands of God.**

If a person has no foundation for belief or a specific set of values, they will in turn believe anything and any behavior will be acceptable to them. This is a very dangerous prospect. Man's actions must be guided by an established set of objective values or chaos and violence will result. This established set of values is the very thing we see lacking in the societies around the world today; chaos and violence are also becoming more and more prevalent in our own country.

What a person believes determines how they live. What a person believes about God will determine what they believe to be the meaning of life. Theology is the study of who God is. What a person understands or believes about God, because of what he thinks he knows to be true about God, is called philosophy.

Many people have a philosophy about God that is not based upon what God says about Himself. This is faulty philosophy not based on sound theological study. Belief systems are formed much the same way. A person either forms a belief system based upon what they think they know, or from an authority. Human beings must receive clear instruction from God to have a correctly constructed belief system.

The following diagram illustrates the order for understanding the basic concepts that form a proper belief system. Each concept is the foundation for the next. Each concept can only be understood as it relates to, and builds upon, the previous concept.

God
Creation
Purpose
Accountability
Instruction
Obedience

Having the proper concept of God determines the Belief System we will have. Many people give little or no thought to their belief system. Proverbs 4:23 says,

> "Keep thy heart with all diligence; for out of it are the issues of life."

What we believe about God determines what we believe about creation. If we do not believe God created man, we will not believe there is a purpose for man to have been created. This in turn affects our belief about accountability.

If there is no purpose for having been created, we will not believe we are accountable to God. If we believe we are not accountable to God, we will not believe that God has given us instructions about how to live a life that is obedient to Him. Accepting or rejecting God's instructions will determine whether we will be obedient to God. If we are not obedient to God, we will not have His blessings, which will in turn cause great instability in our life now and ultimately prevent us from living with Him throughout eternity.

It has been our experience that it is necessary to begin any program to help addicts with these basic principles and concepts. This is the foundation on which to lay all other teaching. Many addicts have no concept of God whatsoever. Any concept they may have is distorted and confusing to them. The absence of Biblical leadership and role models in the life of an addict contributes to having the wrong concept of God.

> **What a person believes about God will determine what they believe to be the meaning of life.**

Let us look at these concepts in their proper order. In a world where people have the right concept of God, there is an understanding of how each of these concepts relates to the previous. When a person believes in God, they also believe God created them. The next logical step is to believe that God created them for a purpose.

If God created a person for a reason, then that person is accountable to God for that purpose. Since God did create man for a specific reason, and man is accountable for that purpose, God gave man instructions for fulfilling this purpose in their lives. These instructions are the Bible, God's Word.

Since we have the instructions necessary for man to fulfill the purpose for which he was created, all that remains is for man to be obedient to the instructions that God gave to him. This is where we find the meaning of life. Obedience is the vehicle by which man experiences happiness and fulfillment in his life.

Happiness is not found in fulfilling the desires of one's self; it is in fulfilling the desires of the Creator. Man was made to fellowship with the Creator. The only way man can be happy is to be in fellowship with the Creator. The only way man can have fellowship with the Creator is to be obedient to the Creator's commands.

This is the difference in secular programs and Christian programs. Secular programs say the addict needs only to clean himself up because he is only accountable to himself. This is why man is not happy and cannot find fulfillment. This is why many are seeking fulfillment in and through sins of addiction. The problem with this kind of "belief-system-thinking" is that it leaves out the consequences of sin.

In a chaotic society, there is no concept of God or one's responsibility to Him. This results in freedoms removed instead of freedoms granted. The Bible says in 2Corinthians 3:17,

"Where the Spirit of the Lord is, there is liberty."

Contrary to what those who deny Christ want us to believe, there is no freedom or liberty apart from knowing God. The very life of an addict proves this. An addict may think or say, "I do what I want." However, in reality, they do what the drugs and alcohol or any other sin of addiction tells them to do.

We refer to a person controlled by sins of addiction as being a slave to and in bondage to that sin. This is the opposite of freedom. The Lord Jesus Christ makes men free. He alone can free them from the bondage of sin, including sins of addiction; not reforming, not going to meetings every week, not a twelve-step program, or even self-determination. None of these things will bring freedom to a person.

A person may be clean and sober from drugs and alcohol and still be in bondage to them. We have all heard stories of people who were clean and sober for many years and suddenly relapse into greater addiction. Why is this? Why could this person not stay sober after having been sober for so long?

No one can free *himself* from the bondage of addiction. It requires that someone other than himself free him from that bondage. When a person is a slave to and in bondage to sin, they are not capable of freeing themselves from this captivity. It becomes necessary for someone else to free him. This is one of the main points where most people fail to see the truth; either because they cannot see it or simply refuse to admit it. Consider these verses of the Bible found in Romans chapter six that deal with the bondage of sin:

> "What shall we say then? Shall we continue in sin, that grace may abound? God forbid. How shall we, that are dead to sin, live any longer therein? Know ye not, that so many of us as were baptized into Jesus Christ were baptized into his death? Therefore we are buried with him by baptism into death: that like as Christ was raised up from the dead by the glory of the Father, even so we also should walk in newness of life. For if we have been planted together in the likeness of his death, we shall be also in the likeness of his resurrection: Knowing this, that our old man is crucified with him, that the body of sin might be destroyed, that henceforth we should not serve sin. For he that is dead is freed from sin. Now if we be dead with Christ, we believe that we shall also live with him: Knowing that Christ being raised from the dead dieth no more; death hath no more dominion over him. For in that he died, he died unto sin once: but in that he liveth, he liveth unto God. Likewise reckon ye also yourselves to be dead indeed unto sin, but alive unto God through Jesus Christ our Lord. Let not sin therefore reign in your mortal body, that ye

should obey it in the lusts thereof. Neither yield ye your members as instruments of unrighteousness unto sin: but yield yourselves unto God, as those that are alive from the dead, and your members as instruments of righteousness unto God. For sin shall not have dominion over you: for ye are not under the law, but under grace. What then? shall we sin, because we are not under the law, but under grace? God forbid. Know ye not, that to whom ye yield yourselves servants to obey, his servants ye are to whom ye obey; whether of sin unto death, or of obedience unto righteousness? But God be thanked, that ye were the servants of sin, but ye have obeyed from the heart that form of doctrine which was delivered you. Being then made free from sin, ye became the servants of righteousness. I speak after the manner of men because of the infirmity of your flesh: for as ye have yielded your members servants to uncleanness and to iniquity unto iniquity; even so now yield your members servants to righteousness unto holiness. For when ye were the servants of sin, ye were free from righteousness. What fruit had ye then in those things whereof ye are now ashamed? for the end of those things is death. But now being made free from sin, and become servants to God, ye have your fruit unto holiness, and the end everlasting life. For the wages of sin is death; but the gift of God is eternal life through Jesus Christ our Lord."
(Romans 6:1-23)

We must see sin as the greatest problem in the life of the addict, and the root cause of all addictions. This is not popular in the secular institutions and even in some "Christian" programs as well, because they have bought in to the idea that addictions are caused by environment and upbringing.

Many Christian institutions use material that promotes what man can do for himself, rather than what God must to do in the life of the addict. Our society has placed such a premium on self-assurance and self-esteem many people no longer feel any need to admit that they are a sinner in need of the Saviour. No one wants to be confronted with the prospect of being sinful.

The very mention of the word sin is offensive to people. Our society blames addictions on a disease or illness. Society says it is the "disease" of addiction that forces a person to satisfy the lusts of the flesh. Denial of sin has permeated even our churches to such a degree, that we send our members to the AA meeting instead of to the altar. Some say we are cruel and uncaring for confronting a person about their sin. I say we are compassionate. God convicts us of our sin because He loves us. He does not condemn us. He wants to save us from our sinful condition.

> John 3:17 "For God sent not his Son into the world to condemn the world; but that the world through him might be saved."

There is deliverance from sin - Lasting deliverance is found in the power of the Gospel of Jesus Christ! Why would we want to withhold this deliverance from people? God, through His one and only Son, and our Lord, has given us the opportunity to accept the gift of salvation.

> **No one can free *himself* from the bondage of addiction.**

By accepting Jesus Christ as our Saviour, we have the same power over sin and death that Jesus has. This power frees us from the bondage of sin, all sin; this freedom is not temporary, it is forever. The freedom we have in Christ is as eternal as God is; it is as complete as is the plan of salvation itself.

The Bible tells us that when we are in Christ (which means we have been born into the family of God) we have a new nature. We saw this already in 2Corinthians 5:17, where it says,

> "Therefore if any man be in Christ, he is a new creature: old things are passed away; behold, all things are become new."

Verse 21 also says,

> "For he hath made him to be sin for us, who knew no sin; that we might be made the righteousness of God in him."

Scripture says very clearly we are no longer to be a slave to sin and that our new nature is one in which we desire to please God with our actions, our thoughts, and our life.

A person controlled by drugs or alcohol is a slave to and in bondage to those sins. This is the opposite of freedom. Permanent freedom is available to all who will place their faith and trust in Jesus Christ. Man must come to God on God's terms; therefore, this faith is not for being free from addiction, but for dealing with our sinful condition.

God makes men free. He alone can free men from the bondage of sins of addiction, not a commitment to weekly meetings, a 12-step program, or sheer determination. John 8:32 says,

> "And ye shall know the truth, and the truth shall make you free."

Verse 36 says,

> "If the Son therefore shall make you free, ye shall be free indeed."

Many people say "I couldn't make it without going to the meetings." While this may be true to remain sober, we need to understand that just being sober or clean is not the ultimate goal. The goal is to be obedient to God and to live in such a manner that pleases Him. If a person must go to meetings in order to stay clean or sober I would submit to you that, they are simply trading one life-controlling habit or dependency for another.

There can be no real hope in this "meeting" type of thinking. The person who is afraid to, not go to meetings, is never truly free from the addiction. Many people who are going through this will tell you they are afraid they will relapse. If a person, who has a chemical dependency problem, realizes that he or she has a sin problem instead, there is hope because God forgives sin. This is not to say that the weekly meeting has no place in the recovery process. Meetings are useful, but only as a supportive role to a main curriculum taught through an addiction recovery program. The Bible states in 1John 1:9,

> "If we confess our sin, He is faithful and just to forgive us our sin, and cleanse us from all unrighteousness."

This verse is saying that each time we as believers come to God and confess our sin, whatever that sin may be, he will forgive us and cleanse us. It is like being able to press the "clear" button on a microwave oven. There are definite consequences for our actions. Even though there are consequences of sin in this life, God forgives us each time we confess our sin. He not only forgives us of our sin, but the Bible says in Psalm 103:12,

> "As far as the east is from the west, so far hath he removed our transgressions from us."

Hebrews 10:17 says,

> "And their sins and iniquities will I remember no more."

Not only does God forgive us of our sins, but also once they are under the blood, He does not remember them any longer. Let us apply these things to our belief system. We know that because man is sinful in nature he is not trustworthy. On the other hand, God is entirely truthful and trustworthy. Knowing this, why would a person follow man's guidance and not God's plan for freedom from addiction? Man does not have the answer.

There have been millions of dollars spent in research and treatment with very little progress made toward an effective solution to permanent addiction recovery. This is what is happening in "meetings" all around the country. The meetings themselves are not bad. It is what is being taught at some of the meetings that is harmful. The unsuspecting people who attend these meeting do not know the truth. I would submit that the people teaching in most of these meetings do not know the truth either.

Sources of belief systems

The Belief System to which a person holds, whether recognized or not, is a result of the influences or lack of influences from parents and/or authority figures during early childhood experiences or their formative years. The concept a person has of God is created by these authority influences and will determine a person's belief system. An incorrect relationship with authority figures can affect that person's relationship with God. The relationship a person has with their parents or those who rear them is one of the most powerful factors that shape a person's views of God and their ability to relate to others.

> **If a person, who has a chemical dependency problem, realizes that he or she has a sin problem instead, there is hope because God forgives sin.**

Strong Authority Figures in one's life will have the opposite effect. This is because God established authorities in our life to give us instruction. The type of authority a person has in their early childhood development also contributes a great deal in shaping many other aspects of their thinking. The Home, School, Church, and community are some of the most common sources of instruction early in a person's life.

The Home is the most influential place of instruction in the early years of a person's life. This is because parents and guardians are the first sources of instruction in the life of the child and are given the responsibility from God to train the child correctly. They are the first influences upon the thinking processes and behavior patterns of the individual.

Because they are responsible for the child's wellbeing and the child is completely dependent upon their care, parents or guardians have a tremendous amount of influence upon the formation of the child's values and behaviors. This, in turn, places a tremendous amount of responsibility on the parents to be the right kind of examples.

Aunts and Uncles can also be a great influence on the life of a child. Time spent with certain members of the adult family can have a lasting influence on the thinking and behavior of a child. It is important to know where and what the child is doing at all times. Most family members are trusted to do what is right, but do not always do what is expected.

In School, there are many influences on the thinking processes of the child. The teacher in the classroom and the coach on the sports field has traditionally had more influence outside the home than any other group of authorities in the lives of children and teenagers. The students view these people as consistent and safe. They become role models to many young people, and this role model position carries a great responsibility.

The Church also has the opportunity to influence a young person's life. Young people instinctively know who cares for them and who does not. Many times, they will seek out the relationships of those in a church because they know it is supposed to be a place of safety and a place where they will be told the truth. Pastors and Youth Leaders have a tremendous responsibility to reach out to these young people. By telling the truth in love, the young person can be reached with the Gospel of Christ at an early age.

The Business Leaders in a community also have a big responsibility to conduct business in a manner that is honest and forthcoming. The community many times looks to the business leaders as examples they want their children to follow. This places a tremendous responsibility on the business leaders to act according to the standards of traditional Biblical values.

The influence authority figures have in the early years of one's life greatly affects one's concept of God and man's purpose of existence. Many times authority figures give the wrong type of example in the early years of development. As a person in this situation matures into adulthood, guilt and blame can result.

Guilt and blame can also distort one's concept of God. We see this very vividly in the Biblical account of Adam and Eve in the Garden of Eden as recorded in Genesis chapter three. Because they were guilty of breaking God's command, they felt they should hide from God. In essence, their concept of God changed to one where they felt God could not see them. Because of sin, they chose to blame others for their sin rather than admitting their own guilt.

Their concept of God changed to one in which they believed God would accept their blaming another in response to their guilt. We can see through this story of Adam and Eve that guilt can definitely distort our concept of God and His laws to such a degree that it allows us to blame others for our moral failures. The greater the degree of guilt, the greater the amount of blame placed on other people and circumstances.

This can even reach a level where an individual views himself as a victim of society, instead of accepting responsibility for the choices he makes. We have seen this take place many times in our own society. While we do make choices, as just mentioned, we need to understand that addiction problems are not the result of poor choices only. The Bible gives us examples of how sin can take control of a person. Romans chapter seven is perhaps the most commonly known passage that deals with the struggle between the flesh and the spirit.

We know that in our flesh we are capable of doing anything that is wrong in the eyes of God. There is no limit to how low even those who are believers in Christ can sink. God desires that we come clean with Him and confess our sin and guilt. By doing so we are showing humility which allows God's grace to be extended to us. The Bible says in James 4:6,

"God resisteth the proud, but giveth grace unto the humble."

What is grace? Grace is God's unmerited favor on our lives. The right concept of God allows us to see Him as the ultimate authority in our life. God has given us examples of authorities such as parents, teachers, pastors, government officials, and others to be examples to us of Christ.

God has ordained that there be authorities in our life that we may receive instruction from them. God intends for these authorities to be good examples of holiness, discipline, and love. Unfortunately, many times these authorities fall short of God's intended example. Even though this may be the case in one's life, the Lord Jesus Christ has given Himself to us as the perfect example for us to follow. We learn about Him through a consistent study of Him found in the Bible.

> **The Home is the most influential place of instruction in the early years of a person's life.**

God's Word never changes. Therefore, we can have complete confidence in what God tells us in His Word. We can have confidence that the Bible's teachings and principles are true and trustworthy because they come from God Himself. They are just as relevant for us today as they were thousands of years ago.

Because we have God's instructions for living a life that is pleasing to Him, even if a person does not have what would be called "proper" influences in his or her life, they are still just as accountable to God to live in obedience to Him. We must make the choice whether to use less than ideal upbringing as an excuse for sinful behavior or choose to change the improper behaviors to one's that are based upon the principles of God's Word.

Our life is either an example for others to follow or an excuse for others to copy. Of course, the proper choice is a life that is lived in obedience to God, which leads others to a saving knowledge of Jesus Christ. The relationship a person has with Christ and their obedience to the Word of God are the tools God uses to change a faulty belief system into one that is pleasing to Him. It is through obedient living that we bring glory to God. This is the ultimate purpose of our existence as human beings.

Chapter 9

Creation - Choices

Once we understand the concept that what we believe forms our personal response to circumstances, we also realize that with these circumstances, we choose what action we will take, whether this action is right or wrong. To understand the addiction recovery process, it is necessary first to understand clearly not only man's origin, but also his responsibilities, in the choices he makes, to God, his fellow man, and to himself. As created beings, we must understand how to fulfill our purpose for having been created. This purpose results in having peace with God, value as a human being, and significance in this life and throughout eternity.

> Psalm 8:4 "What is man, that thou art mindful of him? and the son of man, that thou visitest him?"

What is Man?

Where did man come from? Why does he exist? These questions have been asked for thousands of years. I would submit that these are questions that are asked more and more as time goes by. Man is not getting smarter as some people believe. Are these questions worth knowing the answer to? What effect do the answers to these questions have on our life? Many people ask the question,

"What is the meaning of life?" Would the right answer to this question be worth knowing?

Ask yourself this question, "What is the meaning of your life?" Does it matter to you whether or not your life has a meaning? Is there value in having significance in life? If so, what value would that be? Our society today is teaching people that they have no real value or significance, either personally or otherwise.

How does it make you feel to know that society believes there is no value, worth, or significance in a human life? We see the results of this belief every day. Because people are taught that they have no value and purpose in life, there is no real meaning to living. This is reflected in the number of murders and suicides we see each year in our country alone. Add the total number around the world each year, and the number is staggering.

The absence of value and meaning in life is also reflected in the way certain individuals mutilate, pierce, and tattoo their bodies. Because they feel there is no real purpose for living they might as well do as they want to themselves. We could not go without mentioning the number of planned abortions that take place each year. The murdering of innocent, unborn lives is reflective of the decay and decline of the perceived value of life itself. In place of life having value is the "anything goes" mentality of the society in which we live.

There is an absence of purpose and value in the societies of our world because Satan has attempted to replace God and creation with evolution and humanism. According to this false theory, man is nothing but a higher animal. Therefore, man should have the right to act like an animal; and some do.

God teaches us in His Word that man was created as a unique and totally different being. God Himself makes the distinction when He said in Genesis 1:26,

"And God said, 'Let us make man in our image, after our likeness: and let them have dominion over the fish of the sea, and over the fowl of the air, and over the cattle, and over all the earth, and over every creeping thing that creepeth upon the earth.'" God created man with a definite purpose.

Choices

The choices we make in our life affect how we live our life now and where we will live after death. Our experiences are different from one person to the next. Therefore, we must have a fixed point of reference by which to make our choices and decisions.

God has given us a fixed point of reference. It is the written Word of God. We cannot trust our emotions because they change from one minute to the next. We cannot trust our senses because they can be fooled. We must trust God and His Word alone.

Man was created in the image and likeness of God. Therefore, man has a soul and spirit not just a body. In fact, it is better to understand that man is not a body that has a soul, but rather, a soul that has a body.

Trees and plants have only a body. Therefore, they are only reflections of God's creativity. They exist only in the present. They have no past or future. They have a beginning. They live for so many years and then cease to exist, returning to the elements from which they came.

> **There is an absence of purpose and value in the societies of our world because Satan has attempted to replace God and creation with evolution and humanism.**

Man on the other hand, has a soul and body that is given to him by God. He only lives for so many years in that body, but he has a soul that will live forever. While man's body is living, his mind is actively functioning by making decisions and choices that effectively change his present and future.

The choices a man makes determine whether the man is fulfilling the purpose for which he was created. If a man does not fulfill the purpose for which he was created, he is unhappy and has problems that affect many other circumstances around Him. If a tree had a will to choose and it chose not to produce oxygen it would affect many other parts of creation would it not.

Consider this: Man is the only part of creation that has the ability to choose not to fulfill the purpose for which he was created. We will see what this purpose is in a following chapter. What does this have to do with truth and objective standards as they relate to addictions and recovery?

Truth does exist regardless of what some may say; truth is found in the form of objective standards, which exist in and of themselves. The most important revelation of truth is found in the person of Jesus Christ. According to John 1:14, Jesus Christ is the Living Word. Jesus says in John 14:6,

"I am the way, the truth, and the life: no man cometh unto the Father, but by me."

Jesus Christ is truth. He is God, therefore, He exists in and of Himself. He is our Objective Standard that does not change. The Bible says in Hebrews 13:8,

"Jesus Christ the same yesterday, and to day, and for ever."

We must make a conscious decision to follow Christ in obedience. This is an act of our will. By following Christ, we are fulfilling the purpose for which we were created and our lives can become what they are supposed to be.

When we base our decisions on what matters to Jesus Christ, and what He commands, we are obedient to the ultimate Objective Standard. Therefore, there is no subjectivity or subjective reasoning in these decisions. This is the standard by which the addict should learn to make decisions and choices. Once the addict learns that making choices that are obedient to God is the right path, it becomes a simple matter of his will to train himself to be obedient to God. By creating habits that are obedient to God after salvation, the addict in-turn creates actions that are constructive to a healthy and happy life and not the destructive choices he has made in the past.

Any society will result in chaos that base their actions on subjective reasoning. For example, traffic lights are designed to maintain order and unity. If a person in vehicle approaches a traffic light and does not understand the law regarding the colors, or simply the meaning of the colors, they will not know what action they must take.

In a world where truth is subject to experiences and emotions, instead of being objective in nature, the colors of the traffic light could mean, as many different things as there are people who drive through the intersection. Imagine the chaos and resulting consequences due to this kind of thinking. Without this objective standard, i.e. the colors of the traffic light, many injuries, and deaths would occur.

> **Man was created in the image and likeness of God.**

God created man a perfect being with a conscience and will to choose between right and wrong; which means to make moral judgments. God created man to be what is called a "free moral agent." Man, in his natural state, is a product of all the choices he has made in his lifetime.

Man has a responsibility to glorify God with the mind and body He gave us. The truth is, we do have very significant value to God both in this life and for eternity. The "Key Verse" for this chapter is Psalm 8:4 and it says

> "What is man, that thou art mindful of him? and the son of man that thou visitest him?"

This question is answered in the next two verses, which read,

> "For thou hast made him a little lower than the angels, and hast crowned him with glory and honour. Thou madest him to have dominion over the works of thy hands; thou hast put all things under his feet:"

And in Genesis 1:27 the Bible says,

> "So God created man in his own image, in the image of God created he him; male and female created he them."

There can be no mistaking the fact that God is the Creator and that He created humanity as well as all things. In the New Testament book of John and in the first three verses of the first chapter it says,

> "In the beginning was the Word, and the Word was with God, and the Word was God. The same was in the beginning with God. All things were made by him; and without him was not any thing made that was made." In addition, in verse fourteen, it says, "And the Word was made flesh, and dwelt among us."

Because we were made in the image of the Creator, our lives have both value and significance. So much significance, in fact, that God's Son, Jesus Christ, gave himself to die in man's place to satisfy God's demand for the payment of sin. Romans 6:23 says,

> "For the wages of sin is death; but the gift of God is eternal life through Jesus Christ our Lord."

For man to, not fulfill the purpose for which he was created, is to disregard or waste this value and significance. We understand very clearly from these verses that God created us and we were created in His image. Being created in His image gives the life of every human being very personal significance and purpose.

Because man was made in God's image, and created with a specific purpose, man is also accountable to Him and must obey the laws of God. This obedience is necessary to bring glory to God and for man to enjoy fulfillment. In observing nature, it is very evident that all other members of God's creation are in obedience to the purpose of their existence.

God also made a way for man to live obedient lives within the veil of sinful flesh. This is true in the life of a person who has been born again into the family of God. As stated earlier, when a man accepts Christ as his Saviour he becomes a new creature. The hidden part of man, his soul, becomes alive in Christ. As Christ lives both in and through a person, that person becomes more and more obedient to God and His laws. Just as disobedience to God is a choice, being obedient to God is also a choice that men make.

> **Man has a responsibility to glorify God with the mind and body He gave us.**

Understanding this concept of choice is critical to recovery. When people make excuses for their choices, all they are doing is denying their responsibility for their behavior. For example, when a person uses the excuse of a loved one dying, to drink or use drugs, they are in reality only doing what their flesh dictates that they do - Hoping others will excuse their behavior because of the loss of the loved one. Many times this is just an attempt to make themselves look like a victim in order to gain sympathy; in this way they can excuse their own behavior.

Once a person reaches a certain age they become the product of the choices they make in life, not a victim of circumstances. We see an example of this graphically portrayed in Luke 15:11. In this story, the young man chose to take his inheritance and leave home. He disregarded all he knew that was right.

He found himself feeding the hogs in the field and was so hungry he wound up eating the very thing he was feeding to the hogs. He came to his senses and decided to go back home and ask if he could just be a servant in his father's house. The point is, the young man found himself in this terrible position because of the choices he had made not because of circumstances. The same holds true for the addict. They are in trouble because of choices to satisfy their flesh rather than God.

For most addicts, the ability to choose is a curse because they have learned through destructive habits to choose the wrong things for their life, but it can be just the opposite. With the right counsel and training, and by receiving tools by which to change, the addict can turn the ability to choose into a blessing. Ultimately, it is still the choice of the individual.

Chapter 10

Purpose - Significance

The world's key motivation for living and working in this world is to have a purpose for which to exist. Purpose and significance are elusive goals that most people rarely understand how to reach. The topic of significance has a high premium in the motivational speaking world today. While it is true that without a singleness of purpose, man wanders aimlessly through life and has no real reason to live, but anything man does that has any significant meaning must first begin with God. God must have His rightful place in men's hearts and lives.

Purpose begins with God's purpose in the world. That purpose is transferred to those who are saved. Our duty is to find our place in this purpose. Purpose for life begins after salvation, not before. The meaning of life is God bringing us to Himself. We are here to know God, not to accomplish some great work or live for self-gain. The greatest accomplishment we could ever have is coming to know the Lord. 2Timothy 1:9 says,

> "Who hath saved us, and called us with an holy calling, not according to our works, but according to his own purpose and grace, which was given us in Christ Jesus before the world began,"

Before we can know our purpose in this world, we must understand what God says about our purpose. There are many books written today about purpose in life. Many people are trying to find purpose for their existence. They are searching in places where they believe they will find purpose, but without exception, when this search is apart from God's Word and God's plan for their life, it results in disappointment and failure.

> **God did not create this world and humanity without having a purpose for doing so.**

God did not create this world and humanity without having a purpose for doing so. Knowing this truth gives us hope and comfort. We are assured through God's Word (and He cannot lie) that if we trust in Him and put our faith in Him he will direct our lives into the things that will be for our good and His glory. Ephesians 3:11 says,

> "According to the eternal purpose which he purposed in Christ Jesus our Lord:"

God gives a clear explanation in this verse as to why He has created purpose to be a significant part of our lives. He has given this purpose to those who love Him. The reason God has given to all men purpose is Jesus Christ. The Scripture says in John 17: 7-9, 11, 22, and 24,

> "Now they have known that all things whatsoever thou hast given me are of thee. For I have given unto them the words which thou gavest me; and they have received them, and have known surely that I came out from thee, and they have believed that thou didst send me. I pray for them: I pray not for the world, but for them which thou hast given me; for they are thine…And now I am no more in the world, but these are in the world, and I come to thee. Holy Father, keep through thine own name those whom thou hast given me, that they may be one, as we are…And the glory which thou

gavest me I have given them; that they may be one, even as we are one:"

Let us be clear about this, Jesus Christ is the reason as well as the source of purpose and significance. He cannot be separated from these two at any level. Therefore, it is necessary for us to look first to Him for the meaning of both purpose and significance.

We must understand that Christ determines our purpose, and why having a purpose is necessary. We also need to know why the Holy Spirit must lead us as opposed to being driven by purpose. We need to learn how God defines purpose, and how to determine God's purpose for our life. Before we begin our discussion on these, we will deal briefly with the topic of significance. It is my firm belief that in order for us to have a purpose in our life there must first be something that is significant enough to give us this purpose.

The definition of purpose is "that which a person has set before himself as an object to be reached or accomplished; the end or aim to which the view is directed in any plan." The definition of significance is "meaning or importance."

The world's definition of purpose and significance is the following: Logically speaking, in order for a person to establish something worthy of significance, there must indeed be an object of such significance by which to generate sufficient motivation. In other words, the prize must be adequate for the struggle. The carrot must be large enough to motivate the horse to pull the wagon. The world establishes certain "tradeoffs" as a result.

This can be a very dangerous application in a person's life if not guided properly by the Word of God. While this philosophy is used in motivational seminars and in motivational techniques, many Christian counselors also apply this to their patients as well. It is easy to apply purpose and significance in a humanistic fashion, but in the content of this book, we are looking purely at the spiritual applications of how the object of our purpose must precede our motivation in having a purpose in the first place. Christ is the motivation for this purpose. Christ alone must be the object of significance for the right purpose in life to exist.

Why must Christ alone be the object of significance for the right purpose to exist? Why cannot something other than Christ be the goal? The reason Christ must be the object of significance is that man can only come to God through a personal relationship with Christ. Man possesses an innate knowledge of the Creator. Man responds to this knowledge in only one of two ways: a desire to know the Creator more or to rebel against the Creator and attempt to block out the reminder of the existence of the Creator. This choice determines the course of a person's life.

The choice to accept God's truth regarding purpose and significance leads to a life filled with joy and peace. Knowing early in life the significance God has placed upon humanity, brings great peace and contentment even at an early age. Not recognizing this significance generates insecurity and improper characteristics that lead to a very unsettled and unstable life.

A person that struggles with life-controlling habits, for the most part, have not had a clear presentation of who God is and man's significance to Him. People, who do not know man's significance and importance to God, typically follow the path most likely to gain them acceptance by the strongest forces in their life at the time. The strongest forces in people's lives are usually peer pressures. Because they have not learned what it means to be accepted by God, they have inadvertently chosen to be accepted by their peers instead of God. This is the type of person in which all individuals struggling with addictions can relate.

Because of this choice, this individual is more likely to be dominated by sins of addiction. The question, "How may a person who is dominated by sins of addiction find deliverance from such things?" will be answered later on in this chapter. Once it is established that there must be significance before there can be purpose, and that this significance lies in the love God has for His creation, we can then understand that the purpose of life becomes very clear. The clear purpose of man is to bring glory to God. Because God created man in His image, man's life has sanctity, value, and significance to Him as the Creator. In glorifying God, man fulfills the purpose for which he was created.

How do we learn to glorify God? God has given us clear instruction in His Word on how to learn to glorify Him. 2Timothy 2: 15 says,

"Study to show thyself approved unto God,…"

What is it that God wants us to study? He wants us to study His Word, the Bible. This is so simple many refuse to believe it. Yet this is exactly what God wants us to do. The rest of this verse says,

"…a workmen that needeth not to be ashamed, rightly dividing the word of truth."

Not only are we to study the Word of God, but we are also to put to work what we have learned. How do we do this? We put what we have learned to work by getting involved in reaching others for Christ.

> **Christ alone must be the object of significance for the right purpose in life to exist.**

As we learn what to do because of studying God's Word, we also learn that everything we do should be to the glory of God. He tells us this in 1Corinthians10:31 where He says,

"Whether therefore ye eat, or drink, or whatsoever ye do, do all to the glory of God."

This means even the small things we do every day should be done in a way that glorifies God. The Bible says we are to be "workmen that needeth not to be ashamed." God is saying to us that there is no reason at all that we need to be ashamed. Ashamed of what? Ashamed of bearing the reproach of being a Christian in a dark world and having an answer to give to a questioning world of the hope that lies within us. There are many Christians who are ashamed to be identified with Christ when it comes to taking a stand for what is right, either in the workplace or with lost friends. What a real shame this is!

Jesus said, "If you are ashamed of me before men, I will be ashamed of you before the Father." I do not want my Saviour to be ashamed of me. By studying God's Word and being obedient to it, we have the strength not to be ashamed to be a Christian as well as live a life free from addictions. God loves us so much that He has made it very simple for us to follow Him. This does not mean that the Christian life is an easy life, but it is the best life a person can live. Is being in bondage to terrible sins an easy life? Are the tragedies of people losing their lives because of addictions a better life? There is no easy way to be a follower of Christ. The world hated Jesus Christ when He was on this earth, and the world hates Christians now. Nevertheless, it is still a better life.

The Bible says, "And ye shall know the truth, and the truth shall make you free." The truth is, when man chooses of his own free will to follow God in obedience, God gives that person, through the power of the Holy Spirit, the ability to live a clean and sober life. Bondage to sin is voluntary slavery.

To overcome this bondage, there are a couple of things that need to happen. First, the person must place their trust in Jesus Christ for salvation. The next thing is to be obedient to the truth which they learn in God's Word. Obedience begins in following Christ in believer's baptism. As this person is obedient to the Lord, the Lord will reveal more truth to him. This cycle will continue yielding growth and strength in the life of the Christian.

The Bible says, "If ye walk in the Spirit, ye shall not fulfill the lust of the flesh." God has said this and He cannot lie. Our reason for being created has determined our purpose in life. This reason is defined and designed by God himself and is necessary to bring Glory to Him. Even though we make a general and broad statement that man's purpose is to glorify God by being obedient to his Word, how do we apply this to our individual lives?

We quote a passage of scripture throughout this book out of Proverbs chapter three verses five and six. We see from these verses that God clearly has a path for each one of us to follow. In order for us to follow this path, we must first be following Christ and "Looking unto Him."

The Bible also says, "The steps of a good man are ordered by the Lord." Since we know that no man is good, according to Romans 3: 10, the only way a man can be good is to be in Christ or to have received Christ as his Saviour. Therefore, Christ is living in him. Then, God says his steps are ordered. This means they are already established. People who have trusted Christ as their Saviour have a plan for his or her life that God has already established. All we must do is believe and accept this and follow Christ. He already knows each step of the journey. All we must do is trust Him and follow Him in obedience.

As we grow in Christ and our relationship becomes stronger, we see and hear more and more of His voice leading us and guiding us. When we place our trust in God, the outcome becomes His responsibility. There is such a freedom and liberty in this knowledge. The truth does indeed make us free. As we grow spiritually in this freedom, we realize that God is a much stronger force in our life. We are able to recognize that the object of our affection then becomes the reason for obedience. Let me explain.

When a person accepts Christ for the forgiveness of their sins, and begins walking this path of obedience, love for God increases over time. The more a person realizes exactly what God has done for them in giving His Son, Jesus Christ, to die in their place, for placing them in the family of God, and that God the Holy Ghost is present with them to help them walk the Christian life, their love for God grows.

This love grows to such a significant level to where the person desires to please God above all other things. When God becomes the object of a person's affection, it gives that person the motivation to do things that are pleasing to God and not things that are pleasing to self.

God has already given individuals a purpose for their life. All that is necessary is to embrace this purpose and make an honest decision to follow Christ. Once a person has made this decision, the rest is in the Lord's hands.

The following is a simple outline of the steps a person must take in order to be free from addiction, free from fear of relapse, and free to live a happy and fulfilled life.

> 1. Recognize that this addiction is sin and not a sickness. This realization is at the heart of the recovery process. It is important to believe that God can, and will, forgive sin, if a person will ask God for forgiveness.

> 2. Place their complete trust in Jesus Christ, the resurrected Son of God, for the salvation of their eternal soul. Once this miracle has taken place in a person's life they must make their profession known publicly by following in obedience to Christ's command in baptism.

> 3. Begin a daily time of prayer and study of God's Word. A person who has struggled with addiction must be devoted to spending time with God in order to be free from the addiction and fear of relapse. It is very difficult for a person who has a close relationship with God to have the desire to be disobedient to God's commands. His desire rather is to please God through obedience.

> 4. Become a member of a good Bible preaching church and become active in the church ministries, especially the soul winning outreach. It is important for people to share what God has done in their own life with others. By doing so, the

addict will find this will strengthen not only their faith but also their will and desire to live a clean life. True healing can only take place when a person focuses on others instead of himself.

Addicts should also understand that most of the time all trust in them has been destroyed. It takes a very long time to rebuild trust that has been destroyed through the activities associated with life-controlling habits. Patience is needed. The addict does not destroy trust overnight, and it cannot be rebuilt overnight. The key here it is humility. A person who is trying to regain normal relationships must realize that it is a very difficult task, but it is well worth the effort in the end.

> **When we place our trust in God, the outcome becomes His responsibility.**

Many addicts feel it is easier just to keep using than to try to rebuild their life. This is an irrational conclusion that is derived from false logic or disrupted thinking processes created by the addiction. Regardless of the past, living a Christian life is the best life a person can live on this earth. Nothing can match the peace and joy a person has when they have a right relationship with the Creator. There is no better living than a transformed life!

It is well worth the effort to be humble enough to bear the ridicule of some, the lack of trust from others, and the difficulties in rebuilding a life after addiction. One of the most important things to remember is there are many people who will help through this whole process. The right kind of Pastor and church membership will welcome a recovering addict into their church and help them be accountable in this new life. The right kind of friends will give constant support and help throughout this rebuilding process. Most importantly, the Bible says in 1John 4:4,

> "...because greater is he that is in you, than he that is in the world."

This verse tells us that we are not alone and that we have the very power of God at our disposal. Without this power in the life of a people, no one can do right. Jesus said in John 15:5,

"For without me ye can do nothing."

This includes me, you, and everyone else. We must have the grace of God in our lives to live the kind of life that is pleasing to Him. Obtaining the grace of God is why we must yield to God everything about us and in us; our present abilities, our desires for the future, and our past mistakes.

It is also suggested that a person who is recovering from addiction not be alone for any extended period, but rather spend time in positive reinforcing activities. It can take anywhere from 18 to 36 months for certain drugs to be cleaned from the body's system. This is assuming proper diet and exercise. This time can be much longer if a proper diet and exercise program are not followed.

Accepting Christ as Saviour, following the Lord in baptism, becoming active in a good local church, having Christian fellowship with supportive friends and family, proper diet and exercise, a humble attitude, patience with those who may still mistrust them, consistent daily prayer and Bible reading, and time, are all essential to a full and lasting transformation from a life of addictions to a life that brings Glory to God. This is the ultimate purpose in life. It can be achieved only through the power of God in our lives. We receive this power from God as He says in Philippians 4:13,

"I can do all things through Christ, which strengtheneth me."

The Object of Our Affection
It is impossible to have any kind of meaningful relationship with a person without spending time with them. When a young man and young woman meet, they desire to spend time together. This is necessary to discover whether they are compatible in critical areas of personality, background, and goals in life. As the relationship

strengthens, so does the affection they have for one another until they each become the other's object of affection.

This change takes place over time. As a young couple learns more about one another, over time, their friendship and commitment turn into love and devotion for one another. This is a normal process of learning to love someone and being devoted to their wellbeing. This process also creates the desire in a person to please the other.

Understanding our purpose in life may not be learned at an early age for some people, but it can still be learned at any age. Many people do not have a Christian upbringing or the right kind of influences in their life that convey the idea that God is love and that He loves us unconditionally. Therefore, it would be unrealistic to expect a person with this background to understand this concept. The love of Christ demonstrated in the life of a Believer is one of the best ways to convey the truth to others that God is love.

> **Recognizing that Jesus Christ should be the object of a person's affection gives them a real purpose for their life.**

Once the concept of the love of Christ for us is conveyed to the program participant in the context of Christ dying on the cross, as us, and for the payment of our sin, they will either accept Christ or reject Him. It is the responsibility of the Holy Ghost to convict a person of sin and draw them to God. It is important for the Christian worker to understand the power of the Gospel so that he can be a witness for Christ without fear or apology. Romans 1:16 says,

> "For I am not ashamed of the gospel of Christ; for it is the power of God unto salvation, to every one that believeth..."

Giving the Gospel of Christ to the addict is the main purpose of the addiction recovery ministry. Giving a person knowledge to overcome a life-controlling habit, is secondary to this.

Many people who realize what Christ has done for them, will accept Jesus Christ as their Saviour, and establish Christ as the object of their affection. They will desire to live a life that is pleasing to God. This is the true recovery process. When a person realizes in their heart that they should and want to please God, they will adjust their behavior accordingly. This does not mean that they will never stumble or fall, but it does mean that they will strive for this goal.

As the new convert grows in spiritual maturity, their love for God also grows. As spiritual things become more dominant in the life of a Christian, there are fewer things in their life that are displeasing to God. This is called the process of sanctification. The process of sanctification brings about an understanding of the true purpose in life.

Chapter 11

Accountability - Relationships

The reason we deal with accountability and relationships is to help people understand their accountability toward God and Man and how their conduct and behavior are affected or controlled by their motives. If we have lived in obedience to God's Word, when we stand before Him at the judgment, our works will have been of His will and choosing, our lives of His making, and our relationships of his desire. Ecclesiastes 12:13-14 says,

> "Let us hear the conclusion of the whole matter: Fear God, and keep his commandments: for this is the whole duty of man. For God shall bring every work into judgment, with every secret thing, whether it be good, or whether it be evil."

It has often been said, "No man is an island." We use this quote many times to illustrate man's relationship to one another. This statement shows that there is a responsibility each human being has toward another. This responsibility is natural, but from where did it come?

Consider the following series of questions as we attempt to generate thought on this subject. Is there a beginning to this well-accepted, unspoken rule that we have responsibility one to another?

What is the origin of this concept of accountability? We can take it another step further and ask the question, "What is accountability?" Are there limitations to this accountability? If so, who sets these limits and boundaries? How do the relationships we have with other people affect us? How does the relationship we have or do not have with God effect our relationships with others?

What kind of relationship, if any, are we supposed to have with God? What characterizes this relationship? Many questions like these are answered in one way or another during the lifetime of a person. We need to explore the answers to these questions. We also must know why the answers to these questions are important to us.

Even though these questions are answered over a person's lifetime, many times they are answered in the wrong way or with the incorrect conclusion. As a result, there are destructive behaviors that are prevalent in the life of an individual. It is our intention in this chapter to answer these questions from God's perspective. We find this perspective directly from the Word of God. Since He is the One who created man, who better to understand the relationships in which man is involved?

We will begin with the basics of human nature and human need. We will then progress, using God's Word, to a conclusion that will help us in many different ways, not just in dealing with sins of addictions. Through this chapter, we hope to discover the true nature of man's relationship with God.

It is my conviction that when a person settles these questions many of life's problems can be corrected. God has uniquely created each person. Individuals possess unique characteristics that belong to them only. This includes the area of personality as well as physical characteristics.

Every person has certain basic traits that can be categorized into recognizable groups, although each person retains their own individual uniqueness. We see this throughout all of God's creation. The simple snowflake is a well-known example of God's creativity.

The fact that each person's fingerprint, voiceprint, DNA strand and the shape of the eye's cornea is different from any one else in the world is evidence of God's diversity and creativity. His plan for each of our lives is also uniquely different.

It is differences that God uses as different colored threads to weave a beautiful tapestry of humanity through time. Knowing that God has a definite purpose for each person reveals the love He has for His creation. This purpose begins with one truth, which affects all other aspects of our life. It is the true that God created man for fellowship and to glorify Him. This truth determines whether a person successfully accomplishes his purpose for being.

> **Knowing that God has a definite purpose for each person reveals the love He has for His creation.**

We also see a similar pattern of relationship all through creation. God exists in eternity past, present, and future. We learned in previous chapters that God created man, which has the unique quality of self-will, and the ability to make choices regarding every area of his life, even if that choice is contrary to what God knows is best for him.

We also learned that this ability to choose is referred to as "will." Another descriptive definition is "having the ability to make moral judgments." Therefore, we are called "free moral agents." Along with this ability to choose are the consequences of those choices. We are responsible for the choices we make. Because these choices most often affect other people, we are therefore accountable to our fellow human beings.

The choices we make in life affect other people in various ways. To conclude that one's choices in life affects no one is simply a refusal to acknowledge the truth. It does not change the outcome. This is why we must recognize that when we sin against God, through sins of addiction or any other type of sin; we are creating a circumstance in which someone, somewhere, is affected in an adverse way.

How do we know this to be true? Other than the testimony of nature itself, the Bible tells us because of the sin of one man all men are separated from God. Romans 5:12 says,

"Wherefore, as by one man sin entered into the world, and death by sin; and so death passed upon all men, for that all have sinned:"

This clearly shows that one person's actions or choices affected many more people than just himself and with devastating consequences. When there was a conflict with the first two sons born to man on the earth, which resulted in the murder of one, we see the very Creator Himself holding the remaining son accountable for the other's death.

His accountability was emphasized even though the living son tried to deny his responsibility for his actions. We read of this account in the book of Genesis, the fourth chapter. Here we find the origin of our responsibility to our fellow man.

The story of Adam sinning against God is also found in the book of Genesis, and in the third chapter; this is the origin of our accountability to God as the Creator. In both accounts, we understand that man cannot live to himself only. Man is accountable both to God and to his fellow man for his choices. Understanding this accountability helps guide our motives for our conduct and behavior.

Realizing that we are accountable to God produces a reverence and respect for God and the things of God. Reverence and respect for God is called, "The fear of God." This "fear" is not a cowering or trembling fear we would associate with a moment of terrible crisis or disaster. This fear is rather a humble reverence at the realization of who God is. Proverbs 1:7 says,

> "The fear of the Lord is the beginning of knowledge: but fools despise wisdom and instruction."

In Matthew 10:28 Jesus said,

> "And fear not them which kill the body, but are not able to kill the soul: but rather fear him which is able to destroy both soul and body in hell."

We see here that a humble fear of God will bring about behavior that is obedient to Him. What man believes about God will determine whether he will live for Him. If a man has no fear of God, he is a fool. Psalm 53:1 says,

> "The fool hath said in his heart, There is no God."

What a man believes in his heart to be true about God, will determine how he conducts his affairs with his fellow man as well as with God. This belief will determine the choices a person will make concerning his relationship with others.

If a person fears God and believes that he is accountable to God, he will make choices that reflect that belief. He will recognize his responsibility to others and not make selfish decisions that will be harmful to those relationships. Therefore, if a person has the right kind of relationship with the God who created him, he will also have the right relationships with his fellow human beings.

Relationships

How does a person have a right relationship with God? Because God also desires us to fellowship with Him and to have the right kind of relationship with Him, He gave us instructions on how this can take place.

We find written in the Bible, in the book of Hebrews, chapter four, verses 14 through 16,

> "Seeing then, that we have a great high priest, that is passed into the heavens, Jesus the Son of God, let us hold fast our profession. For we have not an high priest which cannot be touched with the feeling of our infirmities; but was in all points tempted like as we are, yet without sin. Let us therefore come boldly unto the throne of grace that we may obtain mercy, and find grace to help in time of need."

We learn from Hebrews 4:14-16 that Jesus Christ, as our High Priest, desires that we come to Him with our problems. He not only understands them, but He is moved to action because of his compassion for us. This lets us know that He is reachable. The Bible also says in John 6:37

> "All that the Father giveth me shall come to me; and him that cometh to me I will in no wise cast out."

We see here that when we come to Jesus, He does not refuse to receive us. And in 1Peter 5:6-7,

> "Humble yourselves therefore under the mighty hand of God, that he may exalt you in due time: casting all your care up on him; for he careth for you."

These verses let us know that He has compassion toward us. We know that God knows what is best for us. In Proverbs 3:5-6 He says,

> "Trust in the Lord with all thine heart; and lean not unto thine own understanding. in all thy ways acknowledge him, and he shall direct thy paths."

We know that he knows what is best for us because he would not be able to direct our paths without this knowledge. Even though the Lord knows what is best for us, it is necessary for us to trust in Him with all our heart to benefit from His knowledge. If we will place all of our trust in Him and live by faith in His Word, we will follow the paths in life, which are for our good, and his Glory. There is such a freedom and peace in this. It gives us confidence that no matter what we face in life the Lord is in control. This is especially important to the person whose life is out of control because of sins of addiction.

God knows that when we place our trust in something or someone other than the Lord Jesus Christ, that trust is in vain. The life that is controlled by an addiction is a life in chaos; there is no peace or joy. Nothing is more devastating in a person's life than to be controlled by a chemical substance or other sin of addiction. This type of life brings only hurt and destruction to one's self and others around them.

> **Man is accountable both to God and to his fellow man for his choices.**

Why is this true? Why cannot a person live a normal life while being controlled by outside influences other than God? It is because God, as the Creator, has established certain laws of nature and life that must be followed. He is the Sovereign One. He makes the rules. When He says, "The wages of sin is death," then we can rest assured that sin will bring death. When he says, "The wringing of the nose bringeth forth blood," you can have confidence that if someone wrings your nose it is going to bleed.

If God says it, it is true! Therefore, when He says, "Submit yourselves therefore to God, Resist the devil, and he will flee from you. Draw nigh to God, and he will draw nigh to you," we can have complete confidence that if we will obey in these matters, God will fulfill His promise.

How do we live in a way that pleases God? We simply learn from God's Word what our responsibilities are and to be obedient to what God tells us. For us to have a right relationship with God we must first have a relationship with His Son, Jesus Christ by placing our trust in Him alone for the salvation of our soul.

We can then come to God and learn about Him. We can come into his presence, and fellowship and commune with Him.

We can speak to Him in prayer as He speaks to us from His Word. He then leads us down the paths of his choosing and he is glorified by it. We are happy because we know we are now fulfilling the purpose for which we were created. If we have obeyed God, when we stand before Him at the judgment, our works will have been of His making, our lives of His choosing, and our relationships of His desire. Here lies the key to being at peace with God. For this is truly the "conclusion of the whole matter."

Unless we have a clear understanding of what God's commandments are, we cannot hope to be obedient to them. God's word teaches us that our relationship with Him is characterized by His faithfulness, mercy, love, patience, kindness, giving, and understanding.

Faithful:
In the book of 1John chapter one and verse nine it says

"If we confess our sins, he is faithful and just to forgive us our sins, and to cleanse us from all unrighteousness."

The word faithful here means "every time." There is never a time in which God will not forgive if we confess. 1Thessalonians 5:24 says,

"Faithful is he that calleth you, who also will do it."

Hebrews 2:16-17 says,

"For verily he took not on him the nature of angels; but he took on Him the seed of Abraham. Wherefore in all things it behoved him to be made like unto his brethren, that he might be a merciful and faithful high priest in things pertaining to God, to make reconciliation for the sins of the people."

In order for something or someone to be faithful there cannot be a time of unfaithfulness. For example, in order for someone to be faithful to their spouse they must be faithful 365 days out of the year, not just 364 days.

Merciful:

Next, we see that He is merciful. In Psalm 37:26 David says of the Lord,

> "He is ever merciful, and lendeth; and his seed is blessed."

In 1Chronicles 16:34 it says,

> "O give thanks unto the LORD: for he is good; for his mercy endureth for ever."

Then in Lamentations 3:22-23 it says,

> "It is of the LORD's mercies that we are not consumed, because his compassions fail not. They are new every morning: great is thy faithfulness."

Loving:

God does indeed have a great love for us. In John 3:16 the Bible says,

> "For God so loved the world, that he gave his only begotten son, that whosoever believeth in him should not perish, but have everlasting life."

In Jeremiah 31:3 the Bible says,

> "The LORD hath appeared of old unto me, saying, yea, I have loved thee with an everlasting love: therefore with lovingkindness have I drawn thee."

Patient:

We also see that God has great patience. In Romans 15:5 the Bible says,

> "Now the God of patience and consolation grant you to be like minded one toward another according to Christ Jesus:"

Here we see that God is exhorting us to be Christ-like by living patiently with one another just as God is patient with us. Living this way is possible only when we are like-minded in our belief that Jesus Christ is our Lord.

Kind:
We see that God is not just faithful, merciful, loving, and patient, but He is also very kind to us. This kindness is described in many places as more than just kindness. It is described as "loving–kindness." This loving-kindness goes much deeper than just kindness does. It is a deep commitment to the welfare of the recipient. God has this kind of commitment toward us. In Psalm 36:7 the Bible says,

> "How excellent is thy lovingkindness o God! Therefore the children of men put their trust under the shadow of thy wings."

Psalm 63:3 three says,

> "Because thy lovingkindness is better than life, my lips shall praise thee."

Giving:
We must recognize that God is also a very giving God. Not only did he give the most precious gift of all, His Son Jesus, for our redemption, but he continues to give to us as his blessed children. James 1:17 says,

> "Every good gift and every perfect gift is from above, and cometh down from the Father of lights, with whom is no variableness, neither shadow of turning."

Ecclesiastes 2:26 says,

"For God giveth to a man that is good in his sight wisdom, and knowledge, and joy:"

Understanding:
Finally, not only is God faithful, merciful, loving, patient, kind, and giving, he also understands what we face in our lives every day and has compassion toward us. Job 28:23 and 28 says,

"God understandeth the way thereof, and he knoweth the place thereof. ...And unto man he said, Behold, the fear of the Lord, that is wisdom; and to depart from evil is understanding."

God expects us to have the characteristics of faithfulness, mercy, love, patience, kindness, giving, and understanding, in the relationships we have with other people as well. How does this happen? How can we have these same qualities in our relationships with others? There is only one way, the Holy Spirit of God living in us and through us.

Paul said in Romans 7:18,

"For I know that in me (that is, in my flesh,) dwelleth no good thing:..."

In addition, he said again in Philippians 1:21,

"For me to live is Christ, and to die is gain."

Christ living in us enables us to have the right kind of relationship with others and with God. We must recognize that this happens by choice. God does not force His will upon us. We must choose to humble ourselves under the authority of God. We must also submit to the plan that He has for our life. This is called surrender. To surrender one must wave the white flag and yield to God's purpose in their life.

We have examined from where our accountability comes and how to have the right kind of relationships. We have also seen how God gives us examples of right characteristics present in his relationship with us. Now let us explore why having the right kind of relationships is important. We will begin with why we should have the right kind of relationship with God.

God Desires a Right Relationship with Him.
The right foundation for our relationship with God is found in recognizing that it is His will for it to be so. Man was created in the image of God, by the will of God. It was God's design to create us as a reflection of Him. This reflection is deeper than just the visible form of man to include his soul and spirit. It is God's will for man to follow Him in obedience; as we obey Him, our faith in Him grows. This pleases Him and is the basis for all other relationships. In Hebrews 11:6 it says,

> "But without faith it is impossible to please him: for he that cometh to God must believe that he is, and that he is a rewarder of them that diligently seek him."

Therefore, it is important that we live a life of faith. How do we obtain this faith? Romans 10: 17 says,

> "So then faith cometh by hearing, and hearing by the word of God."

Why then is faith so important? Romans 14: 23b says,

> "For whatsoever is not of faith is sin."

We have already established that sin separates us from God. If we are not in fellowship with God, we are not fulfilling our purpose for which we were created. Obedience to the Word of God produces faith. However, in order for the Word of God to produce faith in our lives, we must have His Word in our hearts. We hide God's Word in our hearts by reading it, studying it, meditating on it, and memorizing it. David said in Psalm 119:11,

"Thy word have I hid in mine heart, that I might not sin against thee."

In verse 105,

"Thy word is a lamp unto my feet, and a light unto my path."

In verse 165,

"Great peace have they which love thy law: and nothing shall offend them."

Our relationship with God is important because it is His desire that we worship Him.

Our Relationship with God brings Fulfillment

Just as a watch or clock was created to tell us the time, a car was created for transportation, and a pen for writing, we are created for fellowship and to have a relationship with the Creator. A watch cannot be used for transportation or a ladder for telling time. Each has its own place and purpose, as do we.

We see this clearly in nature. Trees put off oxygen for us to breathe while we put off carbon dioxide for the trees to breathe. When everything is as it should be

> **To surrender one must wave the white flag and yield to God's purpose in their life.**

in nature, there is harmony and peace. When we live in obedience God, we have peace and are able to fulfill God's purpose in this world. I am not saying we do not have struggles - We certainly do. However, it is each struggle that make us stronger. We should accept them as a normal part of life. Many times though, we have struggles that we were never meant to have; these struggles are of our own making.

God does not intend for us to carry even burdens of our own making. Just as He will not force his will up on us, He also will not interfere when we are causing ourselves more problems and burdens because of our disobedience. He is merciful, however, and will help us through all problems and struggles, even those of our making.

God extends grace to us, even though we do not deserve it. He simply loves us so much that he shows us favor, although, many times we are without this favor because of pride in our hearts. Pride is the opposite of humility. God says in the Bible that He resists the proud, but gives grace to the humble. The definition of pride is, "Reserving for one's self the final say in any matter." The Bible has a lot to say about the wrong kind of pride; God must have the final say in our lives. Proverbs 29:23 says,

"A man's pride shall bring him low; but honor shall uphold the humble in spirit."

Why are we talking about pride? We talk about pride and selfishness when dealing with relationships because pride and selfishness are the root sins of idolatry that open the door for addiction behavior resulting in destroyed relationships.

We have been discussing accountability and relationships, and have learned that selfishness and pride are catalysts for all sins of addiction. We have also recognized that sins of addiction are the most destructive to relationships. We have seen in this chapter a very simple explanation of our accountability to God and our fellow man, and that accountability and relationships go hand in hand.

What a person does in their response to these truths is what matters most. It is one thing to know and understand these concepts, but it is a completely different thing to use this knowledge to correct the behaviors that are harmful to relationships. There must be a conscious decision to choose God's way over our way if we are to have the kind of relationships that are pleasing, first to God, and secondly, that bring true fulfillment in our personal lives. Our obedience to the commands of God concerning accountability and relationships will bring the peace and happiness we seek in all relationships that are a part of our lives.

Chapter 12

Instruction - Obedience

Because we are accountable for our actions, we need to understand where instruction comes from, why it is important, and how obedience affects our lives.

> "Take fast hold of instruction; let her not go: keep her; for she is thy life." (Proverbs 4:13)

Instruction

There is a humorous remark we sometimes make when trying to assemble a piece of lawn equipment or other such item we have purchased that goes like this: "If all else fails, read the instructions." We always laugh at this little remark because its meaning is so universally understood. I suppose its use is a commentary on how we, especially men, like to try and accomplish things on our own. I believe this to be a natural part of human nature.

While this is a funny little quip to a not-so-serious circumstance, it is unfortunate that this is exactly the same approach people take with their life. Their belief is that they have the ability in themselves to make things happen that will bring them fulfillment and joy. Satan is a master at deception. He will lure people into things that satisfy the lusts of the flesh for a season, but bring no lasting peace or joy and only destruction in the end. Therefore, these people bounce around in life from one relationship to another, from one to experience to another, from one fix to another, all the while thinking they are in control of their life.

One-day people wake up and realize their life is really out of control and everything they have worked to accomplish is in vain. They are not happy and they have no real joy. They soon realize that they are not in control of their life, but instead addiction is controlling their life.

> **God has given us clear instruction for how to live our lives in a manner, which is pleasing to Him...**

Why is this true for so many people? The answer is "they have failed to read the instructions." We have seen in the previous chapters how that God is the Creator of all things. As the creature, we have a responsibility to be obedient to God as the Creator. God did not just leave it up to us to figure out the right way to live. Proverbs 14:12 says,

> "There is a way which seemeth right unto a man, but the end thereof are the ways of death."

Proverbs 4:19 says,

> "The way of the wicked is as darkness: they know not at what they stumble."

Just as this verse speaks of the wicked not knowing at what they stumble, so does every person who does not accept instruction from God. God has given us clear instruction for how to live our lives in a manner, which is pleasing to Him and fulfilling to us - Which fulfills the purpose for which we were created. What is "Instruction from God?" Where do we find this instruction? Why is instruction important? Why must it come from God and not from some other source?

History of instruction

What is instruction from God? There is an assumption made at this point that the reader believes in God as the Creator. Having made this assumption, let me ask the first question, "What is instruction from God?" We see all throughout Biblical history how God spoke verbally to people whom He chose to use in a specific way. He gave these people clear instructions concerning want to do according to His will to accomplish His desired purpose in their personal lives and throughout the world.

God gave Adam and Eve clear instructions about being fruitful and multiplying humankind, and having dominion over the earth. He instructed them in how to be good stewards of what He created. God also gave them clear instructions in which fruit of the garden could be eaten and which fruit could not be eaten. God even told them what would happen if they disobeyed Him by refusing to follow His instructions. The Scripture is very clear that Jesus Christ was and is the eternal Word of God. John 1:1-2 says,

> "In the beginning was the Word, and the Word was with God, and the Word was God. The same was in the beginning with God."

This passage of Scripture teaches us that the Word existed in eternity past. Note the use of the proper name capitalized - Word. This tells us that the Word is a person. Further passages in John 1 tell us that this person is Jesus Christ, that He created all things, and that He "was made flesh, and dwelt among us."

Before Jesus Christ came to this earth as the Word of God in a robe of flesh, He was in the world as the Word of God in a different form. Prior to Pentecost and the ascension of Jesus Christ after His resurrection, the Holy Spirit dwelt *with* man. After Pentecost and Christ's ascension to heaven, the Holy Spirit dwells *in* people who are in the family of God, who have been saved by accepting Jesus Christ as their Saviour.

We must recognize two things. One, that God did not just place man on the earth without giving Him instructions for carrying out his responsibilities. In addition, because man had a choice to obey or disobey there were either positive or negative consequences for those choices. Because man chose to disobey God's instructions, the resulting consequences were devastating.

Where do we find God's instructions?

At the time of Adam and Eve, God's instructions were given verbally. It was not until many years later that God used the written Word as His means of instruction. One of the first examples of the written Word is seen when God wrote the Ten Commandments on the stone tablets and gave them to Moses.

> **God reveals to us in His Word as much about Himself as he desired.**

Moses broke the original tablets when he saw the wickedness of the people upon returning from the mountain and from the presence of God. God gave Moses another copy of the Ten Commandments also written in tablets of stone. These tablets were later kept in the Arc of the Covenant along with Aaron's rod that budded and manna. God chose to give written instructions so that it could be read to the people and passed on from one generation to the next. The Bible says in Psalm 119:89,

"For ever, O Lord, thy word is settled in heaven."

This gives us assurance that God preserved His Word for all humanity and that we may have access to it to receive His instructions. In writing the Bible, God used over 40 different writers spanning a period of 1500 years, with all content and themes in agreement. We find written within the pages of the Bible exactly what God intended that we should know about life on earth and life after death. God reveals to us in His Word as much about Himself as he desired. He tells us what we need to know about surroundings, our eternity, and ourselves.

He has revealed humanity's past, present and future as they pertain to our relationship with Him. It is through a careful study of the Bible and time spent in prayer we find a lasting and meaningful relationship with God's Son, Jesus Christ. This relationship in turn brings us peace, joy, and great satisfaction in this life and assures us of being with Him throughout eternity in life after death.

God's Word gives us instructions concerning how we are to treat our fellow man, how we are to respond to those who mistreat us, and how to fulfill the purpose for which we were created. It tells of God's love for us; that his love for us is so great he sent his Son to the earth, in the form of a man, to pay the death penalty of sin for every man. The Bible instructs how sinners, separated from God, can be saved and returned to fellowship with God.

The importance of Instruction

There are no errors or omissions in the Bible. God gave us in His Word exactly what He intended for us to have. The Word of God teaches us how to love God in return for how much He loves us. We demonstrate our love for Him by being obedient to his commandments. God's written instructions are historically and scientifically accurate. It is for all people, for all time, for every race and nationality. His instructions are for not only how to live, but how to die as well. Having God's instructions available to humanity is one thing; reading and heeding those instructions are quite another.

Just because a model car, a lawn mower, or a bicycle has instructions included does not mean anything until these instructions are read and followed. The same is true of our lives. God's instructions affect our life whether we are willing to study and obey His instructions or not. The reason we study and obey God's instructions is to please Him and open our life to His blessings. The Bible tells us "But without faith it is impossible to please him." We can only be people of faith as we hear the Word of God. God gives us instructions for living through His Word, the Bible.

The baseball game got underway after the "Star Spangled Banner" was sung and the guest pitched the first ball to the catcher. Everyone greatly anticipated the game that night because it was the debut of a new major league team. As the first batter came to the plate, he was dressed in blue jeans and a long overcoat. The crowd began to laugh and shout at the batter. Why was he dressed in such ridiculous clothing?

After a few seconds of conversation between the coach of the new team and the head umpire, the game resumed. As the pitcher threw his first pitch, the batter swung and missed the ball, but ran straight across the infield to second base. The crowd went crazy, shouting all sorts of insults at the batter. This kind of behavior repeated itself with each new batter and with all the players on the field. The game was in chaos. People went to the ticket counter demanding a refund of their money. Many people left without even bothering with a refund.

As the people began leaving the stadium, the traffic came to a standstill because there were cars going the wrong way. Instead of following the arrows showing the "one way" direction to the exit, people were driving in whatever direction they thought would get them out of the stadium. This caused several accidents and a consequent gridlock.

The reason the ball game went the way it did and the traffic came to a halt is because the participants did not follow the instructions they were given. Therefore, they failed to respond appropriately to those particular circumstances. This simple illustration may seem silly, but it demonstrates a very important principle. When a person is born into this world, they are not born with the knowledge necessary to carry them through life. Every newly born person is an empty sponge, ready to soak up what information is provided. It is important that the right information be given at an early age because it is this information that will have the most influence on the person through the rest of their life.

While learning is and should be on-going regardless of age, the information gathered in these early years will be the basis for the decisions made early in life that will affect the rest of that person's life. Therefore, it is critical that the right instructions be given as early as possible. Without the proper instructions, there will be chaos.

When dealing with the soul of man, there are instructions given in God's Word that tell us exactly what is necessary for man to be in a right relationship with the Creator. Without this instruction, there is chaos in the spiritual life of the individual that spills over into the daily life as well. Learning and following this instruction from God is where real life is found.

Why must the source of instruction come from God?
Let us pretend for a moment that you are an inventor. You have invented the most marvelous device in history. In fact, your invention has never been equaled in all history and will never be duplicated in the future. This invention is of such usefulness that everyone must use it. It is so important that everyone needs it. You are so generous that you will even give it away freely at no charge. The only requirement for its use is that the user must properly follow the instructions you have given.

> **There are no errors or omissions in the Bible. God gave us in His Word exactly what He intended for us to have.**

Keep in mind that no other inventor has what you have invented. You are the only person who really knows how it works. There are others who have tried to write instructions for its use, but they have all failed. It then becomes apparent that everyone who wishes to benefit fully from your invention must get his instructions directly from you. You are the creator of the invention. When they try someone else's feelings or opinions of how it should work or they simply refuse to read the instructions you have provided, the outcome is always the same - Failure.

In fact, you know of people who have had your invention a very long time who have tried everything except your instructions and every time they tried, it ended in failure. You have given them clear instructions on how to use your invention and are willing to answer any questions they may have. They just cannot seem to bring themselves to the place where they realize they need your instructions.

There are also competitors who are constantly trying to keep people away from your invention, or from reading your instructions, or even calling for help because they are filled with jealousy of you. They are trying everything they can to keep people from enjoying what you have invented and made available to everyone free of charge. They do not have what you have and they never can so they want to hurt you by keeping others from having your wonderful invention.

You are very saddened because even though your invention is so wonderful and it is free, many people do not want it or if they have it, they will not read your instructions so they can benefit fully from it. This is exactly the same thing people are doing with their lives. God created a wonderful creature called man. God desires that man reaches his full potential. The Psalmist David recognized this potential when he said in Psalm 139:14,

"I will praise thee; for I am fearfully and wonderfully made."

The only thing necessary for us to receive the full blessings from the Creator is to believe what He says concerning his Son, Jesus Christ, and follow the instructions in the Bible He has given to us concerning life. It sounds simple because it is. If you wanted to work on your Ford car, you would not go out and buy a Honda manual. That would be silly. The same thing applies with us. The reason why it is God's instructions we must follow is because He is the one who created us. He is the Inventor, if you will. He knows exactly what each of us need, and loves us with an everlasting love.

As we are obedient to Him and the light that he gives us, he reveals more truth and light to us. This process continues as long as we are obedient. As a child, we are taught to be obedient to our parents so we can learn to be obedient to God as an adult. It is because of this obedience we are able to receive the blessings of the Lord.

God's Word is the source of all instruction; however, God uses various means by which to instruct us. The first we see is through authority. There are three areas of authority God chose by which to give us instruction. These three areas correspond to the three earthly institutions he has ordained: family, church, and government. We also receive instruction from nature and the Holy Spirit.

The Family
God has ordained the head of the family to be the man. The man's role in the family is as husband and as father. These two roles are roles of authority. It is necessary that the man know what God's Word says about his responsibilities as husband and father so he can give proper instructions to those under his authority. When man does not accept his responsibility to give instructions to his wife and children, there is a breakdown in the family, and consequently, in the other two institutions as well.

The strong Family unit makes a strong Church and Nation. The husband and father must realize that instruction is not just given verbally but also by example in how he lives his life. Children will do what they see their parents do before they will do what their parents say. It is critical that children see their parents living holy and obedient lives toward God and His commandments.

The Church
God has also established a man, the Pastor, as the human authority in the local church, and the Holy Ghost who is the ultimate authority must lead him. According to God's design given to us in the Bible, this position is that of an overseer of the work of God. The Pastor's authority is more benevolent in nature and comes from

a close relationship with the Lord, following the Holy Spirit's leading for the direction of the ministries in which the local New Testament Church is involved, and in how to take care of the flock or Church members.

This position comes at the request of the people who make up the local church body or assembly. It is at their discretion, having followed God's leading and direction in calling the man God desires to lead that particular local church assembly that the Pastor becomes the "under-shepherd" of the flock. God established only two offices in the church. These are the Pastor and Deacons.

The Pastor's responsibility is to ensure that all activities entered into by the church are in obedience to God's Word. The responsibility of the Deacons is to help the Pastor. Under this authority, the Pastor sees that proper instruction is given throughout each ministry of the church. The Pastor must select those who are qualified to teach to carry forth this instruction in the proper manner.

The Government

God has also established government as an authority to instruct citizens in the laws of the land. In our form of government, we elect politicians who we hope will write laws that reflect the moral character of God's law, the Bible. Unfortunately, many times this does not happen.

> **The strong Family unit makes a strong Church and Nation.**

Authority is also given by our government to certain individuals to uphold the laws of the land. These authorities are called "law enforcement officers." These law enforcement officers only uphold and enforce the laws that are written. It is the responsibility of every citizen to learn the laws of the land. As the saying goes, "Ignorance of the law is no excuse." We have seen how God has ordained three separate institutions to give people instruction by authority. God has given us five sources of instruction: Family, Church, Government, Nature, and the Holy Spirit.

Instruction from Nature

God also uses nature to give us instruction. In 1Corinthians 11:14-15 the Bible says,

> "Doth not even nature itself teach you, that, if a man have long hair, it is a shame unto him. But if a woman have long hair, it is a glory to her: for her hair is given her for a covering."

In Psalm 19:1, the Bible teaches us that nature reveals to us the wonderful works of God when it says

> "The heavens declare the glory of God; and the firmament sheweth his handywork."

God also instructs us through examples from animals and insects. God used the ants in Proverbs 6:6 to teach a slothful person the error of his way when He said,

> "Go to the ant, thou sluggard; consider her ways, and be wise: Which having no guide, overseer, or ruler, Provideth her meat in the summer, and gathereth her food in the harvest."

Instruction From The Holy Spirit

We see in 1Corinthians chapter two that the Holy Spirit instructs those who are born again of Him. Verse 12 says,

> "Now we have received, not the spirit of the world, but the spirit which is of God; that we might know the things that are freely given to us of God."

We know by these verses that God chooses to instruct those who are saved by His Spirit.

Instruction Offers New Choices

How do we apply these principles to someone who is struggling with sins of addiction? Most every addict, whether they admit it or not, has an overwhelming desire to be free from the clutches of their particular addiction. No one naturally desires to be controlled by a besetting sin of any kind.

We speak of human beings as free moral agents making independent moral judgments. Our emphasis should be placed on "free." Freedom is desirable for all people. Freedom to make choices is one characteristic that separates us from the animals God created. Animals act instinctively and with impulse upon learned behaviors and patterns, while man has the ability to choose which behavior is appropriate for any given circumstance.

While there are many scientific studies available on the subject of the addictive brain disorders and illnesses, there remains a single separate truth which exists with every person who has, of their own volition or choosing, took that first pill, drank the first drink, looked at pornography the first time, or bought their first lottery ticket. The truth is they made a choice to do it whether by persuasion, coercion, curiosity, or personal desire.

Perhaps these individuals were not as fortunate to have had a good and proper upbringing. Perhaps we could say that society failed them in some way. Saying this may make certain segments of society feel better about their rehabilitation programs, but it does not address reality.

Humans possess a natural inhibition concerning harmful circumstances. This inhibition is called, "self-preservation." The reality is, every person offered an illegal drug or participated in some illicit behavior knew that there were dangers and risks associated with their choice. Making choices contrary to the instructions God gives us in His Word result in freedoms being taken away. The reason God gives us instruction is so we may be able to enjoy the freedom that obedience to His instruction gives.

Obedience

Self-preservation is one of the strongest instincts present in human nature. People must overcome the self-preservation instinct to place themselves in jeopardy. Therefore, when a person uses a controlled substance they must overcome this natural instinct of self-preservation. The addict decides that the feeling they receive from the addiction behavior is worth the negative consequences. The addict feels that it is more desirable to feel the effect of the addiction, regardless of the consequences, than to live a normal life. We call this false logic. Disruption of proper thinking processes brought on by addiction, results in abnormal thinking or false logic.

The lack of education may predispose some individuals to substance abuse, but clearly, it is still a choice the individual makes. No one is free from this truth; man has chosen to have his way since the beginning of time. When God created man with a will to choose, He enabled man to make choices that are bad for him as well as those that are good.

> **Self-preservation is one of the strongest instincts present in human nature.**

We do not pretend to ignore the effects or physical consequences of bad decisions. The scientific and medical community still does not understand why people choose to involve themselves with drugs, alcohol, gambling, pornography, or other life-controlling issues. However, as Christians, we understand these choices to be the result of idolatry, lusts of the flesh, and rebellion toward God and His command to love and obey Him.

We understand that certain personalities are more susceptible to a continuation of harmful activities than others are, but we must not forget that man has a will to choose. We also understand there are physiological changes that occur in the person who abuses drugs and alcohol over a period. We also understand there are some drugs that have an immediate devastating effect upon an individual. We need to recognize these physiological changes in order to effectively deal with the individual from the proper perspective.

What does this preceding information have to do with instruction and obedience? It is crucial to have a clear understanding of the changes that occur in the human brain and body when trying to instruct a person with an addiction or besetting sin problem. The necessary approach varies with the individual. Many individuals have not received help simply because the program counselor did not fully understand the condition of the program participant.

Instruction is only as effective as the participant is able to assimilate and understand the information. The manner in which the information is delivered depends greatly upon the degree the teacher understands the participant's condition. It is unrealistic to expect obedience from a person who does not have a clear view of exactly to what they are supposed to be obedient. In this sense, instruction and obedience cannot be separated. Any program wishing to effectively help a person, must first assess the mental, physical, emotional, and spiritual condition, before beginning a regimen of treatment.

> **Freedom is the result of obedience.**

Our main emphasis should be on the spiritual condition of an individual, because it is our conviction a person must change from the inside out. While this is our conviction, we recognize there are physical conditions that impair the individual from clear thinking processes. Overcoming physical impairments require a healthy diet, exercise, clean living, and obedience to instruction in righteousness. These things take time to recondition the body and reconstruct the mind. However, the Word of God must not be overlooked in this process

There are many factors which affect this process of healing: physical condition; emotional condition; amount of support from friends and family; the type of addiction; the length of time subjected to the life controlling issue; and the level of desire or commitment of the person themselves to a program that deals with the problem and not just the symptom. After an individual has had time to regain some physical and mental faculties, there can be an expectation of progress from a spiritual standpoint. It is wrong to assume that all that is needed is to give someone a Bible and tell them to read it, expecting instant results.

While it is our conviction that the Bible *is* the source of change in a person's life, there must be a certain level of physical awareness for the Word to have an effect. Many times the life-controlling addiction prevents a person from thinking and understanding clearly. Reading the Bible is necessary for holy and righteous living, but the person must be in a condition to receive the truths of Scripture. Once a person has reached the place to receive instruction, we can begin to require obedience.

Obedience Equals Freedom

We have all heard the saying, "If no one follows, you cannot lead." The same is true with obedience and freedom. Without obedience, there cannot be freedom. Obedience is the essential part of instruction. This is not to say that instruction is worthless without obedience, but that instruction without obedience will not yield freedom.

Take the ball game mentioned earlier. The ball players were not obedient to the proper instruction in how to conduct a game, and the drivers were not obedient to instructions in how to drive. Had the players been obedient in the game, and the drivers obedient in how to drive, things would have gone much smoother and there would have been much more enjoyment for all.

Since both parties were given proper instructions, and they simply chose not to obey, no one would argue that they were simply being rebellious. There should be an outcry for someone to change the minds of the players and the drivers. In fact, everyone would agree that there should be consequences since the parties did not obey the rules.

What most people want is to have it both ways. They want to do what they want, when they want, and not be held accountable to anyone for the consequences. This is absurd, as most would agree. However, this is the same logic used by addicts and those who try to make addictions a strictly clinical or medical issue rather than a conduct, or spiritually speaking, a heart issue.

When the players of the game and the drivers are obedient to the established laws and rules, there is freedom for all. The players were able to play the game and the drivers were able to get to their destinations. Is not this the same desire for the addict? The addict simply desires to have control over his life. This cannot be accomplished, without the rules being obeyed, and God sets the rules.

We must understand that there are laws made by man and laws made by God. We are to obey every law of man that does not conflict with the laws of God. We are to obey every law and command of God given to us in His Word.

There is no mystery in this. Freedom is the result of obedience. The only way we can freely drive across the country using the interstate and highway system our nation has created, is to obey the traffic laws. This obedience keeps us, and others, safe from harm and allows free movement.

The more we follow the laws of the land, the more freedom we have to conduct our affairs with other men and live productive lives for the benefit of our society. This also pleases God because He established the institutions of government, and did so for our benefit.

When we are obedient to God, there is freedom. This freedom allows us to live productive lives in the sight of God. As we are obedient to God in our spiritual lives, He gives us more understanding of how to follow Him closer by doing His will and living more like His Son, Jesus Christ. The closer we follow God, the more He directs our lives in the right paths.

God desires to give His children good things, but receiving many of these things depends on obedience to Him and His Word. God has a purpose for giving us instruction and requiring our obedience. This obedience brings glory to Him and is for our benefit.

God said His desire for us to obey Him is stronger than His desire for us to worship Him. This is given to us in 1Samuel 15:22-23 where it says,

> "And Samuel said, Hath the LORD as great delight in burnt offerings and sacrifices, as in obeying the voice of the LORD? Behold, to obey is better than sacrifice, and to hearken than the fat of rams. For rebellion is as the sin of witchcraft, and stubbornness is as iniquity and idolatry...."

Only through obedience to God's instructions can we find purpose in life and peace with God. This is real significance.

Our Response

Chapter 13

The Ministry of Recovery

John came home early from work one day and told his wife, Jane, that he had been let go from his job. He said there was a layoff and he had the least seniority, so he was let go. John had given the company six years of his life. He had always worked extra hours any time they asked, even on weekends for special projects. He was supposedly one of their best employees. She was so upset with the company that she just had to call and give them a piece of her mind. Outraged and ready for a fight, she dialed the number of the company and asked to speak with John's boss.

When John's boss came to the phone, Jane proceeded to tell him what was on her mind. When she finished speaking and finally calmed down, John's boss very kindly explained to Jane that he had no choice but to let him go because John had improperly used the company's computers for personal use and that it had nothing to do with layoffs.

What John did not tell his wife was that he was fired from his job because he had been looking at pornographic web sites on his computer at work. The company had sent out memos over the past year, warning employees of improper use of company computers. John had not heeded their warnings. This particular morning John's boss came to him and told him that the IT Department had traced some pornographic web site information back to John's computer.

This was not the first time John was caught looking at these types of web sites. He was warned two other times about this activity - the last time with a write-up in his permanent record. The most recent event was the "straw that broke the camel's back." John's boss had no other choice but to fire him. Devastated, Jane hung up the phone and sat slumped over in her chair sobbing with her face in her hands.

How could John do this to them? Now they had no income, and with a baby on the way, how could they make ends meet? What could have been so bad that they would have to fire him over it? As she thought about these things, she remembered the nights that John would stay up late on the computer and say he was doing research for the company. She had even once found a magazine in the curbside garbage cans when she had lost a very important bill, and had to go out to the street and rummage through the garbage cans to find it. When she asked about the magazine, John said it must have been a stranger walking by that just put it in there since the cans at the street were convenient.

She had no reason to disbelieve his answer, so she passed it off as the truth. From time to time, there had been purchases made that were unusual and she could not figure out what they were. These were not large purchases, only a few dollars, but they were from places that she did not recognize. John had no explanation for these either. There was not that many, just a few over the past year, so it was not that big of a deal. As she thought about these occurrences, it dawned on her that there might be a much larger problem in John's personal life than what lay on the surface. She was unsure when and how she would confront him.

How would she approach John about this? How would he respond if she questioned him about these things? Would he be angry? Does he have a problem that might possibly need professional help? If her fears turned out to be true, where would they get the money for such treatment? She decided to approach John about this immediately, regardless of his reaction. To her surprise, he came clean about the problem he had been having over the past year. He said that there was this person at work that showed him a web page one day that had pornography on it. At first, John was embarrassed and left the person's office immediately.

Over the next couple of months, this same employee would make jokes about the web sites and act as if John was not up with the times if he left or said anything negative about it. Over time, this wore John down until he actually started becoming curious about these web sites himself. He had to admit that he enjoyed looking at the pictures, even though it made him feel like he was betraying his wife somehow.

The more he looked at the pictures, the less he felt this way. He reasoned within himself that if it was not hurting anyone, what was the problem. He always did it in private. No one was the wiser. As he explained this to Jane, he realized that he had fallen into a trap. His actions had created a habit that would take control of his life and hurt the people that loved him.

> **Recovery from addiction can only come from a daily, meaningful relationship with Jesus Christ.**

This trap was extremely subtle. He really did not realize that what he was doing was affecting him until he lost his job over it. Now he realizes how much this addiction has affected more than just him. It has hurt his relationship with his wife.

They had been married for seven years, and have always had a good relationship. He decided to come clean with Jane by telling her everything. As John revealed to his wife the terrible things he had allowed into his private life, she realized that John would need more help than just coming clean would give him. This had become an addiction for John.

She remembered the advertisement on the radio from the church in their community that has an "Addiction Recovery" meeting on Friday nights. Jane was not sure exactly what "recovery" meant, but from the information in the advertisement, it sounded like it might be something that would help John. She talked to him about this and he agreed to go to one of the meetings. Even though he was embarrassed about his problem, he continued to attend the meetings faithfully.

After six months of going to the meetings, John, his wife, and their new baby girl is attending the church regularly and John has had the opportunity to facilitate some of the classes from time to time on Friday nights. He has a new job, one that does not involve computers, and is doing well. They decided there should be accountability with one another, so neither of them can go on the home computer without the other present, and they have invested in a "Content Blocker" program for the Internet. They are happy together and look forward to rearing their little girl. They are thankful that the church offered the "Addiction Recovery" classes. They do not know what they would have done without them.

While this story is fictional, stories like this are duplicated thousands of times in communities across our country. Unfortunately, most of them do not end as positively as this one. Too few churches offer this kind of program as a mission outreach to their community. The need is greater than most could imagine. There are families that are destroyed by addictions of various kinds with every week that passes. What is the real answer? How are those that are in bondage to addictions going to find the truth? The Bible says in I Timothy 3:15,

> "But if I tarry long, that thou mayest know how thou oughtest to behave thyself in the house of God, which is the church of the living God, the pillar and ground of the truth."

How is the Church of the Living God supposed to behave themselves? They are supposed to tell the truth in love. The truth is, addiction is sin. Recovery from addiction can only come from a daily, meaningful relationship with Jesus Christ. This relationship begins with a person acknowledging the truth found in the Word of God. The Church is supposed to deliver this message of truth to the world. This includes giving the truth to people who are in bondage to addictions. The most effective way to reach addicts with the Gospel is to have a church ministry that reaches out to them.

Recovery Ministry

Recovery: A return to normal state; a gaining back of something lost. Recovery is often referred to when defining the process of gaining freedom from a life controlling circumstance or addiction. The term recovery has evolved over many decades into its current meaning. When the word recovery is most often used in context with drug or alcohol addictions.

The very use of the word recovery denotes a sense of sadness and at the same time hope. Sadness in that something has been lost, and a hope that things can be different by regaining what was lost. Something terrible has taken place that has robbed a person of their sanity, dignity, even their normal life. This terrible thing is addiction. For many people, sadness is all that they will ever feel, because there will be no recovery of what was lost.

Others will have a hope that things will return to normal, but instinctively know that the journey back will be long and painful. The ones that have hope also know all too well the price to pay for the return to a normal life. They also know that a full and complete return to normalcy is, quite possibly the most difficult thing they will ever do.

Many times addicts fear that as hard as they try, and as much as they desire for things to be normal, there is a chance that there will always be something just around the corner that will cause them to slip back into the addiction. There is a strong nagging in the back of their mind that says, "It's not really over, and relapse could happen at any time." The knowledge, that everything that has been done to find recovery is all in vain, if relapse occurs, is a frightening possibility.

The prospect of starting over at square one is almost more than they can bear. It is almost not even worth trying to seek recovery in the first place. Sometimes they think they would be better off just giving in to the addiction until everything is lost; then there would not be any more pain of loss.

Once everything is gone, what difference would it make? There develops an actual sense of relief in the thought of death, almost to a point that it makes more sense to give in to the struggle than to try fighting it. It certainly seems much easier just to give in to the addictions.

> **An addiction recovery ministry should not be viewed any differently than any other mission outreach of the Church.**

This kind of addiction thinking is normal, and is the reality in the mind of addicts. Once the addict is firmly in the grip and bondage of a particular addiction, there is a transfer of reasoning that moves from the logical to the illogical. In other words, the logical becomes illogical and the illogical becomes logical. This phenomenon is referred to in other parts of this book as "False Logic." How can this cycle of thought be broken? What can the addict do to assure there is complete recovery from such devastating choices?

Many addicts attend meetings and programs; they try this remedy and that remedy, they check themselves into rehab after rehab, all with the same results - Relapse. Family members are tired of spending thousands upon thousands of dollars for treatment, only to have their loved one slip back into the addiction after only a few short months of sobriety. Why do the programs, that cost so many thousands of dollars per month, not offer a permanently effective solution to addiction recovery?

There is illusiveness to recovery that is seldom discussed or brought into the open. The reason for this is not many people are willing to accept the truth about most rehabilitation programs. The truth is most programs do not work. I believe this is one reason why there are so many programs in existence today. The director of one state-run program admitted to me personally their program was not working and consequently referred a man to our program where he did receive help.

The methods employed in most recovery programs today are useless in terms of a permanent resolution to the addiction problem. The best that can be hoped for is a temporary reprieve of the addiction. Many program directors view permanent recovery as being impossible to attain. They are satisfied and content with offering a temporary solution. Their attitude is, "Some freedom from addiction is better than none." I have actually heard one program Director say, "Well, at least they will be sober while they are here." This kind of attitude reveals the true intent of the provider having a program in the first place.

This attitude is also reflected in their program methods and content. Addiction recovery is a multi-million dollar-a-year "business" that may be considered by some to be a "growth industry." Many programs give the appearance of professionalism and quality, but have a very humanistic approach to their program.

Some residential recovery facilities even allow the program participants to use tobacco products while in the program. What is the point of addiction recovery when a program facilitates more addiction? In my opinion, these kinds of facilities may be simply operating in an attempt to make money. If their motive is truly to help people, they are going about it the wrong way.

Anyone who finds it necessary to seek help through a residential recovery facility program needs to beware of the type of facility mentioned above. It is important to investigate the program very thoroughly, including staff credentials and experience. The Church is the center for all ministries. An addiction recovery ministry should not be viewed any differently than any other mission outreach of the Church. The addiction recovery ministry should have the same consideration, as does any home mission program.

Primary Reason for Recovery Ministry

Why do most programs fail to bring about a permanent change in the life of the addict? The answer to this is rather simple. Most recovery programs do not understand the cause of addictions. They do not understand the cure because they do not understand the root problem. They treat the symptoms instead of the cause. Therefore, they try everything possible except the true cure.

They think the problem is with man's actions or environment instead of his heart. Therefore, they try everything they can to change man's external behavior or environment, to no avail. This is why people continue to have addiction problems. This is why those who seek help skip from one treatment facility to another, never finding true deliverance from the addiction.

Because God created man, God has the answer to life-controlling habits and any other problem man may have in his life. Let me illustrate this very plainly and respectfully. God is the Creator, the Designer, and the Engineer, if you will. When something in His creation is broken, He has the necessary knowledge to fix it.

When a Builder finds a flaw or something wrong in the construction of a building, the Engineer or designer of that building is called upon to fix it. This is because the Designer or Engineer has very intimate knowledge and understanding of his creation. It is no different with God and man.

God's creation (man) was perfect, but he was created with a will to choose. When the choice was made to disobey God, man became "broken." Because God is the Designer, He has the knowledge necessary to fix the problem. All we must do is follow God's instructions on how to fix the problem. These instructions are found in His Word, the Bible.

His creation became broken in the Garden of Eden. There is no way that man can be "fixed" again. He is forever broken in this life, because of sin. The penalty for this brokenness, or sin, is death. God "fixed" the problem by sending His Son Jesus to die in our place, so that we would not have to die. Man must accept this gift to be "fixed." It is through faith in Jesus Christ alone that a man gains freedom from the bondage of addictions.

There is a much more effective type of program that is available to addicts today that has the proper view of addiction and recovery. These are programs created as an outreach ministry of a local church. Because the Church is the "Pillar and ground of the truth," it is in a unique position to offer lasting help to the addict. This help is found only through obedience to the Word of God.

> **The Church must realize that the program they develop for helping addicts is not just another addiction recovery program, but rather an opportunity to change lives.**

If the Church will take this responsibility seriously, there can be a tremendous difference made in the life of the addict and their loved ones. It is our desire that no one be enslaved and in bondage to addictions, but who is going to help the ones that are? Secular programs are not the answer. The world's view of man's problems will not lead a person to freedom from addictions.

God has the answer to addictions and desires that the message, that He wants the addict to be free and has given everything necessary for freedom, be delivered to them. Someone has to deliver the message! This responsibility belongs to the Church.

The Church must realize that the program they develop for helping addicts is not just another addiction recovery program, but also an opportunity to change lives. This way of life must be pleasing to God. This is the primary reason why the Church should have a ministry to people with addiction problems.

Secondary Reason for Recovery Ministry

Although the main reason for creating an addiction recovery ministry in the Church is so people with addictions can know the Lord in salvation, and to live a life pleasing to Him, there is a secondary reason as well.

It is one thing to lead someone to the Lord, but it is another thing all together to disciple them in the ways of the Lord. The purpose of discipleship is to teach the convert truth so they will be able to teach others the truth. This is true in every aspect of the Christian life.

Imagine what could be accomplished if those with addiction problems in their life could, after finding deliverance from their addiction, turn around and help others like themselves do the same. People relate to other people. This is why the concept of discipleship is so important.

How did Jesus relate to different people? Jesus recognized the individual characteristics of each person and the potential for each person to serve Him. Any curriculum used in an addiction recovery ministry should include clear character building precepts. Each addict is different. Each has a different personality and set of attitudes and behaviors that they bring with them to the program.

The recovery teacher must recognize this in each person and deal with that person based on his or her individual strengths. The recovery program must present Jesus Christ as the Saviour of man and as the Forgiver of sins. Presenting Him merely as another "religion" is a mistake.

Christ must be presented to the addict in terms of "relationship." He desires a relationship with each of us as individuals. Every person needs God's presence in his or her life; not just presence, but ruling presence. He must have preeminence.

The place we give God in our life will determine the place everything else has in our life. Having the correct view of God in the ministry of addiction recovery will ensure that the recovery program will be administered from a purely Biblical point of view. This view will be vitally necessary when dealing with the challenges faced in this type of ministry outreach.

Getting Started

There are many different avenues of involvement a local church can take when developing an addiction recovery ministry as an outreach to their community. The avenue of choice a local church takes depends upon several considerations and variables that determine how engaged they would be in their community. I will only deal with getting started here, but will deal with other aspects and considerations in a later chapter.

There is not a right or wrong level of engagement or involvement when deciding how the church will build their addiction recovery ministry. The correct approach to this and perhaps the most obvious is; what is the need in the community? Although there are more people affected by life-controlling habits than most people realize, some communities have less of a problem than others do. Some communities are fortunate enough to only deal with the occasional addiction or problems that we would consider weights rather than addictions. If this is the case, then perhaps scheduling a monthly open door counseling service at the church is all that is necessary.

Other communities have a far greater need than just one church could possibly handle on its own. For these areas, a cooperative approach may work better for reaching the people in need. The cooperative approach is not meant to be ecumenical in nature, but rather churches of like faith and doctrine banding together to respond to the need in their community.

For the church that is not sure what the need is in their community, there is a simple way to determine the number of people that may need help. With technology advancements and the ability to research just about anything on the World Wide Web, the level of need for an addiction recovery ministry in any particular geographical area is easily ascertained.

The search engine we know as "Google" has many tools that are available for gathering information. Google created a keyword tool that helps advertisers understand the request of the person searching the web. Any person can use this tool to research how many search requests there are for a particular word or phrase. The search results for a particular word or phrase is both worldwide and local to the person's "ip" address and is displayed in a spreadsheet type format for viewing. The number of requests reported by this keyword tool is displayed in numerical form for each individual word or phrase searched by the public and includes all related keywords and phrases for the requested search. Advertisers and business owners use this tool to find out what people are searching for on the World Wide Web so they can adjust their marketing plans accordingly.

A local church can also use this tool to see how many people are searching for an addiction recovery program or rehab center in their geographical area. It may be surprising to see how many people are searching for a program for a loved one or for themselves. This is a good litmus test for whether a ministry is needed in a particular area.

Once a local church determines there is a need for a ministry to addicts, the church must decide what level of involvement they wish to have with their community. Some churches may want to provide a full range of services such as a residential facility, while others may only wish to provide two hours one night a week for a class on addiction recovery. Another church may only wish to establish a service of Biblical counsel to addicts by allowing a church staff worker or qualified layperson to use available office space once a week for sessions. Any of these choices can be beneficial to the surrounding community, and has the potential to bring people to Christ and assist others in their spiritual growth.

Chapter 14

Counsel and Restoration

Of all the activities surrounding an addiction recovery ministry, giving Biblical counsel would be one of the most important. I did not say *counseling* for a reason, and I will reveal why in a moment. Because Biblical counsel is so important, it is necessary to maintain a purely Biblical perspective within any written material or content, and in any formal counsel given verbally to a person needing advice.

To do any less would immediately defeat the whole purpose of offering the counsel in the first place. Why do people seek counsel? People seek counsel because they are looking for a truth by which to make a decision.

God is truth and the source of all truth and therefore a person should first seek counsel from God's Word, the Bible. God said in His Word that the Church is the pillar and ground of the truth, so people should secondly seek counsel from their Pastor, who is the Under-Shepherd of the congregation or flock. The Pastor's love for the "sheep" (people) and the discernment God gives him are only two of the many reasons why a person should seek counsel from their Pastor.

The Scriptures do not prohibit seeking counsel beyond the Pastor. In fact, the Scripture says in Proverbs 11:14,

> "Where no counsel is, the people fall: but in the multitude of counselors there is safety."

We see here that it is actually wise to seek counsel from many sources. However, the choice of sources from which a person seeks counsel can make a tremendous difference in the outcome of the decisions made because of the counsel. Isaiah 30:1 clearly explains the difference:

> "Woe to the rebellious children, saith the LORD, that take counsel, but not of me:"

While it is wise to seek counsel from many people, a person must know that the people from whom they seek counsel are people who are godly, spiritually mature, and who will have no personal agenda. Otherwise the motives of those who do not meet these qualifications would dictate that their interests be served above the person seeking counsel. There are many examples in the Bible where a young ruler acted upon the counsel of his peers instead of mature men, and the consequences of those actions resulted in death.

> **People seek counsel because they are looking for a truth by which to make a decision.**

Why do people need counsel? People need counsel to arrive at a truth. Truth must be learned from sources of authority. In other words, counsel is the expression of truth in word given to a person or persons who need specific direction and guidance. This truth is neither subjective nor irrelevant in nature. On the contrary, true counsel is both objective and relevant to the context or purpose for which it is given.

There is nothing in a person's life in which the Word of God is not relevant. Every experience, action, need, or decision in life, should be a result of a life that is lived according to the Word of God. Living apart from the Word of God creates instability, uncertainty, and insecurity in the life of the individual.

Counsel

Where does counsel fit into the addiction recovery ministry? Does counseling have a place in the same ministry? Counsel begins in the heart and life of the person giving counsel. They must surrender to God just as the person seeking counsel. When God has His rightful place in the heart and life of a person, then and only then do they have the privilege of giving counsel to others.

A strong daily prayer life and time of studying God's Word are necessary when giving counsel to another person. This ensures an open communication between the counselor and God, giving him the discernment and wisdom to give godly advice. Without wisdom and discernment, the counselor is in a tremendously dangerous position of giving inappropriate or harmful counsel.

Godly discernment and wisdom are the most important traits in a person who gives counsel, and there is no substitute for these two qualities for effective counsel. Psalm 33:11 says,

> "The counsel of the Lord standeth forever, the thoughts of his heart to all generations."

Discernment and wisdom come from the Word of God as it is applied to the life of the Believer through the enlightenment and teaching of the Holy Ghost. When we begin with God and His Word, we receive what He can accomplish in the lives of people in need. This is all a person needs because God knows everything about a person and exactly what is needed for them to be what they should be in every area of their life. If we rely on our wisdom, our counsel will fail men. Proverbs 19:21 says,

> "There are many devices in a man's heart: nevertheless the counsel of the LORD, that shall stand."

Once a counselor understands the importance of having God's wisdom, and they rely on discernment from the Word of God, they can begin to help people who are in need of counsel.

Counseling

Many churches and institutions rely heavily on protracted counseling sessions with people who are in bondage to life-controlling habits and behaviors. I believe this type of activity actually gives the person cause to continue their behavior instead of ending it. Godly counsel is critical to helping people overcome life-controlling habits, but on-going counseling sessions only continue placing their problem in front of them instead of putting it behind them.

On-going counseling sessions can cause the addict to rationalize their addiction, thereby giving legitimacy to their behavior. Colossians 2:8 says,

> "Beware lest any man spoil you through philosophy and vain deceit, after the tradition of men, after the rudiments of the world, and not after Christ. For in him dwelleth all the fullness of the Godhead bodily. And ye are complete in him, which is the head of all principality and power."

No other power is necessary. Protracted counseling could also be interpreted as the counselor needing validation that they have something worthwhile to give to the addict. The Scripture takes care of this for us when we realize the importance of godly counsel as opposed to counseling. What is not being said here is that counseling ministries and churches that utilize counselors are wrong in doing so; they are not as long as their methods are Biblical. The methods used in an addiction recovery program must be just as Biblical as the message. To have less than Biblical methods is to weaken the strength of our message.

The Biblical method given many times throughout this book is to teach the addict how to have a daily, meaningful relationship with Jesus Christ. The message is the Gospel of Jesus Christ applied to the heart of the addict in salvation and forgiveness of sin. Thank the Lord for any ministry that has a burden for people in bondage to life-controlling habits, but for those ministries to be effective, their methods and message must be completely Biblical. We must do things God's way to receive what God can do in the life of the addict.

The problem with many ministries today is that, without realizing it, they have built their programs around methods that are humanistic. We are a result-driven society. When we do not get the results we think we should have, we change our methods to reflect a "new" approach we hope will bring about the desired results.

When we use a humanistic approach in the recovery program, we take the responsibility for the results of the program out of the Lord's hands and place it in our own. Instead of studying, memorizing, and meditating on the Word of God, many programs require the participant to learn a number of "steps" that supposedly will give them the ability to remain clean and sober. Dependency upon any "step" program is the most humanistic approach. This type of program leaves the addict with false hopes of remaining free from the life-controlling habit to which they are in bondage.

> **When God has His rightful place in the heart and life of a person, then and only then do they have the privilege of giving counsel to others.**

The problem with this kind of thinking is that we have allowed ourselves to change from God's methods to our own, and in doing so, we have marginalized our results instead of increasing them for the positive. Let us remind ourselves that God's way is far better than our way. God's methods are the only methods that will bring about lasting change and freedom from addictions.

Many extended counseling sessions are patterned after the world's psychiatric therapy sessions and therefore many times have the same results; the person is worse off in the end than in the beginning. There is only so much ground necessary to cover in any counsel session. Once the facts are established, going beyond a few minutes of counsel is unnecessary and subject matter starts being repeated. This is a waste of both people's time, energy, and resources.

The Biblical purpose of counsel is to convey the mind of Christ to a person so they can make their decision based on an accurate and authoritative truth about the action in question. Once the Biblical counsel is given, it is up to the person being counseled to make the right choice based upon the counsel given. Proverbs 12:15 says,

> "The way of a fool is right in his own eyes: but he that hearkeneth unto counsel is wise."

Proverbs 1:7 says,

> "The fear of the LORD is the beginning of knowledge: but fools despise wisdom and instruction."

Life is full of choices, and those choices have consequences. Helping a person make the right choices based upon the Word of God is what Biblical counsel is all about. To go beyond this is to inject man's thoughts and ideas, which can lead to more confusion in the mind of the addict.

What is the correct approach to counsel and advice? Whether the Pastor of a church, or a layperson who is working in a ministry of the church, the approach to giving counsel is the same. As stated earlier in this chapter, the counsel first begins in the heart of the counselor. For instance, for a person to be a witness (verb) for Christ, they must first be a witness (noun) of Christ. In other words, a person would have to be born again before they can tell others what Christ has done for them.

The same holds true for the counselor. Before a counselor can effectively convey needed advice, the counselor must have the knowledge, experience, and discernment from God firmly planted in his or her own heart and life. This does not mean that the counselor must have the same experiences as the person being counseled, but only the principle or precept is needed through maturity and the study of God's Word.

Many times the person being counseled may feel the counselor should have experienced the same life controlling habit as they in order for the counsel or advice to be legitimate. If this were true, Christ would not have been able give counsel to those with which He dealt in His earthly ministry. Christ was tempted in all points as we are, yet without sin, the Scripture tells us. Neither would Christ have been able to redeem fallen man if He were guilty as we are. It is not necessary for the counselor to have experienced the same life-controlling habit to give effective counsel concerning the habit because the Word of God is sufficient to deal with any issue of life.

> **Helping a person make the right choices based upon the Word of God is what Biblical counsel is all about.**

The second requirement for giving godly counsel is prayer. It has been said that every failure in our life is a prayer failure. I believe this to be true. We must solicit help and wisdom from God to effectively deal with people who have life-controlling habits. Prayer also places the counselor in the right frame of mind by creating humility.

Protracted counseling is relevant to people who have psychiatric problems resulting from trauma, illness, and unsolicited circumstances in life. However, problems in a person's life that are the result of sinful behavior must be dealt with from the standpoint of sin. The distinction is that the person, whose problems result from no fault of their own, is not responsible for their condition, where the addict is responsible for their condition and must accept responsibility for their actions.

Restoration by Transformation

Many addiction recovery programs teach the addict they have the power within themselves to permanently overcome their life-controlling habits, as long as they follow a prescribed set of steps and go to a meeting every week. This could not be any further from the truth. Even many Christian organizations teach this same philosophy. This is a huge mistake on their part.

The best results obtained through a program such as this is a marginal reformation of the outward behaviors and activities of the addict. There could not be any lasting help or hope for complete recovery from the addiction because we cannot "pull ourselves up by our boot straps" as they say. None of us has the power within ourselves to overcome life-controlling habits permanently. The reason for this is that we are born in sin and we have a sinful nature that controls our desires and behaviors. We must combat our sinful nature every day, and we simply do not have the strength or power within ourselves to resist the temptations of our flesh.

Some people are strong emotionally and have a measure of fortitude to control certain desires, but in the end, the flesh will win. Romans 12:2 says,

> "And be not conformed to this world: but be ye transformed by the renewing of your mind, that ye may prove what is that good, and acceptable, and perfect, will of God."

Transformation is a process of permanent outward change that takes place over time, originating from a supernatural change in man's heart by God.

The only way to be transformed by the renewing of our mind is through a supernatural work of God on the inside of a person, otherwise we only have what we can do for ourselves, and this is far too little. God performs this supernatural change in us as we accept Jesus Christ as our personal Saviour. God gives us a new life in Christ, and a new nature. 2Corinthians 5:17-18 says,

"Therefore if any man be in Christ, he is a new creature; old things are passed away; behold, all things are become new. And all things are of God, who hath reconciled us to himself by Jesus Christ, and hath given to us the ministry of reconciliation;"

These verses tell us that when we accept Christ as our Saviour, we are given a new nature with new desires. This can be a gradual process, although some things change immediately with some people. We now have two natures, the old nature, and the new nature that God has given us. Philippians 2:5 says,

"Let this mind be in you, which was also in Christ Jesus:"

We can have the mind of Christ if we desire to have it. The desire to have the mind of Christ is one of the things God gives us when we receive the new nature mentioned in 2Corinthians 5:17-18.

When a person accepts Jesus Christ as Saviour, and they receive a new nature, there is still struggle with desires of the flesh. Because we now have two natures, there is a tremendous struggle that takes place between our old nature and our new nature. The nature that wins the struggle is the nature we feed or allow to have control. This is where the battle of the mind takes place.

None of us has the power within ourselves to overcome life-controlling habits.

Before we received our new nature, it was natural for us to satisfy the desires of the flesh instead of God. Most people that have not been born again into the family of God, have no problem satisfying the flesh because their spiritual man is dead. Even with this new nature, we must rely upon the Holy Spirit, who now lives in us, to live a life that is pleasing to God. However, we can now live the Christian life in the strength and power of the Holy Ghost instead of our own power.

If we want the new man to win the struggles, we must give the new man what he needs to win. For the new man to win the struggles, we must feed the mind with things of God and not things of the flesh. Galatians 6:7-8 says,

> "Be not deceived; God is not mocked: for whatsoever a man soweth, that shall he also reap. For he that soweth to his flesh shall of the flesh reap corruption; but he that soweth to the Spirit shall of the Spirit reap life everlasting."

What a wonderful promise this is! When we have the power of God dwelling in us through the Holy Spirit, we can live clean and sober lives. Titus 2:11-12 says,

> "For the grace of God that bringeth salvation hath appeared to all men, Teaching us that, denying ungodliness and worldly lusts, we should live soberly, righteously, and godly, in this present world;"

Galatians 5:16 gives us the final answer to the question of how to have the mind of Christ and live a pure life.

> "This I say then, Walk in the Spirit, and ye shall not fulfil the lust of the flesh."

It does not get any simpler than this. In the following Scripture, we see a very clear picture of how our flesh controls our behavior. It also gives us the way of deliverance in the same passage. In Romans chapter seven God uses Paul the Apostle's own struggles to demonstrate just how powerful our flesh is. Paul was perhaps the strongest Christian that ever lived, but even he struggled with his flesh controlling his actions. What makes us think we can control our desires through human efforts? Romans 7:14-25 says,

> "For we know that the law is spiritual: but I am carnal, sold under sin. For that which I do I allow not: for what I would, that do I not; but what I hate, that do I. If then I do that which I would not, I consent unto the law that it is good. Now then it is no more I that do it, but sin that dwelleth in me. For I know that in me (that is, in my flesh,) dwelleth no

good thing: for to will is present with me; but how to perform that which is good I find not. For the good that I would I do not: but the evil which I would not, that I do. Now if I do that I would not, it is no more I that do it, but sin that dwelleth in me. I find then a law, that, when I would do good, evil is present with me. For I delight in the law of God after the inward man: But I see another law in my members, warring against the law of my mind, and bringing me into captivity to the law of sin which is in my members. O wretched man that I am! who shall deliver me from the body of this death? I thank God through Jesus Christ our Lord. So then with the mind I myself serve the law of God; but with the flesh the law of sin."

This is not a license to sin, but recognition that our flesh is weak and unable to control itself. Why then do so many addiction recovery programs use a humanistic approach to recovery? I submit that it is all they know. God is all-knowing. The knowledge given to us in the Bible is from God. He is the creator. He created man and He knows what works and what does not work. We must follow his teachings if we are to have freedom from life-controlling habits.

At the end of the preceding passage, Paul gives us the key to deliverance. He says, "O wretched man that I am! who shall deliver me from the body of this death? I thank God through Jesus Christ our Lord." We see here that deliverance comes through Jesus Christ. When Christ is Lord of our life, we have the power to overcome the desires of the flesh. The problem with the addict is that they are in control instead of Christ. Yielding to Jesus Christ is the key to deliverance from addictions.

It is easy for a Christian to think they are immune from addictions or bad behaviors. I know many people who felt they could never be controlled by a habit that wound up having a terrible addiction in their life. How does this happen? I believe it is the results of pride in their life. Galatians 6:1 deals with this very clearly. Galatians 6:1 says,

"Brethren, if a man be overtaken in a fault, ye which are spiritual, restore such an one in the spirit of meekness; considering thyself, lest thou also be tempted."

Let us break this verse down and look at its individual parts as they relate to addiction recovery. We notice first that the person speaking is talking to fellow believers because he uses the term "brethren." The first requirement for helping others overcome a life-controlling habit is the counselor must be a Christian. They must know Christ as their Saviour and have a daily walk with Him. Without this relationship, the counselor cannot have the discernment the Holy Spirit gives to those who study the Word of God.

The second point is that the writer does not distinguish between a Believer and lost person who are overtaken in the fault; he refers to him simply as a man. This is significant because the method or requirement to gain freedom from life-controlling habits is the same for Christians as it is for a lost person. They must first have a personal relationship with Jesus Christ.

The third point of this verse is that the man is overtaken. This gives the idea that the person does not want to be in the position of having the fault in the first place. They have been overtaken or overcome. Any honest addict will tell you that they wish they were not in the condition in which they find themselves. Most addicts began their addiction journey with one event, drink or hit. They never thought when they began they would wind up in the grips of something so terrible. Keep in mind that most addicts are not reared in a Christian home to be given guidance in such matters.

The next point is that it is only spiritual people that can restore a person overtaken in a fault. Being a spiritual person involves more than the space here will allow us to write about, but we can hit a few of the major aspects of being a spiritual person. We see in Galatians 5:22-25 that the spiritual person exhibits one fruit of the Spirit that contains nine graces, which are signs of a spiritual life. The list of graces God gives us is:

Love - Unselfish, benevolent concern for others.
Joy - Gladness of heart resulting from knowing and serving God.
Peace - Surrendering and yielding ourselves to the Lord.
Longsuffering - Forbearance, patience, realizing we are all sinners.
Gentleness - Kindness toward others regardless of what they do.
Goodness - Applying our love for Christ in our daily lives.
Faith - Faithfulness to the Lord in our actions.
Meekness - Gracious, kindly disposition, controlled strength.
Temperance - Restraint or discipline exercised over one's behavior.

The reason a spiritual person is needed to restore a person overtaken in a fault is explained in the next point; that being, in the spirit of meekness considering one's self. The spirit of meekness comes from a heart that is humble and one that recognizes that man is but dust. This attitude is void of pride, which we mentioned earlier in the chapter.

> **...restoration is postponed or stifled when we fall into the trap of prolonged counseling sessions.**

It is this attitude of arrogance that is removed when a person considers one's self, knowing they have the potential to be right where the addict is, were it not for God's grace in their life. Humility declares dependency on God and enables the Christian worker to help the addict by restoring them to God through the Gospel of Jesus Christ.

This humility allows us to show the addict that they are accepted and loved. This is one of the cornerstones of effective Biblical counsel. Acceptance for the person reveals God's love for them and must be complete. We accept the person, not the behavior. The recipient of counsel must understand that God's love for them is unconditional and not based upon their behavior.

Both attributes of acceptance and love produce much needed security in a person's life. Insecurity is the result of a person not experiencing the qualities of acceptance and love in their relationships, especially with parents, guardians, or other authority figures. Adam and Eve's disobedience to God in the Garden of Eden destroyed the ability for people to recognize God's acceptance and love for them. This truth must now be taught from God's Word.

Through events in the Garden given to us in Scripture, and through observation of human nature throughout time, we conclude that gender may dictate a dominate lean toward one attribute or the other. In other words, men tend to need accomplishment to find significance, while women may need security as a primary source of value, especially in relationships. While there is certainly a distinction between males and females, many people exhibit both needs and are the more common.

Counsel and restoration go hand-in-hand, but restoration is postponed or stifled when we fall into the trap of prolonged counseling sessions. In many cases, the counseling ministries of our modern churches are creating more addiction problems than they are solving. The addict does not want to be held accountable for his actions. Therefore, he will use the counseling sessions as an excuse for not facing the consequences of those actions for as long as he can.

Prolonged counseling sessions inadvertently teach the addict to rely upon himself to correct the problems in his life. This process is not intentional, but nonetheless occurs. When a person is encouraged to participate in counseling sessions over time, we are telling them that the Word of God is not able to deliver them from their bondage.

In essence, we are saying that there must be something added to the Word of God to find deliverance. This addition is what man thinks, what man creates, and what man defines. God does not need our puny, man-made efforts to deliver someone from life-controlling habits.

The correct response to counsel and counseling is to provide the addict with advice from God's Word and let the addict know in clear and certain terms that they are expected to follow that advice.

It is the Word of God and the power of the ruling presence of the Holy Spirit that changes the heart of men, and therefore, their actions, not our ideas and formulas. We must submit to God and His authority in dealing with the addict in giving counsel and advice.

Expectations

Because Christ is the source of all wisdom and knowledge, we must recognize the power that exists in relying upon Him for victory over life-controlling habits. Because of this power, we must expect the greatest change possible in the life of the addict. This is our greatest expectation. We expect God to deliver the addict completely from the forces of evil present in the world through the same relationship we have with God.

Therefore, the message we give to the addict participating in our program is one of hope and that the best is yet to come. Jude 24 says,

> "Now unto him that is able to keep you from falling, and to present you faultless before the presence of his glory with exceeding joy, To the only wise God our Saviour, be glory and majesty, dominion and power, both now and ever. Amen."

This power comes from the Holy Spirit of God living in us and through us. The program participant will recognize this help as he grows spiritually in his relationship with the Lord.

Our task, as ministry workers, is to lead the way, to show the love of God through our ministry, to show the addict that there is a better way to live. We talked in chapter four about people needing a desire to see the addict as a person in need of the Saviour. God gives us a great example of how this love is demonstrated, in Luke chapter 10, verses 25 through 37. Jesus tells the story of how the Good Samaritan "saw" the need of the traveler who was beaten, robbed, and left half dead.

In this story, Jesus tells us about two other people that actually came by the beaten traveler and actually looked upon him in his condition, but did nothing to help him. One was a priest and the other a Levite. These two men represented the religious and authoritarian societal members of their day. For them to *not* help this traveler actually meant that they had to break their own law. The Samaritan, on the other hand, was the most unlikely of the three to help. The traveler was without a doubt a Jew. Jews had nothing to do with Samaritans. They looked on them as dogs.

Religion has never helped a person find true freedom from sin. Neither has the law. Both look good to the humanistic eye, but are completely useless in breaking the bondage of sin in a person's life. Religion only soothes the conscience of man for a short period. Legalism only places men in further bondage. It is the "unlikely" that truly heals. The Scripture says about Jesus Christ in Philippians 2:7,

> "But made himself of no reputation, and took upon him the form of a servant, and was made in the likeness of men:"

It was the Samaritan, however, that not only looked upon the traveler's need, but he had to look past all of his own prejudices and fears at the same time to have compassion on him. Not only this, but he evidently helped the beaten Jew sacrificially, as he was a traveler himself and surely had limited finances. This is for our example. How many times do we see the homeless person under the bridge, and the beggar at the off-ramp, but are never moved with compassion for them? It is easy to look on people that are needy, but never see their real need.

"To Reach and Restore" should be the motto of every Christian. We must love the Saviour before we can love the ones whom the Saviour loves. When this happens, the addict will not only see that what we have is real and that they can have the same relationship with God that we have, but that the life we live is a far better life now. "There's no better living than a Transformed Life."

Chapter 15

Challenge and Goals

The Pastor received a phone call just prior to leaving home for the Wednesday evening church service. It was a friend of his and owner of a business located down the street from the Church. The friend had been dating a girl that introduced him to cocaine. It was several months later and he found himself hooked on the drug. The Pastor asked his secretary to call a member in his Church who was the director of a residential recovery ministry. The church member was asked to stay after the evening service and talk to his friend who needed help.

When the service was over the Pastor allowed them to use his office for the meeting. The meeting went very well and lasted about an hour. The friend of the Pastor seemed to have a real desire to gain victory over his addiction problem.

The friend's mother also came with him to lend her support. The church member counseled with the friend, prayed with him, and gave him some reading material that would help him through the recovery process. When the meeting was over, the church member noticed that there were several people on the church staff waiting in the main office. The staff seemed to be relieved when the meeting was over. This simple story reveals several challenges the majority of local churches face today.

There was a phrase in a well-known movie some years back that gained popularity. It was "Who ya gonna call? Ghost Busters!" Evidently, in this movie, when a ghost was frightening a citizen, they could call this group of somewhat goofy scientists that would capture the ghost in a homemade contraption. I know this is not a very spiritual illustration, but it fits. Many churches have this same response to people that have addiction problems. When the Church is not sure how to help the addict and resorts to referring the addict to someone else, the Church loses the opportunity to minister to the addict. When the local church refers an addict to an outside program or institution, it is relinquishing its responsibility of reaching a soul for Christ.

Addiction Recovery: A Ministry Rejected
The mindset of many Church leaders today is that there is a stigma attached to this whole idea of addictions and addiction recovery ministries. This stigma extends not only to addicts, but also those who work in programs and ministries that help people recover from addictions. It is as if this segment of our society is feared and left alone by the Church, for the world to figure out how to deal with them. In many instances, if someone in the community needs help with addiction problems, they are viewed as a nuisance or risk and help is sought outside the church.

This attitude is reflected in the lack of a recovery ministry outreach in many churches. As far as these churches are concerned, addicts are "out of sight and out of mind." This attitude extends toward both the addict and those who are called to help them. In these same churches, the attitude is, people with addictions are second-class, and workers in this type of ministry are not respected for the work they do. They are more or less tolerated, but never desired - Not inside the Church anyway. This exclusionist mentality has stifled the outreach to people who need help and is in contradiction to the direct command of our Lord.

Is it Scriptural to have a ministry outside the local New Testament church? It is my conviction that all ministry outreaches are to be managed through the local church. Unfortunately, I know many church leaders who have the view that addiction recovery should take place outside the church. There should be a "place" to "send" "these people" is the prevailing thought in the mind of many church leaders. It is as if this whole segment of people has leprosy. Why is this kind of ministry so rejected by many churches? I believe it is because of two main reasons: Fear and Lack of Vision. It has been my experience that many churches fall into one of these two categories.

Fear

Fear of the unknown is very real for many people. It has been my own observation that when a person is faced with the unknown it has a way of revealing certain emotional characteristics of the person that are otherwise securely hidden away. These emotional characteristics can be the result of a lack of trust, inward feelings of insecurity, or even unworthiness.

> **The correct vision of the addict is one in which the Church sees people as God sees them.**

For a Christian these unhealthy characteristics can be the means of preventing a close relationship with the Lord. As for addictions, fear is also frequently developed because of a lack of understanding of the cause and effects of addictions. Once a person understands, what causes addiction problems and how to deal with people who have addiction problems this fear is usually alleviated. The peace and grace the Lord Jesus gives to His people cannot be overlooked. II Timothy 1:7 says,

> "For God hath not given us the spirit of fear; but of power, and of love, and of a sound mind."

I have talked with missionaries and ministry staff who are afraid to work with people who have addiction problems. Many times this is due to a lack of trusting the Lord for safety and protection. Those who work with people who have addiction problems should always be on guard for the unexpected. However, the Lord gives sufficient discernment to know when there is a potential danger.

Many churches fail to have a ministry outreach to addicts because of fear of the unknown. With some churches, it is a stretch just to have a jail or prison ministry. At least with a jail ministry the chances of the inmates coming to church are slim. However, it is different with an addiction ministry. They might actually show up at one of the services. This is a poor reason not to have a recovery ministry to the community.

Lack of Vision
Perhaps one of the most harmful characteristics in the Church today is the characteristic of apathy. Proverbs 29:18 says,

"Where there is no vision, the people perish:"

This lack of vision is one of the greatest obstacles in the Church today that prevents having a ministry to people with addictions. The correct vision of the addict is one in which the Church sees people as God sees them. In John 4:35 Jesus said,

"Say not ye, There are yet four months, and then cometh harvest? behold, I say unto you, Lift up your eyes, and look on the fields; for they are white already to harvest."

When Christians see the addict as a lost soul, in need of the Saviour, they will respond in obedience and with compassion. Christians will then make a difference in the lives of people with addiction problems. The most important vision the Church must have is the correct vision of God. Before any local church will have the vision of dying souls, they must have a vision of an exalted Saviour. The Church must see God as the King of kings and Lord of lords that He is.

He must be seen as Isaiah saw in Isaiah chapter six and verse one,

> "In the year that king Uzziah died I saw also the Lord sitting upon a throne, high and lifted up, and his train filled the temple."

We must see the Lord high and lifted up. He must have his rightful place in our hearts and lives in order for us to have the correct vision of this world and the place of service that we have in it.

Challenges to the Church
What does the story at the beginning of this chapter tell us about the challenges faced by the Church concerning addictions? This story is common. It is common because most Church leaders are not prepared to deal with the diverse nature of addiction problems.

There are as many people, by percentage, that struggle with addictions in our congregations, as there are outside our congregations. In other words, the same percentage of people in the world that has addiction problems can be translated over to the Church as well. When I was in the military, we were told that if 10% of people in the world were thieves then you could rest assured that 10% of soldiers were too. This just makes sense. The same goes for the Church. Church leaders must recognize this.

There may not be any "apparent" addiction problems in the members of a congregation, but you can believe they are there.

> **Many churches fail to have a ministry outreach to addicts because of fear of the unknown.**

It would be prudent to teach to our congregations the principles in the Word of God concerning idolatry, lusts of the flesh, and obedience to God's Word. Many Church leaders already do this, but not for combating addictions.

The principles given in this text should be taught, in a very methodical way, to every age group in the Church from young people to seniors. Not only would this help those who may be struggling with some form of addiction, but it may help prevent others from falling prey to addictions as well.

Challenge #1 - Attitude

Perhaps the greatest challenge faced by the Church today, concerning ministering to people with addiction problems, is attitude. There is a prevailing attitude in the Church today that an addiction is just a weakness in the life of an individual. While this is partially true, it is not completely correct.

All addictions begin one of, or a combination of, several ways: peer pressure, curiosity, or force. I could say each of these is a weakness of some sort, and I would be correct. However, the circumstances surrounding each one varies greatly from one person to the next.

Peer pressure

Peer pressure is more commonly the strongest reason why people choose to participate in an illicit behavior. The fellow student or coworker, who offers a hit on a joint, drink of alcohol, or a pill, is one of the most common sources of illicit behavior.

Curiosity

I have worked with many people who simply were curious about how the drug or alcohol would make them feel. This continued behavior led them down the road to addiction. Curiosity is a strong human characteristic.

Force

Unfortunately, there are cases where someone weaker physically or emotionally was forced to take part in an illicit behavior. Although this is more uncommon than the others are, it none-the-less happens. It is unconscionable that someone could stoop so low as to force someone weaker into a life damaging behavior. Once the initial and normal physical and psychological barrier is destroyed, there is a phase of dependency, both physical and psychological, that begins.

While it is true that the addict has arrived at this stage due to weakness, staying in the addiction is not. Many addicts have been in and out of different "programs" in an effort to rid themselves of the addiction. It takes a lot of willpower to continue this path for an extended period. It is much like the obese person who has been on multiple diets; they have very strong will power. They will starve themselves for months and become discouraged because there is very little permanent weight loss.

The proper approach to weight loss is a change of attitude toward the purpose for which a person eats combined with an appropriate exercise program. It is necessary to give them the truth by teaching them how to eat healthy. The obese person must accept himself or herself as they are and allow the changes in their lifestyle and eating habits to take care of the weight loss for them. This is a slow process, but it has lasting effects.

> **Before any local church will have the vision of dying souls, they must have a vision of an exalted Saviour.**

The bottom line to this is, an obese person is given the proper information and the right tools. This is what makes a lasting difference in their lives. The same is true with the addict. They must be given the truth about the addiction and then be given the tools necessary for recovery from the addiction.

Another attitude is one that says, "Let someone else handle this kind of problem." Although this may not be a conscious thought in the minds of some church leaders, it is none-the-less demonstrated by their lack of vision and compassion. Having said this we must be careful not to make compassion the motive. Christ is the motive. Bringing an addict to Christ is the primary reason for helping the addict: Bringing them to Christ in salvation and bringing them to Christ through a meaningful relationship with Him is the main reason for an addiction recovery ministry.

Helping them to live a life of obedience to God is the best thing that can be done for the addict. There should be compassion. It is not the motive however. Having the attitude of letting others, deal with the addict is a very selfish attitude. God is able to take care of anything that would seem to be a trouble spot in having a ministry to addicts.

Some Pastors simply do not want to be bothered with an addiction recovery ministry. This is nothing less than refusal to obey the command Christ gave the Church in Mark 16:15,

> "And he said unto them, Go ye into all the world, and preach the gospel to every creature."

This includes the addict.

Challenge #2 - Qualifications
The Pastor, in the story at the beginning of the chapter, had compassion for the friend who was caught in the addiction yet there was still something lacking. Thankfully, he had enough compassion to arrange a meeting where his friend could receive help, but there could have been more help available to this addict than just the meeting. It could have made more of an impact in this friend's life if there was a ministry already in place in the Church whereby he could have received support through counseling or addiction classes. Having classes available on Friday nights or even a Sunday morning Sunday school class would give the addict the opportunity to hear the truth.

Any outreach such as this needs people who are called of God to be a part of this kind of ministry. There are usually several people in any given church body who would love the opportunity to be involved in a ministry such as this. They simply need to be given the tools, through addiction education and training in how to effectively present material for a class such as this.

This Pastor may not have known how to counsel his friend, knowing the difficulties associated with addiction problems. I believe the Pastor of every local church should be equipped to give appropriate counsel in any given situation. If the Pastor's schedule is of such that he is unable to do the counseling himself, there should at the very least, be a staff or layperson qualified to administer such counsel as needed.

The qualifications for working in a recovery ministry are not as stringent as one might think. Having a genuine love for the Lord, burden for addicts, and the ability to learn and pass on truths, is a good start. Having a strong love for the Lord is all that is required. People who have a desire to counsel addicts on a regular basis should receive specialized training in this field.

> **Bringing an addict to Christ is the primary reason for helping the addict.**

As far as a ministry outreach to people who have addiction problems, it does take some effort on the part of the Pastor to promote the ministry inside the church family. There must also be openness on the part of the congregation to offer this kind of ministry to the community.

Challenge #3 - Facilities

You cannot blame the staff in the story for wanting to go home. Most staff who are involved in the ministries of the church are tired after the services are over. Many churches have lay-people who work a job outside the church and then fill a position of service in the meetings of the church. This may even include the music director and musicians.

Even if the church employs full-time staff to fill these positions, they are tired as well. As much as they love their church, they are ready to go home when the services are over. The point is, as there is need, the church should provide a means where those needing counsel or those attending a recovery class can meet for the time appointed. This does not have to be a separate building. It may be sufficient to have a single room with an attached office.

If a room with an attached office is not available, there may be a room available that is large enough to have an office built inside. This room needs to be available for use at the hours designated for the ministry outreach. If it is a room that is used for multiple functions, scheduling must be closely considered to accommodate all purposes for its use. Along with the room itself, there are other considerations as well.

There should be a place designated to store teaching materials; this material should not be accessible to anyone who uses the same facilities for other purposes. Audio-visual equipment may be shared with other ministries, but it should always be made available for the recovery classes. Most recovery classes utilize DVDs and VHS tapes in conjunction with teaching material from a book. A television large enough for the class to see comfortably and a player is needed for the viewing of these DVDs and VHS tapes. Having an office attached to this room allows for the storage of materials and a place to provide counsel.

Challenge #4 - Curriculum

Just as there are many different approaches to recovery from addictions, there are many different books and materials available for the recovery ministry to use in their outreach program. In order to be fair with all of them I must say, as with anything, there are some good ones and there are some bad ones. Whether or not a specific set of materials is best for a particular program is up to the discretion of the director of that program.

The most important consideration for an addiction recovery program's curriculum is whether the material is Biblical and doctrinally sound. This includes proper context of Scripture passages used in the lessons. There are several considerations when choosing a suitable curriculum for an addiction recovery ministry such as:

1) Participants
2) Teachers
3) Cost

4) Curriculum Content

Regardless of what curriculum is chosen, the most effective application of that curriculum is a one-on-one approach. It is far more effective to allow the program participant to move, at his or her own speed, through the course. This allows for the differences in where the participants are in their life.

Many program directors feel they are unable to accomplish this because it is not feasible logistically. They have only one meeting per week and they use this meeting time to teach the lessons. It is much more effective to allow the participants to work through the material at their home and use the meeting time each week as a follow-up and supportive role.

A one-on-one approach accomplishes a couple of things that are extremely important to the success of the program. First, it places the responsibility for recovery on the participant. This is critical in teaching the addict the principle of taking responsibility for their actions. They must study during the week so that they will be prepared for the weekly follow-up meeting.

Because every person is at a different point in their life, the second thing this accomplishes is to allow the participant to move at their own pace through the course. Some participants may already know Christ as their Saviour, while others may not. This would definitely make a difference in how to teach the program.

Transformed Life has an on-line addiction recovery program that is structured specifically for this purpose. The on-line course enables the participants to work through the curriculum at their own pace and prepare any questions or topics they wish to discuss at the weekly meeting. The online program is an extension of the local church that is hosting the weekly support meeting.

These weekly meetings should begin with a time of devotion and transition to discussion time of the topics on the hearts and minds of the participants. This discussion time should be closely guarded as to not allow time to be wasted on unnecessary subject matter. The participants should feel free to engage the director with any relevant question.

Participants

Questions may be asked to help identify considerations for a particular group of participants:

What is the expected number of participants? This consideration is necessary primarily from a financial standpoint. The administrator of this type of church ministry would certainly want enough materials to allow every person in the program to participate, but care must be taken to not over-do the budget.

> The most important consideration for an recovery program curriculum is whether the material is Biblically sound.

Time and experience will allow the administrator of the program to find the right balance here. Keep in mind that the material is only as good as the person delivering the training. Try to avoid purchasing materials that are expensive and unnecessary and remember the principle of stewardship.

What is the age range of the participants? Few, if any, programs are diverse enough to accommodate each individual age group. For this reason, most curriculums are age neutral. It will be necessary to adjust most programs upon administering the curriculum.

What is the gender of the participants? Even though there are some programs that differentiate between male and female participants, the better curriculums are actually neutral in this respect. The reason for this is that the Biblical principles that pertain to addiction recovery are relevant to both males and females. Once again, it may be necessary to apply certain aspects of the program differently, but not the core principles. (It is not recommended that recovery ministries allow the mixing of male and female participants in the same classes.)

What is the education level of the participants? The education level of the participants will determine how the study material is covered. The instructor of the program will have to assess this in order to know how to present the material.

Few, if any, curriculums are geared toward a specific educational level. It may be necessary for the Instructor to adjust the content of the material to match the educational level of the group. Age may also be a factor in how the program material is delivered by the instructor.

If the Church is located in an area where there is a strong ethnic presence, it will be necessary to utilize people who speak the language of the group being reached. The addiction recovery ministry is a tremendous opportunity to cross ethnic barriers with the gospel of Jesus Christ. The curriculum must obviously be available in the language needed for the particular ethnic group.

One other consideration of utmost importance is the criminal background of participants if any. For the protection of children, teenage girls and boys, etc., careful consideration must be given as to the time and place of the recovery classes offered. The director of the recovery ministry must keep in mind the practical truth that those attending a recovery program are not usually choir members or current pillars of the community. Regardless of the answer to these and other questions, a Bible-based curriculum designed for this specific purpose is crucial for the program to be most effective.

Teachers and Educators
Any person in the Church who has a desire to minister to addicts would be useful in teaching, or helping to teach, a recovery program curriculum. Enthusiasm, a genuine love for the Lord, and concern for the addict, will go a long way in being effective in teaching an addiction recovery curriculum. The teacher(s) must also have the opportunity to receive any available training and

instruction offered by the publisher of the curriculum being used. This is important because the Author/Publisher can concisely convey the areas of the text that need greater emphasis.

If a member of the Church shows interest in becoming more involved with the addiction recovery ministry the Church may elect to provide this person with the opportunity to receive training certifications through the ministry that provides the curriculum. This person could also be utilized in other areas of ministry in the Church as the opportunity arises.

When choosing the correct person to teach the addiction recovery material it is also important that the personality and temperament of the individual be conducive to working with addicts. A person who is not in control of themselves will not be in control of a group of addicts either. The right person is one who is spiritually and emotionally mature.

The qualities of spiritual and emotional maturity are actually more important than credentials and degrees when it comes to working with addicts one-on-one. The Pastor should have the discernment as to which particular member would be right for the job. Keep in mind that any curriculum is only as good as the person who delivers the lessons. This means that the intensity level of the teacher will determine how effective the classes are. There is also a passion necessary for effective teaching of any recovery curriculum material.

Cost

You must use caution in selecting a curriculum that is right for your particular ministry. The cost of some programs prohibits ministries from utilizing their material. As with individuals, the Church must do some homework and shopping around in order to find the appropriate curriculum for their particular need. A typical quality workbook type curriculum will cost anywhere from $18 to $26, depending on the type of binding and print.

Always compare apples with apples. In other words, make sure you are making fair comparisons of durability, ease of reading, content, and good support from the supplier/publisher. Nothing is more frustrating than needing a couple dozen books and not being able to get them quickly.

Look for curriculums that offer teacher's helps. Some Curriculums may offer a package of two or three teacher's packets along with twenty or so workbooks. Usually, buying a package deal can save money as well. Some curriculums offer more for the money than others do. This will be covered in more detail in the following segment. Planning and research are essential to prevent wasted money and wasted time.

The Curriculum Content

The ideal curriculum is one that includes several essential elements. First, it is easily segmented into even periods for ease of scheduling. In other words, it is better to use a curriculum that has twelve chapters of content rather than eleven. This may not seem important at first, but it is a necessary consideration. For example, if a ministry offers a year round program it is easy to use one chapter of the material for each month of the year.

Secondly, the participant should easily follow the material. This means the content of the material is structured in a way that has clearly defined objectives. The content of the curriculum should be written at the simplest level possible so that any participant can understand the concepts and principles being conveyed.

Thirdly, and most importantly, the curriculum material should be Biblically sound. This means it should have two things: It has, at its core, Biblical truths that clearly apply to addictions, and it must be doctrinally accurate.

The curriculum must also have the Gospel of Jesus Christ thoroughly woven throughout the entire length of the content. This ensures that the participant has every opportunity possible, and at every stage of the content, to respond to the Gospel for salvation.

There should also be tools and helps for living the new life in Christ. These tools and helps, once again, are based upon the Word of God.

Biblical Truths and Doctrines

The most important aspect of any addiction recovery program is its dependency upon the Word of God for its principles and assertions. God tells us in His Word that the Church is the "pillar and ground of the truth." This was covered in a previous chapter. In order for the Church to be the "pillar and ground of the truth", there must be a basis of truth on which it stands. The source of this truth is only the Word of God. To exclude the Word of God from an addiction recovery curriculum is a paramount failure to recognize the Word of God as the foundation for teaching the addict how to live a life that is at peace with God, himself, and his fellow man.

There are curriculums that use the Bible in its content, but do not believe the principles found in the Bible to be the final authority on the subject. Many times Scripture is used to support a point of view or ideal instead of the point of view being taken from the Scripture.

> **The curriculum must have the Gospel of Jesus Christ thoroughly woven throughout the entire length of the content.**

Curriculum material should always be drawn from the doctrines and principles found in the Word of God. Doctrines are simply, what we believe, or a body of belief. Few recovery programs have the opportunity to explore in depth these doctrines with the addict. In most cases, there is simply not enough time to cover all the different topics and subjects that would be desired. However, any material that is considered for use in a Church ministry should strictly be Christ-Centered, Bible-Originated, doctrinally sound, and convey Biblical principles in a systematic way.

The Process

As with any project, task, or endeavor, there are many right ways to accomplish the same task. It is no different in an addiction recovery ministry. The manner in which a local church administers their program is not as important as having doctrinally sound material used in the curriculum, having dedicated and devoted staff that love the Lord enough to work in the ministry of recovery, and a program that is cost-effective for the Church.

The right process for an addiction recovery program is one in which the addict receives Biblical training over a period that allows for the natural elimination of any chemical substances from their body. During this time of training, there should be a daily regimen of Biblical truths given that bring the participant to a place where they recognize the real need of their life. I call this a Systematic Teaching of Biblical Principles. The real need in the life of the addict is to surrender to God all the desires of their flesh. This can only be accomplished through the Word of God applied to the heart and life of the addict after they have been born again of God's Spirit as they accept Jesus Christ as their Saviour.

The local church should make a weekly meeting available to the participants of a program. This gives them spiritual support and to have accountability for their activities and behaviors. This meeting is not a substitute for the Biblical training program with a curriculum, only a supplement to the training curriculum. Transformed Life Ministries has produced the only (at the time of this writing) complete, self-paced, modular, and socially interactive on-line program that satisfies all these requirements.

Scripture memorization must be at the heart of any curriculum.

The weekly meetings are a time and place for the program participant to receive answers to questions and interact with other people from their community. The facilitator of the weekly meetings should prepare to give a short devotion each week. It would be best to keep the subject matter of the devotion to a topic or concept that is general in nature, such as a Biblical character trait or even a Bible character with whom the participants can build an association.

When the local church facilitator works in partnership and cooperation with a pre-established program, such as Transformed Life's "The Discovery of Hope" addiction recovery course, this strengthens the learning results for the participant because they are learning daily from the on-line course and gaining support from the weekly meetings at the same time.

The Goal

With proper time spent in prayer, research, and training, the Church can develop a viable and effective Church outreach ministry that is cost-effective and Biblically sound. The program developed from this prayer and research will allow the Church to reach many souls for the cause of Christ.

It is my desire to see an effective recovery outreach ministry in every local church across America. If even a fraction of the churches had this vision it would make a substantial difference in our society. There are already some churches that have this vision and are working faithfully at providing this ministry to their community. They deserve our prayers and support for doing so. The primary goal of any recovery program offered through the local church is two-fold:

1) Teach the addict how they can have a meaningful relationship with Jesus Christ.

2) Teach the addict how they can live a Spirit-filled life, free from the bondage of addictions

As I have mentioned before, the most important purpose that anyone can have in life is to help others come to a saving knowledge of Christ. The Lord Jesus Christ deserves the reward of His suffering. This reward is the souls of men. Christ died for this purpose. Our primary goal is to help people have a meaningful relationship with Jesus Christ, and this begins with salvation. We must work faithfully at bringing people to Jesus Christ through the gospel found in God's Word.

Most addicts are lost and need to hear this gospel message. When the gospel of Christ is given, it is the Holy Spirit's place to convict and bring a person to repentance. Secondly, once the addict has made a decision to put their faith and trust in Christ for salvation, they must be taught how to live for Christ on a daily basis.

This is accomplished through a daily devotional time of reading and studying God's Word and having a strong prayer life. Scripture memorization must be at the heart of any curriculum. It is the Word of God hidden in the heart that enables the power of God to be manifested in the actions of the Believer. When Believers behave in a manner that is pleasing to God, He receives the Glory.

Having a viable and effective ministry outreach to addicts is both obedient to God's command to reach all people and fulfills a great need in most communities. The Church is in a unique position to make a difference in our society by helping to bring the addict to Christ and by teaching them what God says about how to live a victorious and productive life while on this earth. May the Lord richly bless all those who reach out to their own "Jerusalem" with an addiction recovery ministry.

End

About the Author

Garland M. Burgess

Biographical Information

Garland Mark Burgess and his family have been members of Temple Baptist Church in Powell, TN since 2006. Mr. and Mrs. Burgess have four adult children and three grandchildren. Mrs. Burgess is an RN and a Health Care Director with a local Knoxville company and has been in nursing for over twenty-seven years. Since 2006, Brother Burgess has authored several books dealing with a range of topics from addiction recovery to business and the economy.

Ministry Experience

Prior to being called to preach, Brother Burgess served in various church ministries as Deacon, Sunday School Teacher, Music Director, Youth Director, and Bus Worker. Mrs. Burgess has served as Organist, Pianist, and Sunday School Teacher. Brother Burgess was called to preach in 2001, while a member of Gospel Light Baptist Church in Walkertown, North Carolina, Dr. Bobby Roberson Pastor, and surrendered to full-time ministry the following year.

In 1978 to 1981 Brother Burgess had the privilege to work, travel and sing with the late, Evangelist Lester Roloff. He again served there for over a year as the Director of both the Lighthouse and City of Refuge homes for men in Corpus Christi, Texas, starting in 2002, at which time he re-opened the City of Refuge Home for men.

He has worked most recently as the Director of Our Master's Camp, a Residential, Addiction Recovery Ministry where he directed and administered the program from organizational conception to operation; developing curriculum guides, program procedures, promotional material, and standards of practice.

He has also worked in other ministries including the Victory Home for Men in Pickens, SC, Bob Jones University in Greenville, SC, and ACE School of Tomorrow Headquarters in Lewisville, TX.

Education

Brother Burgess served eight years in the US ARMY Reserve Signal Corps, where he acquired multiple military occupational skills with specialty in multi-channel, microwave, and satellite communications. He received a commendation for meritorious completion of training in the US ARMY Signal School at Fort Gordon, Georgia, graduating top of his class as "Distinguished Graduate."

He has successfully held management positions with both ADT Security Services as Operations Manager, and BellSouth Telecommunications as Network Manager. He holds a degree in Electronic Engineering Technology, a Bachelor of Science in Bible, and a Master of Ministry degree (Summa Cum Laude 4.0). Brother Burgess is currently pursuing a PhD in Christian Education, planning to graduate May, 2012.

In addition, Brother Burgess has training and experience in Christian School Administration, Large Project Management, Personnel Management, and Business Management.

Calling of God

God has called Brother Burgess to preach the Word of God. Brother Burgess and his wife have experience in several different areas of leadership in church ministry, and believe the Lord has called them into full-time ministry service. They trust the Lord for His infinite wisdom in leading them as they seek to obey Him and bring glory to Him through their lives.

About Transformed Life Ministries

"There's no better living than a Transformed Life!"

Transformed Life Ministries (TLM) was created as a step of faith and obedience to the Lord's direction in reaching people with life-controlling habits as well as those who may desire additional Biblical training to help them in their Christian life and walk with the Lord.

Purpose – To "Reach and Restore"

It is the intent of **Transformed Life Ministries** (TLM) to collaborate with churches that desire to evangelize their communities and the world with the Gospel of Jesus Christ. Carrying out the Great Commission in obedience to God's command, and doing so through the local church, is part of the vision of TLM.

TLM works through the Local Church as a part of the church's overall ministry outreach in evangelizing their local community. The only part we play in this process is to provide materials and support that better enable the church to reach people for Christ. It is our belief that the local church is the center of all ministry outreach to their community and the world. TLM is simply there to support that role.

We believe that working together with local churches will not only enhance the ministry outreach of those local churches, but will also enable members of that church to grow in the process. Our main desire is to help people come to a saving knowledge of Christ and to help them grow as obedient followers of Christ in their daily lives.

This requires a commitment on both the part of the local church and TLM to collaborate for these common goals.

Transformed Life is a valuable resource for Local Churches and Ministries.

Transformed Life is a complete resource for churches and ministries where members and ministry workers can enhance their walk with God, connect with friends and family, and enjoy resources for Christian growth.

It is the desire of Transformed Life Ministries to play a supportive role in becoming a solid, Biblical, resource for churches and ministries. In keeping with this vision, Transformed Life Ministries has created an online learning platform called **Transformed Life University (TLU)**.

Transformed Life offers courses through TLU (Transformed Life University) that help people experience a closer daily walk with the Lord. Through various courses the Christian can learn more about Biblical stewardship, discipleship, courtship and dating, Bible versions, and much more.

TLU even offers a series of courses to help people overcome life-controlling habits (addictions) as well as train Christian workers how to work in an addiction recovery ministry.

Transformed Life University is a self-paced, online, learning platform that offers a variety of courses to Christian workers, Lay-People, Ministers, or anyone who desires a deeper knowledge of God and holy living.

The times are changing, and education is changing with it. For the average person in a full-time career, participating in a traditional class room learning environment is more difficult than ever. There are even many reports that conclude that the high price of education may not be worth the financial burden it requires.

The logical alternative is to utilize online education. Also called Distance Learning, on line education has gained tremendous momentum as a viable way for people to attain a degree, or to continue their education. Concerns with economic trends and financial uncertainties have created a tremendous demand for new on line learning opportunities. Distance Learning is seen more and more as an affordable alternative to attending traditional classes.

This is the motivation for Transformed Life University. Our desire is to offer substantive course content, delivered via a socially interactive platform, where students can gain value from the experiences of others.

By partnering with educators who not only have the academic qualifications, but also the life experience to go with it, and in addiction to the socially interactive platform, we have created a truly unique learning environment that gives the student a much broader level of education than other online programs.

Role of TLU

While many programs are free to the participant and can be used in various ministries of the church, other programs are fee-based and require the end user's financial participation to take the course. TLU educators administer these fee-based courses. These educators become an extension of the local church that is sponsoring the program courses and work in concert with the person(s) the church has chosen as the director for that particular ministry.

For example, if a church has an addiction recovery ministry and wishes to use the **"Discovery of Hope"** addiction recovery program as its curriculum, TLU educators will work with the participant on line while the church member works with them in weekly meetings.

It is important that the church ministry leader and the TLU educator be of the same mind. This is why we offer the **"Making a Difference"** instructor's course to church members who desire to work in this area of church ministry outreach. It is of utmost importance that all church-designated instructors and TLU educators understand a clear Biblical view of what God says concerning life-controlling habits. In this way we are able to offer a permanent solution to the addictions in a person's life.

TLU is designed as a tool and resource to churches and ministries. Although TLU is available to churches of any size, the Online Learning System lends itself well to smaller churches that may not be in a position financially to offer training for various ministry outreaches. As a partner with TLM, you have complete control and autonomy over your ministry and program. TLU is only a resource that helps you reach people with the Gospel and help them through the process of Christian growth, which may start with addiction recovery for many of the participants.

Through the TLU Learning System a Pastor or designated church member may also develop, and make available, supplemental courses to support the programs already available by TLU and its educators, which reflect the goals of that particular church and ministry. These new courses must also be in harmony with the overall objectives of TLU and reflect TLM's vision and mission to be offered through the on-line learning system.

If you would like your church to become a TLM Partner by using the TLU learning platform, simply email us at **partner@tluonline.org** with your name, your position or function in the church, your Pastor's name, and the church mailing address, and we will begin the process by sending a packet of information to your Pastor. This packet explains in detail the role of the church and TLM in the partnership, the simple process of how to get started, and much more.

For more information about the courses offered through TLU, visit **www.tluonline.com.**

For more information about Transformed Life Ministries visit our website at **www.transformedlifeministries.com**.

Suggested Reading

*Note: Not all the books suggested here are written from a Biblical viewpoint. However, from time to time, I have found them either to be simply a source of information or to produce thought provoking, albeit opposite, views from my own; they may or may not necessarily be in agreement with our own convictions or beliefs. Some of these books are given as sources of information only and should be regarded as such.

Addictions - A banquet in the grave, 2001 Edward T. Welch
P&R Publishing - ISBN: 0-87552-606-3

The Treasures of Darkness, 2005 Clarence Sexton
Crown Christian Publications - ISBN:1-58981-255-7

His Way Is Perfect, 2007 Clarence Sexton
Crown Christian Publications - ISBN: 978-1-58981-350-2

Building a Christian World View, 1986 W. Andrew Hoeffecker Editor, Gary Scott Smith Associate Editor,
P&R Publishing
Volume I - ISBN: 0-87552-281-5
Volume II - ISBN: 087411965-0

12 Steps to Destruction, 1991 Martin and Deidre Bobgan
East Gate Publishers, ISBN: 0-941717-05-4

How to say no to a stubborn habit, 1994 Erwin W. Lutzer
SP Publications, ISBN: 1-56476-331-5

Alcoholism or Abstinence, 1953 C. Aubrey Hearn
The Standard Publishing Company, Cincinnati, Ohio
260

Helping the Alcoholic and His Family, 1963 Thomas J. Shipp

Index

12-Step, 18
AA, 18, 175
absence, 18
absorption, 53
abundance, 58
acceptance, 19, 52, 72, 261
accomplish, 19, 33
accountability, 171
acetaldehyde, 53
achievements, 73
acids, 53
activities, 27, 107
actors, 37
addict, 124, 172
addiction, 17, 39, 180, 190
Addiction Recovery, 240
adultery, 57
alcohol, 27, 49, 93, 241
Alcoholics Anonymous, 18, 77
anger, 71, 107
appearance, 107, 111
application, 97
arguments, 33
artisan, 156
assertions, 20
assessments, 34
attitude, 71, 98, 261, 270

attributes, 261
Aunts, 179
authority, 31, 144, 153, 178, 225, 263
awareness, 27, 38, 60
bank, 108
baptism, 158, 196
Bargaining, 39, 70
baseball, 128
battles, 82
beach, 47
behaviors, 18, 21, 28, 104, 163
Belief System, 163
besetting sin, 230
Bible, 35
Binging, 109
blessings, 29
Bob Jones University, 287
bondage, 17, 18, 26, 161, 172, 242
bookie, 108
born again, 44, 157
boundaries, 51
brain, 121
brotherly kindness, 46
build, 19
burden, 26, 65
bureaucracies, 105
Burgess, 287, 294
business, 84, 179

by-product, 29, 148
calling, 26
cancer, 123
captivity, 173
capture, 46
carbon dioxide, 53
cards, 47
career, 47
catastrophic, 37
cause, 25
celebrities, 130
challenge, 20, 265
change, 19
chaos, 143
character, 86, 126, 153, 167
charity, 46
chemical, 39, 177
Chemical Dependency, 39
children, 66
choices, 185
Christ, 17, 21, 111, 257
Christian, 18
Christian Education, 288
Chronic Illness, 39
Church, 17, 50, 87, 245, 266
cigarettes, 52
circumstances, 29, 153

cirrhosis, 123
citizen, 266
clinic, 118
Codependency, 40, 131
coin, 81
comfort zone, 38
commitment, 25
community, 18, 27, 38, 65, 247
compassion, 26, 208, 268
competencies, 34
conceptual, 37
condemn, 30
condominium, 47
confidence, 19, 73
conflict, 129, 153
conformity, 21, 142
congregational, 37
conscience, 59, 149
consequences, 49, 74, 103, 117, 177, 220, 254
consolation, 212
contention, 30
contradiction, 59
contraption, 266
controlling sins, 96
conviction, 29, 102, 169
corporate ladder, 47
cosmic, 165
counsel, 248, 249
counseling, 28, 249
courts, 38

cover-up, 113
coworkers, 65, 270
Creation, 170
Creator, 34, 78
credibility, 36
crimes, 51, 131
cross, 148
culprit, 34
culture, 130, 131
cure, 17, 130
Curiosity, 270
curriculum, 18, 21, 29, 89, 177, 274
cycle, 50, 101, 112
damage, 52
darkness, 21, 119
death, 110, 122, 242
deceit, 96
deception, 217
decision, 31, 249
dehydrogenase, 53
deliverance, 17, 33, 175, 258
Denial, 70
dependency, 27, 29, 177
Depressants, 53
depression, 52, 72
desensitization, 34
Designer, 244
desire, 21, 29, 96
destitute, 28
destructive, 29, 65
determines, 19

Detoxification (Detox), 40
devastation, 130
devils, 28
devotional, 283
diligence, 58, 170
diminishing returns, 57
disappointments, 26
discernment, 97, 249, 268
disciple, 246
discipline, 103
discriminate, 112
disease, 40, 123, 175
disobedience, 262
disorders, 34
disposal, 25, 28
distractions, 59
diversity, 205
division, 47
divisive, 30
divorce, 57
DNA, 53, 205
Doctrines, 280
drug abuse, 37
drugs, 27, 49
DSM-5, 104
DT's, 40
economy, 28
Eden, 35, 103, 146, 245
edification, 34
Educators, 277
embarrassment, 95
embrace, 198

emotion, 131
emphasis, 19, 29, 30
employers, 136
enables, 29
encouragement, 37
Engineer, 244
enslaved, 20, 37
entertainers, 37
environment, 34, 75, 105, 106, 244
equipped, 273
erosion, 70
escape, 56
esteemed, 34
eternity, 30, 136
ethnic, 277
everlasting, 167
evidence, 168
evil, 56
evolution, 165, 184
exclusionist, 266
expectations, 51
experiences, 46, 54, 163
explosion, 165
exposed, 38
facilities, 18, 38, 273
failure, 19, 27, 85
faith, 28, 31, 46, 261
false logic, 229
family, 175, 226
fantasy, 55
favor, 181
fear, 25, 31, 206

fellowship, 50, 61
financial, 85
fingerprint, 205
fishing, 128
flesh, 19, 29, 85, 127, 257
food, 28
football, 128
foreign, 38, 161
forgiveness, 71, 148, 197
formative, 178
foundation, 29, 36, 169
fraud, 66
free moral agents, 228
freedom, 37, 141
fruit, 103, 145, 260
fulfillment, 172, 215
Functioning Addict, 40
gambling, 27, 48
Garden, 35, 262
gender, 262
generation, 38
genetic, 104
Gentleness, 261
Ghost Busters, 266
goal, 18, 19
God, 65, 170
Godhead, 149
godliness, 46
Goodness, 261
Google, 248
Gospel, 17, 21, 89, 135, 179, 279

government, 27, 38, 117, 133, 144, 226
Grief, 72
Ground, 27
growth industry, 87, 243
guardians, 178
guidance, 32, 177
guilt, 31, 50, 180
habits, 17, 21, 30, 104, 190, 255
Hallucinogens, 53
harvest, 25
health, 111
heart, 31, 170
Helen Keller, 60
hell, 64
higher power, 21
hobbies, 47
holiness, 46, 181
Holy Spirit, 20
Honesty, 79
hope, 31, 64, 114, 190
humanism, 32
humanistic, 18, 253
humility, 71, 180, 216, 261
hunger, 32
hunting, 128
husband, 130
hygiene, 77
hyperactivity, 107
hypocrites, 127
ideals, 18

idolatry, 44, 269
illicit behavior, 270
illness, 106, 175, 255
immune, 259
immutable, 167
impact, 27, 137
inadequacy, 51
incarcerated, 88
independence, 51
indulge, 103
infidelity, 57
influence, 26, 126
infrastructure, 66
ingested, 69
iniquities, 177
inner man, 87
insecurity, 51
insight, 18, 100
institutions, 28, 38, 174, 252
instruction, 19, 32,170, 178, 217, 254
intellectual, 34
intelligent design, 150
interactive platform, 291
intercession, 98
intervention, 40, 78
invention, 223
investigation, 49
jail, 92, 268
Jerusalem, 283
Jesus, 17, 30, 148
journey, 197, 241

joy, 218, 261
judgment, 62, 157
kidney, 123
King, 268
kingdom, 27
knowledge, 26, 46, 99, 254
laborers, 25, 28
language, 161
lavish, 47
lawn mower, 221
laws, 59, 144
layperson, 254
leadership, 128
learning platform, 294
leisure, 48
liberty, 172
life, 32, 95, 111
life eternal, 45
life-controlling, 17, 44
lifestyle, 47
liver, 53, 123
loans, 49
local church, 28
longsuffering, 29
Lord, 19, 30, 268
lottery, 48, 108
love, 166, 198, 261
lumberyard, 165
lust, 44
magazine, 238
mainstream, 20
Manipulation, 41

mankind, 35
manna, 220
manufacturing, 66
material goods, 28
media, 59
medical, 28, 38, 160
medication, 75, 94
meditating, 79, 253
meekness, 260
meetings, 18, 176, 281
memorizing, 32, 79, 253
message, 19
methods, 19
military, 77, 269
mindset, 20, 266
ministry, 20, 30, 125, 265, 268, 283
misconceptions, 17
misguided, 18
missionaries, 267
mocked, 63
models, 33
momentum, 48
money, 28, 85, 107, 109, 153
Mood, 107
Music Director, 91
musicians, 37
mutilate, 184
mystery, 29, 90
naked, 28
nation, 25, 144
Natural Laws, 63

Neurobiology, 33
new birth, 157
new nature, 44
notoriety, 19
obedience, 32, 159, 170, 217
obesity, 123
officials, 181
omnipotent, 167
omnipresent, 167
omniscient, 167
online education, 291
Opiates, 53
optimism, 156
origin, 183, 204
overcome, 19
overdose, 109
overtaken, 260
oxygen, 154
Paranoia, 107
paraphernalia, 107
Participants, 274
Pastor, 125
patterns, 113
peace, 28, 261
Peer pressure, 270
penalty, 35, 62, 147
performance, 107
perish, 29
permanent, 17, 27, 44
perpetrators, 34
perspective, 31, 249
pharmaceutical, 75

philosophical, 33
philosophy, 134, 170
photosynthesis, 154
pierce, 184
Pillar, 27
pioneering, 19
poisoning, 109
poker, 108
police, 133
population, 20
pornography, 27, 49, 81, 108, 228
Poverty, 131
power, 17, 20, 30, 153, 267
prayer, 97, 251, 255
prescription, 75
Pressure, 153
prey, 57
pride, 44, 98
principles, 19, 68, 81
prison, 268
privacy, 55
process, 76, 121
productive, 26, 30, 45, 49
profit, 120
programs, 17, 38
progressive, 34
promise, 29
protocols, 21
psychiatric, 253
psychological, 33, 134, 270

Psychotherapeutics, 53
publications, 39
punishment, 145
purpose, 19, 27, 156, 185
qualities, 46, 166
racing, 128
reality, 55, 142
reap, 63, 258
reconciled, 50
Reformation, 41
reforming, 28
rehabilitation, 38
relapse, 18, 42, 83, 118, 241
relevance, 36
remedy, 242
repentance, 29, 80, 86
reproach, 127, 195
republic, 144
research, 50, 282
Residential Treatment Facility, 42
responsibility, 27, 35, 155
Restitution, 42
Restoration, 249, 256
role models, 179
Roloff, 287
sacrifices, 26
safety, 268
salvation, 35, 118, 147
sanctification, 43, 79, 148, 202
sanctity, 195

sanity, 111
Saviour, 25, 34, 257
School, 179
Scripture, 19, 280
Seclusion, 107
Secular, 31
self-esteem, 174
Self-gratification, 104
self-paced, 294
self-preservation, 228
seminars, 193
separation, 50, 120, 147
sessions, 28
shame, 50
shock, 126
siblings, 66
significance, 183, 191, 262
skills, 121
slave, 173
slavery, 18, 26, 196
smoking, 52
snowflake, 204
sober, 31, 173, 258
social life, 54
Social Networking, 293
society, 27, 30, 117, 129, 172, 187, 266, 283
solution, 33, 76, 177
soul-winning, 20
sovereign, 145
species, 152
Spirit-filled, 282
sports, 27, 128

spouse, 66, 122
stability, 67
standard, 87, 142
statements, 20
stewardship, 28
Stimulants, 53
stumble, 86
Substance Abuse, 43
success, 18, 33, 73, 85
supernatural, 31, 256
symptoms, 114
Systematic, 20, 81, 281
tapestry, 205
tattoo, 184
taxpayer, 106
techniques, 193
technologies, 25
temperance, 46, 261
temptation, 55
terminology, 38
terms, 38
testimony, 128
textbook, 30
therapy, 28, 43, 134, 253
threat, 66
throne, 269
tickets, 48
time, 27, 28, 95, 120
tobacco, 49, 52
transform, 134
Transformation, 21, 43, 78, 256

Transformed Life, 30, 45, 275
Transformed Life Ministries, 281, 289
trap, 19, 67
trauma, 255
treatment, 21, 33, 133, 230
treatment protocols, 34
trenches, 33
turmoil, 25
Twelve Step, 29, 43, 173
under-shepherd, 226
uniform, 111
universal, 142
unreached, 17
US ARMY, 288
Uzziah, 269
values, 73, 179
victims, 34
victory, 17, 30, 136
viewpoint, 31
Violence, 131
virtue, 46
vision, 17, 80, 268
voiceprint, 205
voyeurism, 54, 102, 108, 122
vulnerability, 109
wages, 62
wagon, 83
warfare, 128
watchman, 19
Wealth, 153

weight, 107
will, 29, 32, 155, 214
wine, 67
wisdom, 251, 254

Withdrawal, 44, 109
witness, 26
workbook, 278
workplace, 196

world, 17, 21, 25
wounds, 63
wretched, 259

www.ingramcontent.com/pod-product-compliance
Lightning Source LLC
Chambersburg PA
CBHW070723160426
43192CB00009B/1296